I0797025

AFTER THE FIRE

A NATION DIVIDED:
STUDIES IN THE CIVIL WAR ERA

Orville Vernon Burton and Elizabeth R. Varon, Editors

After the Fire

Richmond in Defeat

NELSON D. LANKFORD

UNIVERSITY OF VIRGINIA PRESS
Charlottesville and London

The University of Virginia Press is situated on the traditional lands of the Monacan Nation, and the Commonwealth of Virginia was and is home to many other Indigenous people. We pay our respect to all of them, past and present. We also honor the enslaved African and African American people who built the University of Virginia, and we recognize their descendants. We commit to fostering voices from these communities through our publications and to deepening our collective understanding of their histories and contributions.

University of Virginia Press

Printed in the United States of America on acid-free paper

First published 2025

9 8 7 6 5 4 3 2 1

Library of Congress Cataloging-in-Publication Data

Names: Lankford, Nelson D. author
Title: After the fire : Richmond in defeat / Nelson D. Lankford. Other titles: Nation divided
Description: Charlottesville : University of Virginia Press, 2025. | Series: A nation divided | Includes bibliographical references and index.
Identifiers: LCCN 2025006438 (print) | LCCN 2025006439 (ebook) | ISBN 9780813953366 hardback | ISBN 9780813953373 ebook
Subjects: LCSH: Richmond (Va.)—History—Civil War, 1861–1865
Classification: LCC F235.R557 L36 2025 (print) | LCC F235.R557 (ebook) | DDC 973.7/38—dc23/eng/20250401
LC record available at https://lccn.loc.gov/2025006438
LC ebook record available at https://lccn.loc.gov/2025006439

Cover art: Richmond, Virginia, ruins of Richmond & Petersburg Railroad depot with destroyed locomotive, April 1865. (LC-B811-3260; Civil war photographs, 1861–1865, Library of Congress, Prints and Photographs Division)
Cover design: Kelley Galbreath

For Elizabeth Carr Stevenson

CONTENTS

ILLUSTRATIONS

AFTER THE FIRE

Prologue

April 3, 1865

The sun rose red and angry, as great sheets of flame engulfed Richmond's business quarter sloping down from Capitol Square toward the canal and the river below. Before dawn, retreating Confederate soldiers set fire to tobacco warehouses and all the bridges across the James River as they hurried toward Lee's disintegrating army. At first, smoke rose straight up in the still, soft air of morning. But by sunrise a powerful wind blew flaming embers onto the doomed wooden rooftops of shops, banks, mills, and factories, setting fire to everything in their path. Frank Lawley, correspondent to the London *Times,* was there. His last dispatch quoted Shakespeare's *Tempest:* "Hell is empty, And all the devils are here." To another observer, the sun shone malevolently through the haze, "like a great beacon of woe, or the awful unlashed eye of an avenging Deity."[1]

By the time the first northern cavalrymen arrived in the Virginia capital and fired a few lazy shots at rebel army engineers fleeing across Mayo's Bridge, the flames were completely out of control. Ammunition stores ignited and sent flashes of flame like the forked lighting of a summer thunderstorm through the dense black clouds looming over the city. Merchants who lived above their stores frantically dragged possessions onto the green of Capitol Square to save them from destruction. Below the state capitol building, Thomas Jefferson's austere Roman temple on a hill, families huddled under the trees, not yet fully leafed out. They were not safe even there. "Men, women, and children crowded into the square," cried a witness, "blinded by cinders and struggling for breath." They had to brush burning coals off their clothing or risk catching fire. Blazing wind-borne sticks and shingles rained down on the scene. Above it all rose Thomas Crawford's grand equestrian tribute to the nation's first president. "Amid this carnival of ruin," remembered a northern soldier, "stood the great statue of Washington, against which firebrands thumped and rattled."[2]

From the veranda of her mansion perched high on Church Hill, Elizabeth Van Lew watched regiment after regiment of blue uniforms stream in from the east. She was a successful spy who had helped prisoners escape to Union lines and sent vital intelligence to Grant's encircling armies. She deplored the destruction appearing before her eyes but welcomed the conquerors. The pall of smoke over the city seemed to her like the sweetest incense. "What a moment!" she exclaimed. "Avenging wrath appeased in flames!"[3]

Thomas Morris Chester, a Black journalist, marched in with those blue-coated soldiers. He had attached himself to units of the United States Colored Troops (USCTs) and shared with them the hardships of life on campaign. His dispatches from the front to his Philadelphia newspaper extolled the African American contribution to the war effort. Although some white residents in working-class neighborhoods came out to greet the USCTs, who were among the first Union soldiers arriving in Richmond, the greatest number of onlookers were Black. With evident pride, Chester praised "the great concourse of American citizens of African descent" who flooded the streets to welcome their liberators. A perceptive white soldier observed that "People generally are glad to see us here, not, I suppose from much of a real union sentiment but because they have suffered so much."[4]

The night before, Richmond's long-serving mayor, Joseph Mayo, and his councilors had sought to destroy the liquor supply for fear that drunken looters would wreak havoc. They failed. Numerous accounts described the wild scene in the hours of darkness as men, women, and even children got down on their hands and knees to lap up alcohol from the gutters. An inflamed mob ransacked shops as social order departed with the last Confederate soldiers, some of whom indulged in pillaging too. Failing to prevent chaos, the harried Mayo rode out to the east to surrender his city to incoming Union forces and urge haste to avert further anarchy.

In the mad tumult of that day, soldiers vied to raise the first American flag over the Virginia capitol. They would argue about who had succeeded for years to come. In fact, a biracial youth, Richard Forrester, claimed that honor, not a soldier in blue. Ominously for the future of race relations, white regiments disputed the claim of USCT men to have been the first into town.

Godfrey Weitzel, at twenty-nine the very young brevet major general who commanded local Union forces, rode in with his staff. They were elated with their good fortune that their entry had not been contested. There would be no battle of Richmond. The major combat had taken place twenty or so miles to the south, around Petersburg, where the larger armies of Grant and Lee had dueled for the past year across a bleak moonscape of forbidding earthworks. Now their cannon fire had faded away to the southwest, and no one in Richmond, including Weitzel, yet knew the outcome. He took up a position on the neoclassical portico of the state capitol. From there, he looked down on what one of his men called "a gigantic crater of fire." He could appreciate the terror of civilians cowering on the lawn: his own wife had died in agony from burns.[5]

A young woman whose house was threatened by flames looked on in horror. It was, she cried, "my idea of the day of Judgement. . . . I feel as if God had hidden his face from us as a nation, and as individuals." By afternoon, one by one, the spans of the two railroad bridges and Mayo's Bridge, the sole link across the James for pedestrians and vehicles, dropped into the river with great hissing splashes.[6]

Edward Porter Alexander, a Confederate artillerist, watched the conflagration from the temporary safety of the south bank of the river. "It was a sad, a terrible & a solemn sight," he wrote years later with a detachment he could not have felt at the time. "I rode on with a distinctly heavy heart & with a peculiar sort of feeling of orphanage." Others stared, transfixed. "I watched those silent awful fires," wrote Mary Fontaine, helpless to do anything. Susan Hoge, a staunch Confederate, conceded that "the yankees put a stop to [looting] & made the negroes work to put the fire out & they worked hard themselves." By afternoon, when flames had eaten through the commercial heart of town and the wind abated, the danger to untouched portions of the city finally lessened. With the bitterness of an eyewitness who had spat untold columns of venom at his northern foes, journalist Edward Pollard remembered an unwonted medieval silence that first night: "a strange quiet fell upon the blackened city . . . the quiet of a great desolation."[7]

When the sun came up the next day, the view from Main Street down to the river, and between Eighth and Fifteenth Streets revealed a stunning vista of blackened walls, smoking ruins, and tottering chimneys. Improbably, that same day, with flames still licking at the charred remains of Richmond's industrial and mercantile might, Abraham Lincoln himself walked through the smoldering ashes. He had been visiting Grant's headquarters downriver at City Point, near Petersburg, and when he learned the Confederate citadel had fallen, he insisted on seeing it for himself. He congratulated his jubilant officers crammed into their temporary Richmond headquarters in Jefferson Davis's former home. Later he toured the center of town and the landmarks of Confederate power that remained. At the base of Crawford's towering bronze Washington, he stopped his carriage and gave an impromptu speech—sadly unrecorded—to the throng of freed people who crowded around him.

For northerners, the gaunt ruins captured by photographers who swarmed over the city in the first week after the cataclysm symbolized the utter and final failure of secession. For Richmonders, April 3, 1865, was forever seared into their memories. The fire overshadowed everything that had happened before in their city and influenced everything that followed for years to come. That day marked Armageddon for Confederates and liberation for African Americans. It meant not just widespread physical destruction but the complete upending of their society, a great inversion of the way they organized and viewed the world.

Emancipation wrought the most sweeping change of the nineteenth century, perhaps in all of American history. What would follow this seismic event? For many months after April, great uncertainty prevailed. It was a time of intense anxiety and tension. For Black residents, anxiety over whether the promises of emancipation would be realized or whether a recession back into some form of bondage might yet occur. For Confederates, anxiety over whether they would regain their political rights or suffer severe punishment for secession and war. These apprehensions heralded a time of profound tension between the races and between civil and military authority. The city's Black and white communities emerged from the conflict with radically divergent interpretations of what the war and its outcome meant. Those perspectives anticipated and underwrote the checkered legacy that has reverberated down the years to our own time.

This is the story of Richmond and its people in the early months after the war, especially during the first pivotal year. It evokes a vanished world of privation, defeat, jubilation, false starts, tribal antagonism, and the lost causes of Confederate nostalgia and of racial reconciliation. The story emphasizes the year of tentative rebuilding after the fire, culminating in dramatic events during April and May 1866 that put on vivid display the contrasting ways Black and white residents remembered the war.

That first year, and those powerful expressions of remembrance, are important because they gave birth to attitudes that predominated in the years to come. Those beliefs informed the tumultuous political changes that followed in quick succession. A compromise settlement finally ended Virginia's prolonged limbo with a new constitution approved in 1869. It readmitted the commonwealth's representatives to Congress and reasserted the ascendancy of the prewar white establishment. But it also enshrined the right of Black men to vote. For the first time, they sat in the state legislature and participated in a fragile interlude of biracial democracy before the curse of intolerance blighted their hopes.

In April 1865, however, all of that was hidden in the future. For the stark immediate present, how would Richmonders put bread on the table for their families?

1

Last Ditch of the Rebellion

April to May 1865

Thomas Crawford's imposing statue of Washington was a recent adornment to Capitol Square. As soon as it was erected, it became the focal point of civic life in the last years of peace. Richmond had prospered during the 1850s, thanks to tobacco, grain milling, iron manufacturing, and the domestic slave trade. To white Virginians, a monument honoring the nation's chief founding father seemed a fitting way to celebrate their achievements, just as Jefferson's nearby Roman temple housing the state legislature had done for an earlier generation. It was, in fact, in Rome, among the ruins of the Baths of Diocletian, where Crawford created his masterpiece. The heavy task of constructing its stone plinth was done by enslaved workers purchased expressly for that purpose. That must have been an embarrassment for Crawford, a friend of Charles Sumner, the US senator and abolitionist. The sculptor's sister-in-law Julia Ward Howe later wrote "The Battle Hymn of the Republic" and was married to Samuel Howe, who helped bankroll John Brown's raid on Harpers Ferry a year after those workmen set the figure of Washington in place.

Crawford died of brain cancer before he finished, but to complete the work Governor Henry Alexander Wise contracted with Randolph Rogers, another ambitious young American sculptor in Rome. At the unveiling in 1858, a vast assembly of Richmond's leading citizens gathered to hear both Wise and his archenemy, US Senator Robert Mercer Taliaferro Hunter, praise the founder of the nation. Three years later, Wise nearly undid Washington's creation. Breathing fire and

Thomas Crawford's equestrian statue of George Washington on Capitol Square at its unveiling in 1858. (Library of Congress)

brimstone at the convention called to address the impending breakup of the Union, Wise almost single-handedly propelled Virginia to secession and war. At the foot of the statue on Washington's birthday a few months later, Jefferson Davis took his oath of office as Confederate president. The statue then presided over a hopeful influx of bureaucrats, soldiers, swindlers, refugees, and fortune hunters who swelled the city's wartime population.

Now the failure of Davis's government lay all around the tall equestrian figure. Evacuation, plunder, and fire had done their worst. Few had foreseen such a Götterdämmerung. With the rebellion a failure, Capitol Square and the business district below it bore grim witness to the calamity. Abandoned state papers and useless bank notes swirled about in the wind, a squall of failed dreams. Heaps of clothing and housewares, family heirlooms and cheap furniture—the detritus of shopkeepers' pitiful efforts to escape the flames—littered the lawn sloping down the square. As the symbol of Richmond's prewar success and now of its defeat, the bronze Washington became a favorite subject for photographers, who used it as a backdrop for proud northern soldiers and for paroled Confederate veterans.

More pregnant for the future, beginning with Lincoln's visit, the statue attracted crowds of freed people. They had not been allowed there before freedom came, and their presence marked the first dramatic way they began to challenge established customs. The statue would soon become a magnet for mass meetings as Black political awareness awakened, a contested site where the definition of who was a Virginia citizen would be disputed. For the moment, though, no one, Black or white, could say how postwar society, civil rights, politics, or labor relations in Virginia would take shape.

Godfrey Weitzel had no time to contemplate statues. After he led his small force into Richmond from the east on the morning of April 3, his men battled the fire into submission that afternoon. He was now beyond reach of the field telegraph back in the siege works facing the city. All was chaos and flux. His first priority was making sure Richmond was militarily secure. He had to reestablish contact with Grant's mobile headquarters. He had to provision his men. He had to attend to the needs of the city's population. And he had to satisfy his military and civilian masters. These tasks he accomplished with varying degrees of success in the ten days he was supreme commander in the defeated capital of his nation's enemy.

Weitzel was the first in a line of many Union generals given the assignment of governing the former Confederate capital. None would find it easy. For both soldiers and civilians, it was a surreal week in the captured city before news of Appomattox came. Not knowing the outcome of the fighting added urgency to Weitzel's task. The son of German immigrants, he looked older than his twenty-nine years, thanks to a bushy black beard, a flat, careworn face, and four years of active military life. He had studied engineering at West Point, where he also taught after he was commissioned at the age of nineteen. Although not an aggressive field commander and considered timid by some officers, he had experience in civil administration in occupied New Orleans. His command consisted of part of the Army of the James, a smaller force from Grant's much larger army. Weitzel's troops had held the line east of Richmond while Grant and Lee faced one another across the trenches at Petersburg. The Black Twenty-Fifth Corps and part of the white Twenty-Fourth Corps gave the young general sufficient force to hold the city. One benefit of being out of telegraphic touch with headquarters was not being micromanaged by his immediate superior, the bluff, impetuous General Edward O. C. Ord, whom he warmly detested.

Weitzel declared martial law and appointed as military governor Brigadier General George Shepley, who trailed a whiff of corruption from his time in occupied New Orleans and Norfolk. From the first day, frightened Confederate women fearing for their property besieged his provost marshal with pleas for guards to stand outside their homes. That badgered officer assured them there was no need but agreed to most of their requests. He warned his men to treat people with respect, forbade disloyal speech, banned meetings, and announced summary punishment for anyone guilty of looting. In subsequent days, from his office in the capitol, he signed the passes required of any civilian wishing to leave town.[1]

Edward Ripley, the twenty-five-year-old colonel of the Ninth Vermont Regiment, relished his promotion to brigadier general and assignment to head all troops on guard duty. He set up patrols at once and on the first night rode with one of them to inspect the city, still lit by dying flames from the fire. In the small hours of the morning, these exhausted soldiers discovered nothing amiss in their ride from one end of town to another. No one was about in the darkness except sentries on alternate street corners. All they could hear, Ripley recalled, was "the clatter of our horses' hoofs and the jingle of our sabres."[2]

Weitzel's sense of urgency did not diminish after the fire subsided. No one could promise him the danger of a Confederate counterattack had passed, and he disposed his infantry and artillery accordingly.

Until they learned of Lee's surrender, engineers worked with haste to construct defensive positions facing out from the city. The army came well equipped to impose stability and order. Weitzel set his men to work clearing wreckage from the river, reconnecting the city by rail to supply lines to the south and east, and reestablishing telegraphic links to the outside world. Within two days Peter Michie, Weitzel's chief engineer, directed his men to throw a line of canvas boats and wooden trestles across the river, from the foot of Seventeenth Street on the north bank to the suburb of Manchester on the south. Within weeks they added a second line of pontoons to permit traffic to flow in both directions at the same time.[3]

Along the docks at Rocketts Landing, the quartermaster employed more than a thousand Black men to gather up abandoned Confederate supplies and load and unload ships, once they were able to put into the port again. Although workers had removed enough debris for navy vessels to come up the James as early as two days after the fire, for many weeks pilots bringing supplies to the city had to proceed with caution. Confederate engineers had planted hundreds of antiship explosive devices, which they called torpedoes. Mine-clearing operations left buoys with tiny scraps of red cloth to mark the presence of defused but still deadly ordnance. A rudimentary steamer service linked Richmond with the outside world within a week. The US Military Railroad Service worked miracles to repair decrepit lines below the city. By the end of the week, two regular passenger trains ran between it and Grant's throbbing supply port downriver at City Point.

In his first hours in town, Weitzel learned he would have to feed not just his own men but most of the residents. Thousands besieged him for rations as soon as he established his headquarters. An assessment later that summer estimated that the fire had destroyed four-fifths of Richmond's food supplies. Without authorization, the general sold abandoned tobacco to purchase food for civilians. There was little coffee and sugar but great quantities of unappetizing hard tack and codfish. Two relief agencies that had provided comforts for Union soldiers, the US Sanitary Commission and the US Christian Commission, drove their wagons into town behind Weitzel's men and lightened the military's burden feeding the populace. The army also welcomed the aid of William Munford, of the local YMCA, whose relief work had aided poor Richmonders during the war. He had made repeated appeals for donations during the Confederacy and continued to do so now. The army organized the Richmond Relief Commission, staffed by white volunteers and led by Lieutenant Colonel Adam Badeau. He estimated that they had fed about fifteen thousand by April 21 and gave out ration tickets to the needy without "distinction of color or political opinion." But Badeau, like many US Army officers, did not like being in the relief business and condescendingly worried about the danger of fostering idleness among recently freed Black Virginians.[4]

From the outset, a vast inflow of people of all sorts complicated the army's efforts to restore order. The population had swollen from sixty thousand before the war to two or more times that number at the peak of Confederate fortunes but had declined since then. The exact number is unknown, but there were perhaps eighty thousand residents in April, evenly divided between Black and white, plus more than ten thousand Union soldiers stationed in and around Richmond. Added to these were hundreds of both races who now tried to reach the capital every day in search of food, shelter, and displaced relatives. A northern soldier remembered that every building and shed was crowded with people seeking refuge. A shopkeeper, George Bagby, grumbled that "our streets are crowded with strangers civilian & military from all quarters of the US."[5]

Hundreds of Confederate soldiers paroled at Appomattox—not just Richmonders but natives of other states seeking transport—streamed in every day, footsore and weary, dejected by defeat but glad to be headed home. The flood of soldiers overtaxed the army's ability to process and accommodate them. The parlous state of railroads and the lack of sufficient shipping meant that for a time the outflow of Lee's veterans from the city could not keep up with the influx. Because most were unparoled, the army set up an office to accept soldiers surrendering themselves, singly and in small groups. Tension between men of the two armies led to occasional fights. Eventually the army banned the wearing of Confederate uniforms in public. When provost guards detained soldiers in violation of this decree, they subjected them to the indignity of stripping off their insignia of rank.[6]

The great phenomenon of the day universally remarked upon was the stream of freed people on the roads. They were going in every direction, but mostly headed to Virginia's capital city in a massive exodus from the countryside. They were in search of food, in search of a new livelihood away from the farms where they had been held in bondage, and in search of lost family members. Emancipation—still ill-defined and inchoate in the early months—was the most extraordinary aspect of the post–Civil War landscape, and the movements of its beneficiaries gave dramatic testimony to that fact. Their hopes for the unknown future contrasted starkly with the spectacle of downcast Confederates soldiers trudging home. John Coles Rutherfoord, a farmer from Goochland County fifteen miles away, had seen the beginning of pandemonium as he boarded one of the last canal boats leaving Richmond just before the fire. He reached momentary safety at his plantation but feared his former workers rushing into town. As they left, one group shouted back to him the threat "that they wd. return to set things right." With that admonition ringing in his ears, Rutherfoord buried his silverware.[7]

Because it valued order and feared social upheaval, the army was as uneasy as former slaveholders about this worrisome demographic flux. Emancipation complicated Weitzel's task even more than dealing with thousands of Confederate veterans. That the army soon chose to conciliate the white population at the cost of disappointing Black Virginians would add to unrest in the coming weeks. Before long, the latter began to worry about threats to their newfound freedom. They could not know if its promise would be realized. And for many months that uncertainty would cloud their hopes for a better life.

Among the myriad tasks the army faced in pacifying the city, managing information was one it dared not overlook. Richmond newspapers had always wielded great power over opinion in the antebellum South. General Grant knew the war had magnified that influence. Even though most newspaper offices had gone up in smoke, he thought it vital to locate and silence Confederate editors still at large. A day after

Weitzel established his command, Grant sent an order to "arrest all editors and proprietors of Richmond papers." That order marked the opening shot in a postwar duel between pen and sword. It was by no means certain who would win in the contest between defiant editors and victorious army commanders.[8]

One journalist who momentarily escaped was the tempestuous Edward Pollard, prone to violence and tetchy about offended honor. He was one of the angry young men at the secessionist *Examiner,* and his desire for revenge for the loss of his cause burned as fiercely as the fires that had consumed his newspaper's presses and melted their lead type. Dressed in shabby black clothes, with his right arm in a sling (the result of his latest brawl), and sporting an unkempt red beard, he strutted unrepentant through the streets of Richmond. After a week of this, the army could no longer tolerate his presence and expelled him from the city. A northern newspaperman on the scene sneered that Confederate scribblers like him "have found the last ditch of the rebellion, and have tumbled into it." Through gritted teeth, Pollard vowed to be heard from again.[9]

With lightning speed, Pollard's northern counterparts descended on Richmond, the biggest news story of the day. The African American reporter Thomas Chester was on hand when Weitzel's Black Twenty-Fifth Corps entered the city even before the fire reached its peak. Others arrived within days despite an unevenly enforced press ban. Soon they were dictating long cables from what seemed to them like a city on the far side of the moon. Their dispatches filled papers throughout the North and crowded out other news, at least until Appomattox. Richmond, one wrote, "has become to loyal Americans in the course of the last four years as strange and foreign a place as Rome or Constantinople." Artists for *Frank Leslie's Illustrated Newspaper* and *Harper's* sketched the ruins for engravers to translate into print for the insatiable northern reading public, eager to learn about the defeated capital. Richmond's *Whig,* which survived the fire and reopened as a Union paper, cleverly colored in the burned areas on a prewar map of the city and sold prints as souvenirs for Union soldiers to take home.[10]

Photographers with the army knew a lucrative opportunity when they saw it. They quickly transported their mobile darkrooms to Richmond to record the charred remains of rebellion. Alexander Gardner was one of the first. He missed by only one day the chance to capture Lincoln speaking to freedmen at the foot of Crawford's Washington. But he, Matthew Brady, and others photographed the capitol rising above the Burnt District, as it became known, the acres upon acres of ashes, and all the principal architectural symbols of the Confederacy that had escaped destruction. More than three hundred wet collodion glass plate negatives yielded images that powerfully shaped the visual impression of fallen Richmond, then and for generations to come.

The northern public thrilled at the sight of these, the South's tangible wages of sin. A favorite photograph, with a dead horse floating in the canal in the foreground, showed how the fire had carved a path from the waterfront up to the border of Capitol Square. At the top of the image, blurred by the slow shutter speed but still distinctive, the American flag flew once more from the roof of the capitol. In one innovative sequence, Gardner stitched together five images in a cinematic panorama of disaster from the capitol down to the canal and the river beyond. These pictures distorted the extent of destruction because only 10 percent of Richmond's buildings burned, but they captured the views the North wanted. And if only a tenth burned, that embraced nine-tenths of the city's businesses, jobs, and wealth.

Prolific war correspondent Whitelaw Reid finagled his way past a ban on press access to reach the city within forty-eight hours. The vessel he sailed on was filled with, in his words, assorted parasites who "wanted to dig for money around the garbage of Richmond." Within days after Lincoln's visit, a stream of notables, including the president's wife and his vice president, went to admire the stricken rebel capital.[11]

Like Confederate luminaries before them, most northern dignitaries stayed at the Spotswood Hotel. It may have been the grandest hostelry in town, but overcrowding meant some guests had to settle for cots in the halls. One complained of ravenous mice, dirty linen, and walls covered with obscene graffiti. Another marveled at the kaleidoscope of characters at the hotel—"gentlemen, fashionable loafers, broken-down chivalry, Union officers, rebel chieftains, eminent visitors, thieves, gamblers."[12]

Especially galling to combat veterans on both sides were the self-important visitors demanding free transportation to outlying battlefields where they could pick up ghoulish souvenirs. "Robbing a battle-field of its bones," growled William Kreutzer, a New York colonel, "is a species of Vandalism not hitherto witnessed in this country." Every day dozens of people combed through the labyrinth of ruins for relics, careful to avoid unstable brick walls and chimneys. Scavengers rooted about for more than a month before the extravagant prices they commanded began to fall. Some visitors took a longer view. The narrative historian Francis Parkman came down from Boston with a bankroll of five hundred dollars in greenbacks and an eye for historical documents. In a short stay, he bought up a hoard of Confederate imprints that were then useless but he hoped would be priceless for future scholars.[13]

Northern soldiers eagerly played the tourist among the ruins. Daniel Nelson, a recent graduate of Harvard Medical School, had just taken a commission as acting assistant surgeon in time to be present at Appomattox. He blithely described his mobile hospital's journey from the surrender through the wreckage of war to the Virginia capital: "Bad hills & dead horses. Paroled prisoners violate their parole & are hung." He barely noted Lincoln's assassination in his diary (merely commenting that Andrew Johnson "must let liquor alone now") because he was much more excited about getting to Richmond. He first caught sight of the capitol building on April 25. His hospital's wagon train bumped across the pontoon bridge the following morning in clouds of dust under a blazing sun. He called it the greatest day of his life, as the garrison welcomed his division with bands playing and flags flying.[14]

After reaching temporary camp north of town, Nelson lost no time riding back to gawk at the sights and comment on the locals with the condescension of a superior outsider. He found the Customs House a foot deep in blank Confederate checks and treasury bonds. There were, he admitted, many beautiful houses, but "they all show Southern sloth & slavery's curse." In any case, he thought all they needed was a bit of Yankee energy to be put right. Even less perceptively, after talking to Richmonders, he failed to detect the depth of their anger and dismay over their loss and professed to see very little bitterness.[15]

Julia Wilbur viewed the city with a more jaundiced eye than the young surgeon from Massachusetts. The Rochester, New York, Ladies' Anti-Slavery Society had sent the forty-nine-year-old Quaker advocate for abolition and women's rights to Alexandria, Virginia. There she taught freed slaves, an experience that lifted the severe depression that had plagued Wilbur in the early war years. When she reached Richmond in May, she, like Dr. Nelson, wanted to see all the sights in the prostrate former rebel capital. Much of her time was spent with Narcissa and Richard Forrester, who showed her around their city. It amused her to eat strawberries and cream from Jefferson Davis's china, which, they said, his house servants had given to the Forrester boys the morning of the evacuation. Richard Forrester was the son of a prominent white attorney and a free woman of color and would go on to a notable role in the city's early postwar years. It was his son who had raised the first American flag over the capitol building.

With the Forresters, Wilbur toured the warren of slave pens and auction blocks in the Shockoe Bottom district along a polluted stream east of Capitol Square. They horrified her. One of the most notorious traders, a violent man named Robert Lumpkin, showed her and her party around his jail complex, where hundreds of enslaved people had suffered whipping, violation, and separation from loved ones. He seemed to think he could ingratiate himself with these northern women by telling them about Mary Lumpkin, the young enslaved woman who lived in his jail and bore his children. Theirs was a complicated relationship: she submitted to him and eventually moved to Philadelphia with their children, accepting his money for their housing and education in the North. Unimpressed by his story, Wilbur and her Black abolitionist friend indignantly berated Lumpkin for his role in a brutal and degrading system. After talking with him, she concluded, "This City has been a complete hell."[16]

After a week, Godfrey Weitzel could be satisfied with the work his men had accomplished. He had achieved his military objectives. The army and relief agencies were feeding a malnourished city. He appeared to have secured at least the grudging acceptance of the white population. But the young general had fallen afoul of his political masters in Washington, DC, and it was all about prayers.

In times of trouble, Richmonders, like most Americans of their day, turned to their houses of worship for solace. They were at full capacity the week after the Confederate collapse. Edward Ripley, the brigadier commanding soldiers on guard duty, thought it politic to summon ministers to discuss reopening their churches on April 9. It would be Palm Sunday, the beginning of Holy Week leading up to Easter. He insisted that they allow no disloyal words to be spoken. He accepted the argument of Dr. Charles Minnigerode, the wily rector of St. Paul's, that Episcopal churches could not change the wording of their prescribed liturgy without permission from their bishop, who could not be reached. Ripley agreed to a compromise. Minnigerode would omit praying for the Confederate president and substitute a general prayer for those in authority but did not mention Lincoln by name.

When Secretary of War Edwin Stanton received a cable reporting on Palm Sunday in Richmond, he exploded. That Weitzel permitted the compromise prayer was a travesty. The young general had angered Stanton before, over his conduct when Lincoln visited the city the previous week. But the prayer issue was too much for the volatile secretary of war. Indignant at being reproached, Weitzel appealed over Stanton's head to Lincoln. The president absolved him, but the damage was done. The general was now a marked man. Stanton gave Richmond's Episcopal churches a choice. They could pray explicitly for the president of the United States, or their doors would remain closed. Because they refused, there were no Easter services for them that year.

Ten days after his army swept into Richmond, Weitzel left, if not in disgrace, then certainly in bad odor with the high command. With his Black Twenty-Fifth Corps, he marched down to Petersburg to a temporary posting at a miserable site with contaminated drinking water. The army then sent them to the Rio Grande to swelter in the Texas heat. He resented the shabby treatment, and it irritated him that the irascible and meddlesome General Ord replaced him as overlord of Richmond. But despite his annoyance with Ord, it was Stanton who engineered Weitzel's dismissal. The general, however, was not entirely wrong when he chose to blame his dismissal on the disgust some haughty members of the First Families of Virginia showed toward his African American soldiers. "But you know," he later wrote with mordant scorn, "the negroes had to leave there, the smell was offensive to the F.F.V.'s." He was not imagining things. Lucy Fletcher, who lost a brother and brother-in-law in Confederate service, loathed the United States Colored Troops and feared them. She thought Weitzel's men looked "like an army of savages & cannibals just imported from Africa." Black soldiers received the same inhospitable welcome as they occupied cities across the South.[17]

With Weitzel out, a triumvirate of generals ruled the city for almost two months. Ord arrived first and instituted a more lenient policy toward the residents than had his predecessor. His wife, Molly, a southerner, came with him, and within a week a relieved Richmonder wrote that she was encouraging her husband in his treatment of Confederates. General Marsena Patrick, the army's chief provost marshal, arrived on April 14 and took over the relief agencies and military police. He was a severe, inflexible disciplinarian who antagonized many of his brother officers. Looking for all the world like an Old Testament prophet with an extravagantly long white beard, Patrick fretted excessively in his diary about security, about controlling Black people and paroled Confederates, and about his hemorrhoids. He complained that Richmond was "full of non-residents, paroled prisoners, refugees, followers of the army, and colored people." He got along with the headstrong Ord but scribbled in his diary, "He is still Crazy Ord. Goes off half cocked." Patrick doubted the administrative talents of the chief army officers in Richmond, each of whom thought he alone was competent to be in command.[18]

The general in charge of civilian affairs over both Ord and Patrick was Henry Halleck, nicknamed "Old Brains." An accomplished writer and businessman but a disappointing field commander, Halleck feuded with his peers while obsessing over the logistical details that made him a pedantic but astute administrator. He would have preferred to be posted back to California, where he had been happy before, but his administrative skills were needed in Richmond. Trying to bring order from chaos compounded the intestinal disorders that plagued Halleck, who treated the added stress with opium.[19]

Soon after satisfying the most pressing needs of feeding the populace and beginning to restore water and gas service, the army took action to rekindle economic activity. It began by requiring an oath of allegiance to the United States from nearly everyone. To import goods, to practice a profession, to execute a bill of exchange, to negotiate a promissory note, to serve as director of a company, even to acquire a marriage license, Richmonders had to sign the oath by May 1. Whether to do so posed a dilemma for die-hard Confederates. Should they hold to their principles or bow to necessity? Elizabeth Munford wrote her absent husband that everyone was taking the oath, which she called "a bitter pill."[20]

The humiliation weighed on many of them, and northern observers doubted their sincerity. When one saw Confederate soldiers swearing the oath, he thought he sensed hypocrisy on their lips. Another mused, "It will be a long time before the United States is greatly beloved, but it will be always obeyed." Every day more residents decided they were ready to swallow Munford's bitter pill and crowded the four offices opened in town for that purpose. Thousands signed the pledge within the first weeks. But doing so did not mean they were ready to forsake their Confederate allegiance.[21]

After a few weeks of military rule, white Richmonders began to entertain some hope. They grudgingly appreciated the army's feeding program and support for rebuilding. They were relieved that Union soldiers did not, as a rule, lord it over their fallen foes. But they also began to think that they might be allowed to restore much of the old structure of society and its familiar racial hierarchy. Standing in the way of such a restoration were the rising aspirations of Black Richmonders, so vividly manifested in their welcome of liberation. Those aspirations would soon clash, and clash dramatically, with that outdated worldview.

2

No Longer Way down in Egypt's Land

April to May 1865

When Union troops poured into Richmond, none was more elated than the Rev. Garland White, chaplain of the Twenty-Eighth United States Colored Troops (USCTs). He had been born enslaved there but had escaped to Canada. He volunteered to fight before the army admitted Black men. When it finally did, he helped recruit a regiment in Indiana. His men often sought the aid of this self-taught parson to write their families in the event they died in battle. Now he entered the fallen Confederate capital as a free man, a liberator of his people on their day of Pentecostal joy. As his regiment marched down Broad Street toward the western side of town, hundreds of formerly enslaved people surged forward to cheer the disciplined files of blue-coated African American soldiers. "It appeared to me," White beamed a week later, "that all the colored people in the world had collected in that city."[1]

They did not just welcome the soldiers but pressed forward to beg for news of separated family members. The USCTs had been recruited from every state, and maybe they had heard of a mother or father torn from their families and scattered across the South by the notorious slave auctions of Richmond. Only when the soldiers reached camp and stacked their weapons did they break ranks and eagerly shake the hands of these grateful people, enslaved only hours before. In this supreme moment of joy, the soldiers clamored for White to address the crowd. He did but got only as far as proclaiming "freedom to all mankind" before he choked up over the emotional scene taking place around him.[2]

The men and women who heard his brief words faced daunting prospects in the strange new world that beckoned. They had few resources and faced prejudice, poverty, and chronic underemployment, but they looked forward with hope. Not knowing what might replace the old strictures of bondage, however, or even whether some of them might be reimposed, tempered that hope.

Apart from the family, the church was the most important institution created by Black southerners before emancipation. No house of worship better showed that achievement than First African Baptist, a large redbrick cruciform structure perched on Broad Street as it sloped down into Shockoe Valley to the east. Because it boasted the largest hall in the city, the Confederate government had used it for mass public meetings. Its membership, more than three thousand on the eve of war, comprised perhaps a quarter of the adult Black population in Richmond. As the law required, the minister was white. Robert Ryland had preached the southern version of the gospel to his African American flock for nearly a quarter century. With his long, thin face and copious white chin whiskers, he personified the stern image of white control over Black people, even in matters of faith. His gospel preached meek submission to masters and contentment with a degraded station in life.

Yet beyond appearances, Ryland allowed the congregation some management over its worship and winked at deviations from strict observance of the law. To circumvent the statute forbidding Black preachers, the thirty-member board of deacons, mostly free Black men but also some still enslaved, fashioned elaborate prayers into miniature sermons. These gave expression to their own hopes and beliefs, not Ryland's. Although the deacons and Ryland usually agreed, sometimes the white minister was outvoted. This taste of self-government undergirded the rapid growth of postwar Black political sensibility. Parishioners also created a distinctive style of music that appealed to their tastes, a form of call-and-response evangelical praise music distinct from that of their white neighbors. Though he did not consider slavery wrong, Ryland did condemn the separation of family members and denounced as sin the law forbidding Black men and women from

Parishioners pose for a photograph in front of First African Baptist Church on Broad Street, a center for Black religious, political, social, and educational activities. (National Archives)

reading the Bible. He even published a slim book called *The Scripture Catechism, for Colored People* and sparred with Mayor Joseph Mayo over this subversive disregard of the law.

The church raised money for indigent members, used strict discipline to instill family values, and crucially for the future, fostered a de facto self-governing structure for the African American community. Indeed, Ryland praised the ability of his church members to manage complex matters of governance. He cautioned that anyone who doubted their talents in that regard foolishly underestimated his parishioners. First African Baptist and the other Black churches that flourished in the antebellum city formed the institutional backbone of the Black community and its nerve center. The churches fostered a tradition of self-help and a network of affiliated social organizations that were largely invisible to white Richmond but that burst forth in the first weeks of freedom. Ryland had garnered the respect of many parishioners for allowing them a real role in the church, but he represented the past. Poignantly conflicted over what to do, the congregation first rejected and then accepted his resignation that summer. Although they turned at first to a northern white abolitionist preacher, eventually they chose a minister of their own race, James Holmes. Ryland had baptized him when he was enslaved, and he went on to serve for three decades at First African Baptist.[3]

Just as they developed their own particular form of sacred music, the church's members also embraced biblical themes that held a special resonance for enslaved people and those nominally free but who existed without rights at the margins of society. They especially cherished the Exodus story. Moses leading the people of Israel out of Egyptian bondage beyond the reach of pharaoh had spoken with great power to parishioners yearning for release from their chains. Now that story had miraculously come true before their eyes. When Garland White and his comrades freed Richmonders from bondage, surely this was the jubilee foretold by biblical prophecy. When Abraham Lincoln walked through the smoldering ruins, freed people imbued that improbable sight with religious meaning and fervor. One euphoric African American woman, on seeing the president, shouted, "I know that I am free, for I have seen Father Abraham." She spoke for them all.[4]

Black Richmonders soon ratified that spontaneous welcome with a more organized program of praise and thanksgiving. Two days later, and still before Lee surrendered, First African Baptist became the site for the grandest celebratory gathering in the city. Even with the largest capacity of any Richmond church, it was filled to overflowing. City residents and USCT soldiers alike crammed the pews and every space to stand. Hundreds spilled outside and craned their necks to listen through open windows to the service inside. The Philadelphia journalist Thomas Chester called the gathering to order and received the congregation's noisy welcome as he saluted them "upon the triumph of liberty in Richmond."[5]

Prayers by northern white clergymen were well received. But nothing could exceed the symbolism of another speaker. No Black man had dared to mount the pulpit before, but Chaplain David Stevens of the Thirty-Fifth USCT claimed the honor to preach on this day. The jubilant congregation sang a hymn with verses appropriate to the moment: "I'm going to join in this army; / I'm going to join in this army of my Lord." Summing it up afterward, one of Chester's white colleagues wrote with evident emotion, "I shall never forget a scene I witnessed, yesterday, at the Historical African Church."[6]

Similar scenes happened at other Black churches. At a jubilee service at Third Street African Methodist Episcopal on April 18, parishioners gathered to rejoice at their deliverance from bondage even as they mourned the death of Lincoln three days earlier. And they did not just celebrate; they ratified their allegiance with their lives. When the army set up a recruiting office in town for the USCTs the day after the fire, Black Richmonders joined the colors at the rate of two or three hundred a day. To wear Union blue symbolized their manhood and their claim to equality.[7]

Even as they celebrated emancipation and flocked to their churches to give thanks for deliverance, freed people had to eat. The quest for food became the paramount concern for all residents of the devastated city. It was not true that civilians were starving under Confederate rule, but they were pinched and hungry. The fire made things worse by destroying much of the meager stocks of food left in town. Citizens of both races and all classes begged northern soldiers to share their rations. A journalist who came into town with Union troops described the "gaunt figures, sharp features and general attenuated appearance" of the people, irrespective of their station in life.[8]

Soldiers began distributing food right away, as did private northern charities and local relief efforts. Confederate civilians sometimes accepted these handouts with bad grace, but their Black neighbors were profuse in their gratitude. "They have a word and a smile for our soldiers," a northerner remarked, "the whites cannot do either." In addition to the difference in the manner the food was received, a disparity in treatment manifested itself at the outset, and Black men and women resented it. They saw that white citizens received free food by petitioning for it, but the army required African Americans to work for theirs. It was they who cleared the debris from city streets and rebuilt bridges and buildings, whereas their Confederate neighbors only had to take the oath of allegiance to receive their daily bread. Weitzel justified the different treatment because the loyalty of white people was suspect. To his way of thinking, the freedmen need not take the oath, but they did need an incentive to work. The difference in treatment rankled, as did the condescension that underpinned it.[9]

Near the close of the war, Congress created, under the War Department, the Bureau of Refugees, Freedmen and Abandoned Lands. Everyone called it the Freedmen's Bureau. Under the guidance of a commissioner and assistant commissioners for each Confederate state, it was responsible for aiding the transition to freedom. At first it distributed clothing, food, and fuel to both poor Black and white people, in coordination with northern charities. Later it assisted in creating schools, reuniting families, claiming civil rights, and negotiating for fair wages. Even more portentous for the future of race relations, it attempted to distribute land that the army acquired during the war for the benefit of the freedmen. But the Bureau would not establish a presence in town for two months after the fire, an eternity for people struggling in the confusion of postwar Richmond. In the meantime, African Americans looked to their own to take care of themselves, as they always had done.

Before the war, southern society divided them into the two categories of enslaved and free. The latter carved out a space for themselves at the margins of society, though their lack of any civil rights tempered this simulacrum of freedom. In Richmond and other towns, a growing number of people had gained permission from their enslavers to hire themselves out. That some enslaved people could negotiate wages with employers and arrange for their own room and board troubled the city's white citizens before the war. Afterward, the independence that freedom gave Black people to regulate their own lives magnified that worry.

Men like Albert Royal Brooks achieved a measure of success in this unfriendly environment. A tall man of powerful build, with a dark complexion, shaved head, and high cheekbones, Brooks made an imposing presence. By hiring himself out to a tobacco manufacturer, he earned enough to buy his own freedom and then that of his wife, Lucy

Detail of a photo of a jury pool featuring Albert Royal Brooks (*left*), who owned a taxi service and exemplified Black entrepreneurship in Richmond; and Lewis Lindsay (*right*), a leading African American delegate in the constitutional convention of 1867–68. (The Valentine Museum)

Goode, and their children. With an instinct for entrepreneurship, he invested in a taxi service, a livery stable, and an eatery. He took his place among the leadership of the free Black community and became a founder of First African Baptist Church. Although his success rested in part on the patronage of whites, his achievement was a testimony to Brooks's drive, industry, and creativity. At the beginning of the war, his firm consisted of ten hacks, or taxis, and twenty-two horses, worth ten thousand dollars. As it did for many of his white neighbors, the war and the fire devastated his livelihood. But with self-discipline, resolve, and tact, he set out to rebuild.[10]

The urban work experience of Black people before the war acquainted them with the rhythms of factory labor and the discipline of the clock, with the use of money and the value of bargaining for wages. Underemployment would remain chronic, but they soon found work in brickyards, with drayage firms, along the docks, and in the coal mines west of town, in addition to iron foundries, markets, restaurants, hotels, and tobacco factories. They were more ready and eager to chart their own course in the free labor market than their white neighbors expected. The most common jobs for African American men, and the best paid, were in tobacco processing. For women, the likeliest occupations were in domestic service. Their energy in applying themselves surprised even northern observers, who expected less ability and motivation from people who had been oppressed by bondage.[11]

Almost as soon as white businessmen struggled to reconstitute the banks, which had all fallen victim to the fire, leaders of the Black community looked to their financial future, too. In June, a representative of the Freedmen's Savings and Trust Company of New York spoke to a gathering at the Ebenezer Baptist Church about the value of establishing a branch in Richmond. He described its benefits and suggested that they consider his proposal and give him their opinion at another meeting. But they told him that was not necessary: they wanted the bank right away. It opened a few months later, and thousands opened accounts over the next few years.[12]

In a memorial written later that spring, leaders of the community described their achievement in spite of the hardships of slavery. They claimed that more than six thousand of their number belonged to churches in Richmond and Manchester, the suburb directly across the James River. The whole Black population attended divine services on a regular basis. They were, they said, a sober and caring Christian people. When heartless enslavers turned the sick and aged out of their houses, the community looked after them. In a dig at the army, they boasted that relatively few of them asked for the government rations "so bountifully bestowed upon the unrepentant Rebels of Richmond." Despite the law, they said, perhaps three thousand could read. Several thousand owned property valued at more than two hundred dollars, some at more than one thousand dollars, and even a few at more than five thousand dollars.[13]

Even under the constraints of slavery, through its so-called secret societies the Black community justified Alexis de Tocqueville's wonder at the distinctive American genius for volunteerism. Little is known about them, except that they provided services such as burial insurance and aid to sick and poor members. With emancipation, the need to conceal their existence ceased, and an efflorescence of these benevolent societies blossomed overnight. The United Sons of Love, a prewar entity, and the Lincoln Union Aid Society, created after emancipation, both supported their members in these ways. The Richmond Humane Society, created later that year, grew out of the prewar church tradition of aid for indigent members. Sometimes the names of the societies and fragmented lists of members are all that remains, such as the Mechanics' Union Society, the Young Men's Golden Harp, Soldiers of the Cross Society, and Young Men's Hope Society. Some were women's organizations, such as the Daughters of Salem and Christian Daughters of Peace. They all created special ranks, badges, and costumes that were on display on ceremonial occasions. After freedom came, they expanded the range of activities for socializing that added to community spirit and gave single men and women an opportunity to meet. They also proved a useful means of integrating newcomers to Richmond into the existing community. The societies had in common the chance for members to exercise leadership and hone their political skills. They were hugely popular in the first months after freedom, and dozens surfaced or came into existence by the end of the year.[14]

If emancipation was the most extraordinary feature of the day, the thirst for education was its signal manifestation. With astonishing speed, schools cropped up throughout town, some before northern teachers began arriving to help. There had always been some secret schooling for a few Black students. (It had been illegal to operate schools for them before but not, as was commonly thought, to teach them individually to read and write.) Within two weeks, thousands were attending schools set up with the aid of six Black churches. Northerners Lucy and Sarah Chase had instructed Black pupils for several years in Union-occupied Tidewater Virginia and came to the capital as soon as they could. At a school they helped church members open at First African Baptist as early as April 18, they were soon teaching more than a thousand. They were astonished at the knowledge of their students and discovered that many could read and some could spell a little. Sympathetic northern teachers who came to Richmond knowing nothing about the resilience and strengths of the Black community marveled at the self-reliance of the freed people and the eagerness of their children to learn. Their passion for education became a hallmark of their aspirations in these early days of freedom and far beyond.[15]

By the time Garland White's regiment reached its objective at the western end of Broad Street on April 3, the chaplain had encountered many people begging for news of lost family members. "Among the densely crowded concourse," he wrote, "there were parents looking for children who had been sold south." His heart went out to them. He could see that, uppermost in the minds of many, even as important as thanking God and Abraham Lincoln for deliverance, was the ache for news of missing loved ones. White caught snatches of queries from the conversations that swirled around him as he moved through the crowd. Some of his comrades heard the questions being asked by one particular woman named Nancy, who was bent from age and toil and who came from Hanover County, north of the city. They brought White through the crowd to meet her. As she quizzed him, recognition dawned when she told the astonished chaplain, "This is your mother, Garland, whom you are now talking to, who has spent twenty years of grief about her son."[16]

White's joyful reunion with his mother, and other encounters that happened that day, were the first efforts to knit families back together. They would engross Richmond's Black community for years to come. In the first months after liberation, thousands of former plantation workers took to the roads of rural Virginia to reach the capital because they hoped to find family members there or at least news of where they might be.[17]

Shortly after Francis Pierpont, the unionist governor of Virginia officially recognized by Washington, arrived in Richmond in May, he received a plaintive letter from New Orleans. "About 16 years ago," wrote Stephen Flemming, "I was sold as a Slave from the State of Virginia." That transaction separated him from his wife, Polly, and his five children. He had not heard from or about them in all that time, and he begged the governor for help. In a neat, literate hand, Flemming spelled out the names and ages of his children. He concluded with the hope that Pierpont would "take a little interest in this affair of mine."[18]

Gradually tiny entries, no more than two or three lines long, began to appear at the back of newspapers asking for intelligence about specific individuals. In June the *Whig* ran a notice that read, "Information wanted of Louisa Johnson (colored), wife of Monroe Johnson. Said woman was sold to go to Richmond, Va., in the Spring of 1862." Caroline Ford placed an even more heartrending plea in the same newspaper: "Information wanted of my three children (colored)—John and James, formerly owned by ____ Epps, of Nottoway county, and Nannie, by Lew. Jones, of Nottoway." Such notices—like that by Mary Brown, who hoped to find a daughter who was sold eighteen years earlier—continued to be published into the next year and beyond with diminishing prospects of success.[19]

Here again, the church played a role because Mary Brown's notice ended by requesting that information be sent to her via First African Baptist. Before the war, Black churches had provided an underground postal service that enabled separated enslaved people to maintain contact. Now such clearinghouses could operate in the open. Once it established a presence in Richmond later that summer, the Freedmen's Bureau joined the church to aid families in their searches.

They did not all achieve the happy resolution given to chaplain White. Perhaps more common was the experience of Charles Maho. Like White, he had been sold away from Richmond, in his case to Mississippi, but had escaped. He joined a Black regiment and returned to the capital searching for his wife, only to discover that she had died many years before. To set against that crushing news, he did find a daughter and lived with her after he found work in a tobacco factory. For many others, especially the thousands of vulnerable minor children who had long been separated from their families, reunion must have been a fraught time of renewed uncertainty.[20]

Under slavery, southern society had not recognized the Black family. Afterward, even sympathetic northerners who went south to educate freed people often brought condescending assumptions with them.

Surely enslaved people, they reasoned, being brutalized by servitude and denied legal marriage, could not have developed the values of thrift, sobriety, industry, and virtue so central to northern notions of family and respectability. Sarah Chase was one northern teacher who did not subscribe to such views. She described the moving dignity of Black family life in Richmond. Despite poverty, she wrote, "the house and family [are] scrupulously neat and tidy, the clothes marvelously mended, and the faces radiant with joy, thanksgiving, and hopefulness; though the larder is nearly empty."[21]

The church had always promoted family ties in spite of formidable obstacles. Now that emancipation had lifted slavery's threat to family life, the church was able formally to ratify marriages that had existed before, though lacking in legal sanction. Even the army gave its support, after a fashion. General Halleck, an inveterate worrier with a patronizing attitude toward African Americans, issued General Orders No. 8 on May 27 to address what he thought was the chief problem. The order instructed clergymen and magistrates to teach Black couples about their familial obligations, especially regarding the support and education of their children, and discouraged them from living together unmarried. He need not have worried. In the first several years of freedom, couples hastened to regularize their vows, sometimes in mass ceremonies. Later, the Freedmen's Bureau helped with marriage registers, and the state legislature belatedly recognized prewar African American unions.[22]

Black Richmonders emerged from the shadow of slavery with a network of institutions that enabled them to construct their own definition of freedom. The churches they had created in the antebellum era gave them experience in self-governance to sustain their community beyond nurturing their spiritual life. Secret societies for mutual support and self-help dovetailed with the work of the churches. Most importantly, the extended families that they had maintained in spite of the separations of slavery supported them with emotional bonds. Now the greatest blessing of emancipation enabled them to reconnect and rebuild their families.

With these assets they embarked in April 1865 on a quiet but relentless transition away from enslavement and the meager legal space accorded even the most successful of antebellum free Black people. Out of the public eye, in a variety of private venues, they began to discard the assumptions and trappings of servitude. While the army was busy cleaning up the aftermath of the fire, dispensing food, and encouraging economic activity, and civilian government had not yet been reconstituted, at first Black people enjoyed greater freedom away from the baleful gaze of white supervision than they had ever enjoyed. That would not last. No one could tell them in the exciting days of early April that that supervision would not reassert itself. What did become apparent quite soon was that control over Black men and women would become the insistent leitmotif of white opinion in postwar Richmond as much as it had been under slavery.[23]

John Oliver returned to Virginia in the early postwar days to see how his fellow African Americans were building a new life amid the ruins of the Confederacy. He had been born free in Dinwiddie County south of Richmond but before the war made his home in the North, mainly Boston. A house carpenter who had also taught for the American Missionary Association, he came to visit but ended up staying the rest of his life. Looking back two years after emancipation, he regretted all the lost opportunities of those early days of freedom, and he laid the fault at the feet of white Richmonders. He said they should have been, as they often claimed to be, the best friends of Black people. He himself hoped that would be the case, but it was not so. White people could not see beyond the pain of their lost cause. "The acute agony of defeat," Oliver wrote in a poignant lament over missed chances, seemed to have been taken out on African Americans. And thus "at the very beginning of the new order of things, they made aliens of those whom they should have allied to their interest by every tie of friendship." Even then, he held out hope that white Richmonders would change their ways and welcome Black people as fellow citizens.[24]

In early April, though, the bleak disappointments to come were hidden from the optimistic eyes of the newly free, who could only marvel at the deliverance that jubilee had wrought. Their wildest dreams seemed about to be realized. But that joy was tinged with a nagging fear that those who had held them in bondage were not ready to accept what complete emancipation should mean. Freedom was a precious commodity, still undefined, still unrealized.

3

You Cannot Subjugate Us

April to May 1865

While he waited for General Grant's arrival for the surrender ceremony at Appomattox Court House, former governor Henry Alexander Wise, now a Confederate brigadier, snarled defiance at an inquisitive Union army chaplain. Wise had wrapped a frayed blanket over his filthy uniform to ward off the rain. With his ragged iron-gray beard and slumped posture, he looked the epitome of loss. The northern minister who quizzed him mistook this haggard outward appearance for inner defeat. He saw none of the famous passion in Wise's now-sunken eyes. This could hardly be the celebrated "fire eater" who hanged John Brown at Harpers Ferry more than five years before and then provoked Virginia's secession in 1861. And yet Wise would not concede. He had been "always opposed to this unholy fraternal war," he boasted. Incredulous, the clergyman rebuked him and insisted that it was Wise and men like him who were guilty and ought to hang. "You cannot subjugate us," Wise shot back, "God is with us. . . . The great heart of the South remains unconquered."[1]

Wise had dominated the protracted debates during Virginia's secession crisis. His long hair and lean features gave him the look of a haunted, even dangerous man. Erratic, conceited, slovenly, dribbling tobacco juice down his shirt, he was, despite a hacking cough, a politician of undeniable charm and a speaker of mesmeric power. More than any other Virginian, he had brought on the war that wrought such destruction in the Old Dominion, nowhere more apparent than in its capital. The war had diminished him but had not cowed him. He would

Former Virginia governor and Confederate general Henry Alexander Wise, a leading advocate of the Lost Cause creed. (Virginia Museum of History and Culture)

not admit to error. Though he would never wield formal political power again, he still commanded widespread attention, as he did with that surprised Union chaplain at Appomattox. That appeal soon enabled him to give voice to the way Confederates viewed the war, its causes, and its meaning for the future. As they moved from disbelief to dismay to defiance, that way of looking at their society would give them strength to face the world that bitter defeat had created. But before that could happen, they had to endure a paroxysm of fear, grief, and uncertainty. What form would the North's retribution for the war take?

Before news of Appomattox reached Richmond, and in some cases even weeks after, die-hard Confederate residents convinced themselves that their cause was not yet lost. Their city in ruins and occupied by the hated enemy, they had watched in silence as Lincoln walked through the streets. One of them spitefully wished Jefferson Davis's house had burned to prevent it being sullied by Lincoln's presence. "Those who lived in the finest houses," observed a northern eyewitness, "either stood motionless upon their steps or merely peeped through the window-blinds." Even then they did not all lose faith. A future novelist of the Old South, Constance Cary, then only twenty-one, remembered that "Through all this strain of anguish ran like a gleam of gold the mad vain hope that Lee would yet make a stand somewhere." Mad, vain, and fatuous.[2]

The sign that all was lost came when artillery began firing salutes the evening of April 9, after news of the surrender flashed down the telegraph wires. It was not, as some fleetingly hoped, the cannons of avenging Confederates returning to drive the occupiers from their city. Hundred-gun salutes repeated the next day and into the week following. Their salvos shattered windows in the capitol and thundered oppressively in the ears of despairing white civilians. "We have certainly been thro' a furnace of fire," moaned Margaret Brown Wight after Appomattox. "Lands laid waste and desolate mills, farms burnt, dwelling houses, servants gone. Nearly all the horses taken. Confederate money nothing but waste paper . . . and all this for nothing, *nothing.*" Distraught and depressed, Fanny Young feared that if she dared think about what it all meant, "I almost go mad with horror & fear. . . . So many of our noble young men perished for nothing!" She and thousands of Richmonders like her looked out at their ruined city and bewailed the war as years the locusts had eaten.[3]

If ecstatic joy defined Black religious services, the atmosphere in most white churches could not have been more different. Even in the house of God, worshippers could not escape the scent of ruin billowing up from the ashes around them. At one service, the sound of weeping permeated the sanctuary in the pauses between the minister's prayers for wounded Confederate soldiers.

On the first Sunday after the fire, heartbroken citizens, mainly women in mourning dress with the acrid taste of smoke still lingering on their tongues, filled St. Paul's Episcopal Church, just west of Capitol Square. German-born rector Charles Minnigerode had ministered to his parishioners throughout the war. He had baptized Jefferson Davis and married and buried Confederate notables. He had just outsmarted the Union army over the prayer controversy. Now, as he peered out at his flock through wire-rimmed glasses, he shared their grief and apprehensions for the future. His own son was missing with Lee's army and feared killed. Uriah Painter, a Philadelphia journalist, was there and described the scene at St. Paul's without sympathy. They knew they were beaten, he wrote: "They have lost their all, but hug their pride closer and closer as their troubles thicken and their relatives and friends are swept away." Diana Corbin, daughter of Confederate naval commander Matthew Fontaine Maury, fervently vowed she would forever after wear mourning to remember "my dead Brother and my dead Country." April 3, 1865, brought the immolation of their way of life, and they could not, would not, forget.[4]

Because more battles had been fought in Virginia than in any other state, the Old Dominion suffered greater devastation than the rest of the South. Towns, houses, and barns burned, farms stripped, bridges and railroads destroyed. Central Virginia suffered the greatest losses. Beyond the physical damage loomed the grievous human cost. If few Richmonders died from fire on April 3, many had lost loved ones in the war. A quarter of the South's white men of military age were dead. Accurate figures are elusive, but perhaps as many as forty thousand Virginians died of wounds and disease, three-fourths of them wearing Confederate gray. In the optimistic spring of 1861, they had come filled with the exuberance of youth from farms and hamlets all over the state to join the colors of the new southern nation. Richmond had been their marshaling point in those naïve, euphoric days and then their rallying cry as the war dragged on.[5]

Four years of struggle had ground their cause to dust. Those who survived came home weighted with the emotions of defeat, a witch's brew of dejection, guilt, and anger that would embitter the outlook of many over the years to follow. Many bore outward signs of that trauma. For decades it would be a common sight to see crippled survivors hobbling down the streets on prosthetic legs or bearing empty, pinned-back coat sleeves. It was not just men in uniform who suffered. Wartime privation, hunger, and disease afflicted the civilian population as well, free Black and enslaved as much as Confederate white. But for those in uniform, the months of boredom in camp and the seconds of horror in battle bequeathed that special camaraderie that only brothers in arms could know.

In a cold, soaking rain on April 15, Robert E. Lee returned to Richmond, a paroled prisoner, as testified by the signed and countersigned scrap of paper he carried. He arrived with his headquarters staff in a tiny caravan of tired horses at the south bank of the James River. As they passed over the Union engineers' wooden pontoons, the river current muffled their hoofbeats. It was Lee's first view of Richmond in ruins. Nearby the fire-blackened piers of Mayo's Bridge and the two collapsed railroad trestles loomed up from the mist. Stretching out before the party, rubble rose in terraced ranks where businesses had once bustled with activity. Despite the steady downpour, thin spirals of smoke still rose fitfully from mountains of ash.

Richmond had expected him, and a crowd gathered along his path. The first efforts to cheer him failed. People contented themselves with waving hats and hands in a sad pantomime of welcome. There by chance to record the spectacle was Thomas Chester, the African American journalist who had entered the city with his jubilant United States Colored Troops (USCTs). He admitted that, as Lee approached his borrowed townhouse on Franklin Street near the outer edge of the Burnt District, spectators finally managed to raise a hoarse salute. Careworn and exhausted, Lee bowed to them as he mounted the steps but paid no attention to their entreaty for a speech and shut the door behind him. Another northern journalist who loathed Confederates as much as Chester conceded the dignity of Lee's bearing. But of the people lining the general's path, he concluded, "It was their blasted hopes, their thwarted ambition, as well as their military idol, that rode through the streets of Richmond today, and it is no wonder the people wept."[6]

It was the same day Lincoln died, though the army somehow managed to suppress news of the assassination until the following morning. Robert Ould, the paroled Confederate commissioner for prisoner exchanges, learned the news at dinner at the Spotswood Hotel. Thanks to his Union counterpart, he had been released from custody. Normally composed, Ould blustered that Lincoln's assassination was the worst blow to fall on the South, even worse than Lee's surrender. To the west of town, Alice Payne, the mother of a Confederate soldier, feared blame for Lincoln's death would fall heavily on the South, and she filled her diary with mournful, choked syllables, "Poor Virginia gone gone forever." Unrepentant Richmonders furtively expressed pleasure at the news. Lucy Fletcher sneered to her diary of her "thrill of horror at hearing of his miserable end." On learning the news, Judith McGuire, who had nursed soldiers in a Richmond hospital, could only fret about northern retaliation and blame Lincoln for shedding rivers of southern blood. Few dared voice such sentiments publicly. When a paroled Confederate officer did so at the Ballard House Hotel, Union soldiers beat him senseless.[7]

Soldiers draped the Customs House at the foot of Capitol Square in black on the day of Lincoln's funeral. Black cloth hung above the doors of the capitol and inside on the railing around Jean-Antoine Houdon's marble likeness of Washington, a smaller, more refined progenitor to Crawford's bronze Washington, standing to the west of the statehouse. The jittery army command refused a request from some civilians to gather for public mourning. On the day of the funeral, cannon fire from minute guns reverberated through the streets of the city, reminding its residents they were pariahs in the eyes of the North.

White citizens of Richmond may have begun to take some hope from lenient treatment by the US Army during the first weeks. But that did not mean they had escaped retribution at the hands of the government in Washington. High-ranking Confederates, even those bearing paroles from Appomattox, feared for their lives. They agonized even more after John Wilkes Booth's shocking deed. From their reading of Roman history, southerners educated in the classics knew the lot of those who lost civil wars. But they had no need of ancient precedents to stoke their anxiety. In their own time only two years before, and to the horror of Europe, Russia had put down a revolt in Poland. The czar hanged dozens of rebel leaders and exiled thousands of others. Confederates had every reason to fear the same fate. After Lincoln's death, Henry Spaulding, an angry Union soldier, said, "Let the army loose, & let every man go in & kill and slay." Another soldier stationed in Richmond denounced "traitors who deserve no better fate than [to] be hung between Heaven and earth for foul birds to pick their bones."[8]

These were private soldiers' jottings, but Confederates could read similar enraged comments in the northern papers that were soon circulating in Richmond. Even before the assassination, the *Philadelphia Inquirer*'s man in town demanded that some sacrificial Confederates must hang or rebels would see treason "as a fashionable amusement instead of a capital crime." Even more chilling were the words spoken by then vice president Andrew Johnson, a stubborn bigot who had little love for the freedmen but who burned with a poor man's hatred of slave-owning grandees. "I would arrest them," he told a crowd in Washington celebrating the fall of Richmond. "I would try them; I would convict them, and I would hang them." Thomas Chester believed high-born Virginians privately lamented that Lincoln would have spared even Jefferson Davis, but they expected no mercy from Johnson.[9]

These were the fears that agitated members of the Maury family as they looked out on their burned city with contempt for their occupiers and despair for their cause. The patriarch, Commander Matthew Fontaine Maury, had been in Britain on a purchasing mission for the Confederate navy and was in the West Indies on the way home when he learned of Appomattox. His family warned him against returning and worried that he had no idea of the danger. "We, and all of his friends, think it is worse than madness for him to think of coming now," one of them wrote. Johnson's threatened punishment for Confederate leaders seemed all too real. "Many will be hanged, many exiled," Maury's cousin insisted. "What good can you do the State by coming here and hanging[?]," he pleaded.[10]

Prominent civilians who did not fear for their lives nevertheless dreaded punishment for aiding the rebellion. Susan Wood Hoge had no such worry for herself but did for her clergyman husband. With a high collar secured by a broach, and her hair pulled back primly from her face, she may have seemed the demure stereotype of a minister's wife, but that modest appearance concealed a stoic, iron personality. Her husband was Moses Drury Hoge, whose sermons from the pulpit of Second Presbyterian Church had thundered righteous support for

Susan Wood Hoge was an equal partner with her minister husband, Moses Drury Hoge, in building Second Presbyterian Church into one of the most vibrant prewar congregations in the city. (Virginia Museum of History and Culture)

the cause. As chaplain to the Confederate Congress, he fled town with Jefferson Davis. Level-headed and practical, Susan remained behind to manage their large household next to the church. On the morning of April 3, explosions from the arsenal broke all her windows, and embers set fire to her house three times. Displaying great composure, she coolly went up on the roof and, with the help of the church's sexton, put out the flames with wet blankets. Three weeks later, she conceded that Generals Weitzel and Ord were polite to civilians but thought Halleck was likely to be tyrannical. She fumed at a sermon preached by the Rev. Dr. Thomas Moore of First Presbyterian because he dared to say Richmond after the assassination was far more grief-stricken than if it had been Jefferson Davis who died.

Susan was of two minds about advising Moses to return home. Writing him formally as "My dear husband" in a neat, tiny hand, she bluntly told him he should expect to find much that was disagreeable.

She resigned herself to the fact of defeat and told him that, if they were to endure the new regime, "we must make up our minds to suffer." He could not adjust as quickly as his pragmatic spouse. His Calvinist certitude seemed to have abandoned him. She thought he looked twenty years older when he returned home a month later, brokenhearted, "crushed & utterly cast down." He admitted he felt like a shipwrecked sailor. Only sleep allowed him to escape his profound sense of humiliation. Exile in England had no appeal. He knew Confederates there would be viewed like those defeated Polish rebels, "the object of pity dashed with contempt and not even of sympathy."[11]

Others did act on the impulse of exile. For a time, the allure of Latin America beckoned. Matthew Fontaine Maury heeded the warnings of his Richmond relatives not to return and instead sailed to Mexico. Short and stocky, with a massive head and pronounced limp from an old injury, Maury had earned an international reputation as an oceanographer and the sobriquet "Pathfinder of the Seas" for his findings. He built up the US Naval Observatory in Washington but resigned when Virginia seceded and joined the Confederate navy. Unwilling to relinquish the secessionist dream of an independent republic, in Mexico he tried to create a "New Virginia" under the auspices of the hapless Emperor Maximilian's immigration scheme. Few other Confederates followed. Even his closest friends could not be enticed. His project collapsed, along with Maximilian's ill-starred French regime. Others tried Brazil; none succeeded. Their failure to re-create the antebellum slave South and their gradual return home dissuaded others from following.[12]

The problems caused by the influx of Confederate soldiers worsened as April wore on. Some arrived singly, some in small regimental groups. Thousands of them congregated in the center of town and sought paroles from the army. Provost Marshal Patrick knew he had to move out the soldiers who were not residents of the city because more would be coming in, at the rate of several hundred a day. The combination of rebel soldiers and emancipated men, women, and children who streamed into town threatened to overwhelm the army's efforts to feed them. At the Spotswood Hotel officers wearing blue and gray occasionally got into arguments. Patrick thought it best to forbid them both from carrying sidearms. A constant stream of Confederate generals from the prewar army called on him, claiming him, he wryly observed, as an old friend.[13]

More poignant were the reunions among family members who had chosen different sides. Sandy Henderson served as chief engineer on the ironclad monitor USS *Onondaga* that helped keep Confederate warships bottled up on the James River below the city. He was the only member of his family to remain loyal to the Union when war broke out. Afterward, he went to his father's house in Richmond, where he found his unrepentant Confederate brother. The engineer secured a three-day parole for him and then took him to the gunboat where he loaned him money and gave him food and clothing. But at the end of the three days, when his brother would not recant his Confederate allegiance, he took him to Castle Thunder, the former southern jail that now warehoused obdurate rebels.[14]

The army's policies for handling veterans of Lee's army complicated matters because they kept changing. A stickler for military etiquette, General Patrick grumbled to his diary, "I have no policy marked out, no chance to establish a policy, inasmuch as it is not known what the policy is to be." General Ord provided transport to those trying to reach northern ports for a connecting passage to the Deep South. Grant criticized Ord's leniency and ordered him to stop helping Confederates. But he was not on the ground in Richmond and could not see the crisis brewing with the great influx of rebel soldiers. Confusion among Union officers over what benefits parole conferred added to the problem.[15]

In contrast to the desire of Confederate soldiers and rural Black people to get to Richmond, some residents were equally desperate to escape. Henri Garidel, a grumpy, pipe-smoking Creole who had worked as a lowly Confederate clerk, mourned the fall of the city. He could not take his mind off being separated from his family in New Orleans. Chronic gastric distress aggravated his dour temperament. Buffeted by the latest rumors about what the victors intended, he confided to his diary that he was going mad. Out of work, penniless, and stranded far from home, he despaired of being able to leave, even if he could get permission. He took petty pleasure in seeing federal soldiers blocking African Americans from congregating on Capitol Square and marveled at the might of the Union army as it marched through town on the way to Washington. After many futile trips to the post office looking for letters from his wife, Lolo, he retreated to his shabby boardinghouse and bemoaned his fate. A devout Catholic, he went to mass nearly every day to pray for reunion with his family. Finally, more than two months later, he secured passage on a steamer out of "this prison of Richmond."[16]

Fannie Taylor Dickinson lived with her husband and children in her parents' house next to an army camp on the western edge of town. Like her minister husband, Alfred, she was a fervent, optimistic Confederate. When she learned that the city would be surrendered, she broke down and cried. Five days after the fire, she learned what the great upheaval in southern society meant for white Richmonders. "Last night on ringing the bell for Millie," Dickinson wrote in her diary, "she was nowhere to be found." Millie was the forerunner. After another week, all of the Black people in the household departed. "Today," wrote Fannie, "our servants have all left. Father offered them higher wages but they preferred to set up for themselves. This is indeed the unkindest cut of all. I cannot write about it." She could not imagine why they might want to be independent of white authority and make their own way in the world.[17]

Many others exhibited the same self-pitying anxiety over the effects of emancipation. Feeling sorry for themselves in their reduced circumstances did not augur well for the future of race relations. "No one who was not here will ever fully appreciate the horrors of that day," Mary Fontaine wrote. "Our Richmond servants were completely crazed," she sniffed. "They danced and shouted, men hugged each other, and women kissed, and such a scene of confusion you have never seen." The sight of Black children playing on Capitol Square, formerly denied to them, distressed Lucy Fletcher, the mother of five who had lost close relatives in combat. "Hundreds of ragged & dirty negro boys are rolling over the beautiful grass," raged this unforgiving minister's wife.

"Throughout the grounds, dirty tents are placed for the sale of cakes & pies, & this is Yankee *civilization!* I hope they enjoy each other's society." Margaret Brown Wight scoffed at former slaves flocking into town from the countryside, saying they were unpleasantly surprised when the army put them to work. The loss of the customary deference they had come to expect from Black people angered women like Wight. They were unprepared for the confident bearing of the United States Colored Troops entering the city, well drilled and not at all the image described in Confederate propaganda. They were right to fear the example that would set for the city's freed people.[18]

Suddenly people who owned property, whether in slaves or land, found all the trappings and institutions of law that protected their privileges stripped away. "We are fearful of opening our mouths," one complained. "We cannot vote. We have no government or organization whatever save the military. We have no courts, no magistrates, no constables, no police, no judges, no notaries public." The effort to restore the elements of local civil society seemed agonizingly slow. As that process began, uppermost in the minds of many white Richmonders was the need to control the people they had held in bondage just days before. That assumption of command pervaded and aggravated relations between the races. It rested on an inequality that African Americans no longer accepted. For the moment, the latter were too busy trying to earn their daily bread to think of politics, but not many days passed before some of them began to campaign for equal rights.[19]

To awe the locals and keep their soldiers occupied when most had only thoughts of returning to home and family, Union commanders staged elaborate full-dress reviews. George Templeton Strong, an indefatigable charity worker from New York, wanted to see the fallen rebel capital for himself. While there he observed a grand review at the end of April that stretched the length of Main Street. In his waspish prose he described "black regiments and white, alternating like the keys of a piano." But that occasion could not equal May 6, a day of beautiful sunshine, when residents witnessed the grand spectacle of a portion of the victorious northern army march through town on its way to Washington. Led by

Major General George Gordon Meade and staff, the long columns of the Second and Fifth Corps broke their camp of the previous night in Manchester on the south bank of the James and surged across the pontoon bridges into town, a blue juggernaut of immense strength.[20]

The Richmond garrison determined to give their comrades a rousing reception on their path through the city. As Meade rode past the escort on Governor Street, drums rolled and regimental flags waved, many bearing the names of battlefields across the South. Meade, the short-tempered commander of the Army of the Potomac at Gettysburg, lifted his hat in salute. The organizers had laid out the line of march to take in the main sites of Richmond so that the veterans who had besieged it could take home memories of the prostrate Confederate capital. When they passed by Lee's house on Franklin Street, a cheer went up from the column. One of the officers told the press that between forty-five thousand and fifty thousand men marched in the parade and took nearly six hours to pass. When one watched that spectacle, mused the depressed Louisiana Creole Henri Garidel, "you are no longer surprised that we were simply crushed."[21]

Beyond Richmond, America moved fitfully toward the end of war. It did not follow a straight line. On April 21, Lincoln's funeral train departed Washington on its sad, slow journey to Springfield, Illinois. Four days later, soldiers ran the assassin to ground in a Virginia barn and killed him. The day after they cornered Booth, on the Mississippi the side-wheel steamer *Sultana* exploded and killed more than a thousand, mostly emaciated Union prisoners returning home from Andersonville. On May 4, Confederate forces surrendered in Alabama, Mississippi, and Louisiana. Six days later, soldiers captured the fugitive Jefferson Davis in Georgia. Two days after that, the last skirmish took place at Palmito Ranch, Texas, a minor, futile Confederate victory. At the end of the month, demobilization accelerated quickly after a grand review of the Union armies in Washington. Private soldiers and general officers alike scrambled to return to civilian life.

Most white Richmonders could not move on with their lives so easily. For four years, their newspapers had demonized the North and primed readers to fear Union victory. A quick succession of emotions limned their reaction to that outcome. Their initial doubts turned to despair when they had to accept the bitter truth of Lee's surrender. Then, in short order, they accepted the outcome but with a cold recalcitrance that would shadow their city for years to come.

Thomas Chester, the Black journalist who marched in with Weitzel's army, saw residents in the fashionable part of town peering out their windows at the conquering foe. "There was," he claimed, "no mistaking the curl of their lips and the flash of their eyes." They did not drop their hostility, even when the occupiers displayed courtesy and sometimes even solicitude for their reduced plight. Once persuaded that Union soldiers were not bent on rape and pillage, Confederate women took pleasure in snubbing them on the streets. When Provost Marshal Patrick's men arrested a woman for wearing a Confederate flag in her hair, he scolded her and sent her home. It is unlikely she was as penitent after that admonition as he believed. A northern visitor described residents like her as "gloomy, sullen, subjugated, in despair of the Confederacy yet hating the Union." The anger would not subside soon. A southern veteran spat at a British visitor some months later, "We have taken the oath of allegiance, & will obey their laws, but we are not going to love them."[22]

It was not the case, as some northerners later claimed, that defeated Confederates were so submissive in the first few weeks after Appomattox that they would have meekly acquiesced in the complete restructuring of southern society. This was the later view of Republicans who advocated a sterner policy toward the South than the one Andrew Johnson announced at the end of May. They wanted to blame him for allowing a golden opportunity to slip away. What this interpretation got wrong was the fact that defeated white southerners were consistently hostile: there never was a chance the victors could recast southern society. An astute northern observer wrote that Richmond's placid surface masked private hatred. The citizens, he said, with the exception of a few hotheads, respected the authority of the army, "but underneath this calm, society is seething and boiling."[23]

If some, like Elizabeth Munford, were willing to take the oath of allegiance and move on, many others could not. Anne Hobson, the twenty-seven-year-old daughter of former governor Wise, bewailed defeat as the realization of what it meant sunk in. "The results of years might not have changed life as much as these six days have done," she cried with selfish anguish after a week. "My God! What have I suffered, what do I not still suffer."[24]

After so much bloodshed and so much enmity, it would take years, in some cases generations, for the fiery hatred of people like Hobson to cool. After the death of their cause and of so many of their young men, they endorsed with hardened hearts the words printed in the *Richmond Dispatch* just before fire consumed it. After the destruction of southern society, the editor raged, "the future unity of America is a dream of maniacs." Matthew Fontaine Maury's cousin spoke for adamant Confederates everywhere when he despaired that Virginia would remain a conquered province. Even so, he would not atone for his actions or disavow his principles. "Our masters are thirsting for our blood," he raged with fury at southern defeat. "Every man's hand seems red with the blood of my brothers and friends. I will not shake them in friendship." That hostility underscored the racial animosity and civil-military tension that characterized the city for months to come.[25]

4
Charred Ruins

April to June 1865

For a year after the fire, residents became accustomed to seeing Peter Michie directing crews of surveyors with theodolites and chains making observations around the city. A handsome officer with dark, wavy hair and ample muttonchop whiskers, he had finished West Point during the war and rose to be chief engineer of Godfrey Weitzel's army facing Richmond from the east. He supervised the construction of massive earthworks and took pride in them, as is apparent from a photograph of a straw-hatted Michie at the bottom of a deep trench in the siege works surveying his handiwork. Two days after Richmond fell, he laid the first pontoons across the James River and later built a permanent bridge to replace them.

Michie's greatest achievement and legacy, however, came after the fighting ended. His map of Richmond and vicinity recorded in the minutest detail what the city looked like at the end of the war. It was not published until 1867, but it preserves a remarkable graphic snapshot of the last days of the Confederate citadel and the fortifications surrounding it. Michie's surveyors drew in every structure according to scale on each city block, including the meanest outbuildings. The curved landscaped paths in Capitol Square appear in painstaking outline, as do islands in the river and the neat rows of barracks in the Chimborazo military hospital. Even the names of individual landowners appear on houses outside the built-up area. But most telling are the many city blocks below the capitol that lack any detail at all, in stark contrast to the finely etched lineaments of the surrounding squares. Here, in

In this detail of the postwar map created by Peter Michie's US topographical engineers, Capitol Square stands out at the top center, with curved garden paths surrounding Jefferson's neoclassical capitol. The great expanse of ashes in the Burnt District, rendered as empty blocks, stretches to the James River below. (National Archives)

acres of cinders and forlorn rubble, unrelieved by any structure, was the bequest of the great fire, a tabula rasa of defeat crosshatched by the mapmakers in undifferentiated gray.

Two days after flames obliterated all those buildings—on the same day Michie's men were stringing their first canvas pontoons across the river—J. B. Jones, a dyspeptic clerk in the Confederate War Department, toted up the mute victims of destruction. "The burnt district," he cried, "includes all the banks, money-changers, and principal speculators and extortioners. This seems like a decree from above!" It would remain the distinctive mark of Richmond for months to come.[1]

Michie opened an office in the Customs House at the foot of Capitol Square, where he could see the expanse of ruins. He groused that exorbitant rents forced him to seek personal quarters two miles beyond the city limits. But he was a diligent engineer with an indefatigable work ethic. During the war he was always ready to be where the fighting was hottest, according to the blunt, pugnacious General Ord. He appreciated that drive in the younger man ("worth his weight in gold as an Engineer") and perhaps saw something of himself in Michie. He candidly told General Grant that because Michie's permanent rank was only lieutenant, he gave him the brevet, or temporary rank, of brigadier because he had to support his mother and sisters. In fact, it was not solicitude for Michie's impecunious family but the understandable desire to keep his exceptional talent within his command that motivated Ord.[2]

Michie would stay in Richmond long after the army sent Ord packing. He began compiling his great work while small fires still flared up unexpectedly amid the mountains of ash. Indeed, they continued to do so as late as the end of June. By late summer, some halting progress in rebuilding had begun. That meant that his map was out of date before it was complete, as new structures slowly began to replace the detritus of loss. Finding capital for rebuilding and stitching together degraded transportation links were necessary steps if the economy was to be restarted. Less promising were the revival of enterprises of questionable value and the resurgence of criminal activity. Moreover, rebuilding shops, factories, and banks took place in parallel with the fraught and far harder work of framing a yet-undefined new social and political architecture for the city.

Richmond is a city of hills, and in April 1865 many of them looked down on scenes of devastation. Capitol Square, the center of the government quarter, occupied the most important one. The view from it, looking to the south toward the James River, encompassed the industrial and transportation nodes that had fostered Richmond's wealth, a view that now took in the void left by burned warehouses and factories. The mansions and churches of the rich who enjoyed that wealth clustered close around the square to its north and west. They all survived the fire.

The land fell off sharply to the east of the capitol into Shockoe Valley, bisected by a fetid creek lined with tanneries and slaughterhouses and their noxious effluvia. To the east of the valley, Church Hill denoted an older quarter of the city, and beyond it the Chimborazo plain and its vast Confederate hospital complex. The working classes mostly lived in the low-lying parts of Richmond close to their places of work, along the river and canal. Large mills and foundries dotted the landscape along those transportation links. In a warren of narrow streets and alleys from Capitol Square to Shockoe Valley, jails and auction halls had supported the slave trade. Bars, brothels, theaters, and gambling dens clustered around them. To the west of town loomed the penitentiary on its own hill, and, west of it, Hollywood Cemetery perched on a high bluff overlooking the river.

The war cost the South two-thirds of its assessed wealth—more if the value of enslaved people was counted—half of its livestock, half of its manufacturing capital. Such abstract aggregates meant little to Richmonders. They only had to look around them to see the grievous state of the city's utilities, transportation, factories, and housing stock. Those losses, and the lack of gainful employment for a despondent people, made the task of rebuilding a challenge of daunting proportions.

Outside the Burnt District, that portion of Richmond the fire had spared turned a shabby face to the world after years of neglect. Few buildings had seen new paint since the prosperous days before secession. Fewer could boast a pedigree more recent than early 1861. Gradually, the sounds of masons chipping mortar from scorched bricks and of carpenters sawing and nailing new lumber resounded here and there through the ruins but not at breakneck speed. Nor, for a time, were the first buildings as substantial as the ones they replaced. Eventually new and better warehouses, mills, and factories would rise in place of those the fire erased. But questions about legal title and dearth of capital caused a maddening delay to rebirth.

Not just businesses burned on April 3. Many people lived over their shops and were left homeless by the flames. Their misfortune exacerbated a preexisting housing shortage. It began during the war and was made worse by the influx of Confederate veterans and rural African Americans after Appomattox. Every space with a roof, it seemed, even the humblest shack, was inhabited. Widespread squalor marred much of the city. High rents bedeviled Richmond and incited protests into the next year. To alleviate the shortage in the near term, the Union army designated former Confederate army camps as temporary shelter for the homeless.

Because the fire destroyed the commercial heart of town along Main Street, for the first months afterward business shifted to the north along Broad Street, beyond Capitol Square. The center of business would eventually drift back to Main, but for the moment, a rash of temporary buildings mushroomed amid the ruins there. These hybrid shanties, favored by the sutlers who followed the army and sold provisions to soldiers, disfigured the cityscape and were criticized as eyesores. Part brick, part wood, part canvas, they called to mind, someone said, the coarse structures in San Francisco during the Gold Rush. Aside from their ugly facades, they were susceptible to fire, something no one wanted to see again.

No serious rebuilding could be possible without a large infusion of capital, and Richmond was broke. William Macfarland, lawyer, bank president, and former member of the legislature and the Confederate Congress, took a leading part in the search for financial backing. Some thought him overbearing and pompous, but others considered him a sympathetic man. A colleague at the bar said he had the habit of shifting as much work as possible onto his associates. Another unkind observer called him a "curly-headed poodle . . . nearly overcome with dignity and fat." But the urbane manners of the sixty-six-year-old appealed to many of his fellow Richmonders, and they chose him for varied positions of leadership. He was a vestryman at St. Paul's Episcopal Church, director of Hollywood Cemetery, and vice president of the Virginia Historical Society. He also had an African American half sister.[3]

There was great excitement on April 25 when officials of Macfarland's Farmer's Bank of Virginia opened a vault they had retrieved from the ashes. The fire had consumed the building along with every other financial institution in the city. The contents of the vault survived intact, but Macfarland knew beforehand that when they opened it, they would find only private papers and a few valuables owned by individuals. He had sent the bank's specie, some $200,000 in coin and bullion, for safekeeping with the Confederate Treasury on the night of the evacuation.

On the day the vault was opened, the gold and silver were still in the hands of Jefferson Davis's fugitive regime, still uncaptured somewhere in the Deep South. A mirage forever disappearing into the distance, that treasure would continue to allure and bedevil Macfarland over the next few years. But for the present, he and his fellow bankers sought more likely sources of funding.

Two weeks after the fire, a group of six local financiers joined with bankers from Washington, DC, to establish the First National Bank of Richmond. The day it opened for business in the Customs House, surrounded by ruins, General Philip Sheridan's cavalrymen clattered en masse through the streets on their way to a grand victory parade in the national capital. Other banks received charters that spring and with First National held the majority of the city's meager deposits. The problem remained: how to attract the much greater sums of new capital required for large-scale rebuilding?

In June a New Jersey real estate agent, J. A. Martin, came to town with a proposal for financing new buildings in the Burnt District. He interviewed General Ord and Macfarland and then made his pitch at a meeting of business owners in the state senate chamber. He told them he could raise $10 million for construction, with real estate as collateral. He said he could attract that much northern money, but only if the real estate was fairly valued, and that was a problem. He candidly told the gathering that after investigating Richmond properties, he thought most owners of empty lots were greatly exaggerating their value. Other attendees agreed and urged property holders to sell their lots if they could not afford to rebuild on them. Martin's plan went nowhere because questions of ownership remained.[4]

An astute outsider observed at the end of April that "the city still continues to wear the same inanimate appearance, business of all kinds being almost virtually suspended." The dearth of warehouses caused by the fire sent commercial rents skyrocketing. Serious impediments stood in the way of a robust renaissance. Most insurance companies lost all their records to the flames. Even greater uncertainty arose not just from lack of capital but from questions of title that would not be resolved until the federal government decided on the fate of Richmond's ruling class. President Johnson delayed announcing his policy for Reconstruction and terms for granting amnesty until late May, and when he did, the uncertainty over who owned Richmond and the right to rebuild it intensified.[5]

The city had been the transportation and communications hub of Virginia in 1861, but four years of war had comprehensively wrecked its infrastructure. The US Military Railroad Service took over and repaired several lines after the army marched into town and turned them over to private owners by summer. Four of the five railroads into Richmond operated for at least some distance outside the city by the end of April. But the old problem of not having connections between lines inside the city persisted. The teamsters and hostelries that profited from transfer of goods and passengers from one railroad station to another remained hostile to such a consolidation, as they did in most cities of the era.

Confederate engineers had done their work too well on the night of the evacuation. Reestablishing links across the James River did not happen quickly. The Richmond & Danville Railroad was able to use the fire-blackened granite piers of its burned bridge to build another and was back in operation in summer. Although service extended to Danville again, engines could only creep along at ten miles per hour because of wartime damage to the roadbed. Bridging the river south to Petersburg took a year longer. Extending north from the city, the Richmond, Fredericksburg & Potomac Railroad confronted numerous burned and damaged bridges. By the end of May, passengers could make a more circuitous route to Washington by riding the Virginia Central line west almost to Charlottesville and then switching to the Orange & Alexandria Railroad northeastward toward the Potomac River. Pedestrians and horse-drawn vehicles that had relied on the Mayo family's toll bridge fared a little better, but at a cost. To replace that burned causeway, Peter Michie's engineers built a new covered bridge by the end of June and removed the temporary bridge. But the pontoons had been free. Now the tolls that had enriched the Mayos were back in place.[6]

The James River was Richmond's original link to the wider world. The US Navy opened passage to the city quickly enough. But hulks the rebels had sunk to deter Union attack and the remains of their own scuttled gunboats had to be demolished to afford safe access to the capital. A year later the wreck of the Confederate naval academy's school ship, CSS *Patrick Henry,* sunk during the evacuation, still threatened vessels coming to the Rocketts Landing wharf. A longer-term problem was the inability or unwillingness of Richmond's government to dredge the river on a regular basis. The James River and Kanawha Canal had offered a waterway to the west before the war but was inoperative by 1865. Lapsed maintenance and Union cavalry raids had left many locks breached and canalboats burned, sunk, or expropriated. The vision of a water passage through the mountains to the Ohio River beyond beguiled Richmonders after the war, as it had done before. They poured scarce capital into reviving that obsolete dream even though railroads had long surpassed canals. They were fortunate, however, that traffic on the canal, slow as it was, had resumed a month after the fire.[7]

Communication with the outside world was as difficult right after the fire as transportation. The tardy restoration of postal connections with the rest of the South slowed the revival of commerce and hindered private correspondence. Although the army had its military telegraph link to Washington, commercial lines were not erected until mid-May. A further private line and two for the press joined the city to Washington by July. The city's water and gas utilities suffered from neglect. When it was repaired, the gas works, near the Rocketts steamboat landing, served public buildings, several thousand homes, and a thousand street lamps. Subscribers complained when service was restored that it cost too much and smelled bad in the bargain. The waterworks west of town escaped wartime damage but fell increasingly behind in supplying enough potable water for the growing population.[8]

Some of the earliest restored economic activity was not what the city's leaders would have desired. Prostitution, illegal liquor sales, gambling dens, blackface minstrel shows, and theatricals of a similar low quality, all of which targeted the more than ten thousand northern soldiers stationed in and around the city, swung into action almost immediately. In all of these mainstays of Richmond's poorly regulated demimonde, racial barriers were blurred. The cash nexus was what counted, not skin color or political allegiance. Gradually the signs over the lowliest bars, picked out in gold lettering, reflected the changing times. Saloons such as the Rebel, the Lee, and the Stonewall were rechristened to cater to Union tastes as the Olive Branch, the White Dove, and the General Grant.[9]

During the war, the New Richmond Theatre had thrived under the direction of an energetic English scapegrace named Richard d'Orsay Ogden. He had entertained Confederate soldiers, was thrown into jail for draft dodging, and earned the opprobrium of Richmond's press. Being accused of making "the temple of Thespis a cess-pool of excrement and foul vapours" apparently only increased his popular appeal. The bite of the humor in his productions sometimes landed him in trouble. He was once set upon and beaten severely by men who took exception to his artistry. Later he got into a gunfight with a journalist who took offense when Ogden claimed he had called a Black man a gentleman.

For actors, it was believed that Richmond and other southern cities were more congenial than their northern counterparts, and so it continued after the war. Ogden convinced the city's new masters to allow him to reopen his theater only two nights after the fire. His success was ensured by inviting General Weitzel and staff, decking out the hall with masses of American flags, and inserting northern patriotic songs throughout the hodgepodge of dances, music, and ballads. At the Varieties Opera House on Franklin Street, Buckley and Budd's United Minstrels and Brass Band had an audience of Union soldiers guffawing over stereotyped blackface characters. They made sure to include plenty of political jokes appropriate to the new regime. A short distance away at Metropolitan Hall, Wray's Combination Ethiopian and Burlesque Opera Troupe served up similar low fare. Musicians, performers, and theatergoers kept up an unholy racket far into the night.[10]

Like the theaters, the densest maze of brothels, in the crooked lanes east of Capitol Square along Locust Alley, next to slave jails and auction houses, escaped the fire. Appealing to a variety of appetites and unconcerned about upholding racial barriers, they were back in business overnight and eager to relieve northern troops of their greenbacks as soon as they set foot in town. A Union surgeon, Norton Folsom of the Forty-Fifth USCT regiment, estimated that one thousand prostitutes plied their trade in as many as one hundred brothels. He tried to institute a system of medical inspection and treatment of those found to have venereal disease. A cure was beyond the reach of medical science in 1865, and infected soldiers were preyed upon by hucksters touting bogus antidotes. A doctor from Washington, DC, boasting of ridding both men and women of certain unnamed diseases, started advertising soon after the army set up residence. Wittingly or not, veterans on both sides took home with them a dreaded venereal scourge that ravaged their wives and sweethearts.[11]

Public health concerns extended beyond the sex trade. Because the city earmarked no money for trash pickup, the stench of rotting garbage and outdoor privies pervaded the streets. Empty lots became dumping grounds and attracted plagues of flies and rats. Abattoirs and tanneries in the low-lying areas along the river and the polluted Shockoe Creek added their poisonous reek to the mix. The fetid aroma of Richmond in the summer of 1865, as well as the sight of its ruins, did not inspire confidence in its future. A month after the fire, the army began a campaign to inoculate all residents against smallpox, free of charge.[12]

Like the bawdy houses and theaters, many gambling emporiums survived the fire. They attracted petty criminals and became so noxious that the army cracked down on faro banks and other games of chance later in the summer. Unwilling to admit that most crime was homegrown, the press blamed flamboyantly dressed young men from the North "who make the bar-rooms and brothels noisy by day and night." A visitor in a nearby boardinghouse sandwiched between two theaters said she could not sleep because of "the noise of the performers, & stamping, yelling screeching, shouting, as if bedlam had broke loose." The papers were filled with gruesome accounts of beatings, drunkenness, garottings, rape, murder, thievery, and other crimes. In their letters home, Union soldiers complained of being preyed on by the locals, Black and white.[13]

The newspapers often exaggerated criminal activity as a way of blaming disorder on freed people, but no one disputed that crimes high and low seemed to characterize Richmond more than they had any time before. Poverty and overcrowding played their part. The great influx of rural Black newcomers, Confederate veterans in transit, and the Union garrison all contributed to lawlessness. To law-abiding citizens, it all seemed to have made their city an increasingly dangerous place. Even junk dealers were suspect. They occupied a gray area where stolen goods changed hands. They found a booming trade in selling scrap metal gleaned from battlefields to blacksmiths and foundries. When that supply dried up, they turned to stealing iron fences and pipes. Infractions of all kinds produced a sad parade of defendants overflowing the docket of the Mayor's Court for misdemeanors.

As the exhilaration of victory faded into the boredom of garrison duty, the army faced its own problems with crime and indiscipline. Garland White, the African American chaplain who entered Richmond the day of the fire and found his mother, saw military justice at its severest. Samuel Mapp, a Marylander recruited by the Tenth United States Colored Troops, had helped eradicate slavery in the Confederate capital only to be executed by a firing squad of his comrades for flouting an order from a white officer. Chaplain White accompanied Mapp to the place of execution and said a brief prayer for the condemned man. As the crash of the volley from twelve blue-coated soldiers died out, White recalled, it was "the saddest spectacle I ever witnessed."[14]

Some shopkeepers, even those dispossessed by the fire, were quick to reopen. Tom Griffin, a free Black restaurateur who had catered dinner parties for well-heeled Confederates, lost two establishments in the fire. He nevertheless opened up in a new location only two weeks later. He rented one of the iron-front buildings on Governor Street and sought a permit from the army to satisfy old customers and new ones with ready northern cash.

John Dooley, a prosperous Irish immigrant, had built a large hat factory before the war. Richmonders were well acquainted with the gilded sign that marked his retail outlet. When ill health forced his discharge from the Confederate army, he founded the Richmond Ambulance Committee. On the night of the evacuation, one of Dooley's sons ran down to the shop to retrieve papers from the store's office before civil order collapsed. He was just in time to lock the door behind him, but that only momentarily deterred looters, who soon ransacked the premises. It did not matter. All of the Dooley establishment, shop and factory, went up in smoke, consuming three decades of work in a matter of minutes. When another son returned from Confederate service and saw the city's ruins for the first time, he could not write about them in his diary and vowed revenge for defeat. His father, however, chose to focus on rebuilding rather than vengeance. He announced the reopening of his hat shop in June, relocated, like Tom Griffin's restaurant, to an iron-front building on Governor Street. It would take longer to rebuild the factory.[15]

Pharmacist Robert Warren Powers was more fortunate. His house was on Broad Street well away from the Burnt District, and his drugstore survived the blaze. Just before the Union army marched in, Powers raced down to his store to collect guns he had stored there and threw them into the river, just to be safe. The next day he received permission from the provost marshal to reopen. His was the first business to do so. From a meager stock of medicine, he compounded a few simple prescriptions and dispensed them free of charge.[16]

Benjamin Lewis Blackford, a twenty-year-old Confederate mapmaker from Lynchburg, could hardly believe his luck. When he reached Richmond in May, few southern veterans could find work. But when General Michie asked him to join the US Army team surveying the city, he seized the chance. Before secession, his parents had advocated gradual emancipation. His pious, humorless mother, Mary Berkeley Minor Blackford, was said to have hidden a copy of *Uncle Tom's Cabin* under her bed. But when war came, the five Blackford sons served the Confederacy. His elders despaired of Blackford's indolent habits, but like other bright, nonchalant boys, he displayed a knack for finding his way in the world seemingly without effort. Now the offer of $1,200 a year in Union greenbacks to continue making maps under a different flag overcame any doubts Blackford had about taking the oath of allegiance. He was, he blithely wrote a brother, "amused at being in command of Yankee soldiers."[17]

Bacon Tait managed the transition to peacetime easily too, all the more remarkable for the unsavory nature of his business. As a young man he had made a fortune in the interstate slave trade, one of the chief props of Richmond's economy. For more than three decades, from a slave jail in Shockoe Bottom he profited from the degrading commerce in human beings. He despaired, however, of ever finding a respectable white woman who would marry him. His profession made him an undesirable choice, even to many families that owned slaves, and he lived a lonely life. Like other successful Richmond human traffickers, he began a marriage-like relationship with a free woman of color, Courtney Fountain, and raised four children with her. Because he was wealthy, he moved his interracial family to Salem, Massachusetts, and shuttled back and forth between there and his thriving business in Richmond. In his absence, his manager Sidnum Grady looked after the slave jail.

Because Tait invested his slave-trading profits in real estate that survived the evacuation fire, his finances emerged largely intact from the ashes of the system that had enriched him. One transaction, among many, illustrated his adroit dealings. During the war he rented out land he owned to a Confederate hospital and then profited from the use of that same property by the Freedmen's Bureau afterward. His manager did not fare as well: Sidnum Grady committed suicide with an overdose of laudanum. Tait passed on his fortune to his children. The oldest, Celine, married a white Salem man; her three siblings moved away and passed for white. Tait and Fountain lived apart after the war, she in Salem and he in the city where he had made his fortune. Though wealthy, he lived modestly at the home of Solomon Myers, his former salesman at the slave jail, and died later of dementia.[18]

Tait, like Blackford, was an outlier. Unemployment and underemployment plagued Richmond for many months to come. In the first weeks, enterprising out-of-work residents of both races found ways to earn a little money from northern soldiers stationed near town. They sold them food to supplement the army's drab fare or martial relics gleaned from abandoned camps. Street stands selling lemonade, cakes, and fruit popped up along the margins of the main streets around the Burnt District. Others hawked bundles of papers and account books scavenged from Confederate offices to be repurposed for commercial use, for wrapping paper, or sold to the mill to make new paper. Hundreds of unemployed men and boys made their way with their poles down through the rubble fields to the riverfront to fish for shad, trout, and mullet. At the markets, their catch was worth, if not its weight in gold, then at least in scarce pennies of the new currency. None of these activities promised a long-term solution to lack of steady work, though they showed the ingenuity of people desperate for income when they had none.

When they had no alternative, the most wretched citizens passed through the city Alms House, a large, Italianate redbrick structure built on the eve of the war near Shockoe Cemetery on the north side of town. On the day of the fire, a neighboring powder magazine exploded, shattering the building's windows and killing eleven of its paupers. The survivors faced a bleak future in the impoverished city, the indigent sick among them being the most pitiable. There were not enough well inmates to help care for those too weak to help themselves. They laid about in filthy rags, listless. The saddest case was a woman whose scrofulous limbs bred maggots. The genial but often drunk doctor periodically removed the latter but did nothing more for her. Women from northern charities who dispensed used clothing reported back these distressing conditions. The city Alms House may have been housed in a modern building, but it lacked adequate bedding, medicine, furniture, and sanitation. "Gave clothes to the dumb, blind, lame, handless, footless, idiotic," recorded one of the charity workers at the end of a disheartening day there. "No end to the misery."[19]

As tentative reconstruction began, the building trades found they were in great demand. Help-wanted ads in the papers charted the gradual growth of employment. Restoring the greatest number of lost jobs, however, had to wait until the three main industries of Richmond could resume operation—the manufacturing trinity of flour, tobacco, and iron.

The largest employer had been the sprawling complex of foundries, smithies, machine shops, and rolling mills that constituted the Tredegar Iron Works along the river. During the war, Tredegar's mills and lathes churned out hundreds of cannon for the South. The fire had burned right up to the company's borders but left it untouched. Explosions in the nearby arsenal, however, shattered nearly all the glass at Tredegar. The Union ordnance officer who later surveyed the firm recommended against reopening armaments production but thought that the works were suitable for making and repairing railroad equipment and farm implements. The army briefly rehired workers to complete ironwork for bridge repair but then shut down the operation. The War Department directed General Halleck to turn over the company to the Treasury Department, and it remained idle while the government decided whether to return the factory to its private owners. Indecision over what to do punished the hundreds of workers, Black and white, who hoped for quick reemployment there.[20]

Through resourcefulness in finding work, Richmond's African Americans disproved the white fable about their supposed innate laziness. Within days of the end of the old regime, they began making agreements with employers, some former enslavers and some new bosses, in dozens of occupations. They made the transition to working for wages, as even biased observers sometimes admitted. The flourishing of Black entrepreneurship showed that they did not need white supervision to engage in productive activity. As they participated in rebuilding their city, they encountered new arrangements in the workplace. Later that year, skilled Black and white workers clashed over jobs. For the time being, they all maneuvered warily to find advantage in the inchoate postwar economy.

Seven weeks after the fire, on Sunday, May 21, a calamity of another kind punished Richmond. After a day of oppressive heat, black clouds blotted out the late-afternoon sun. In a matter of minutes, a violent thunderstorm flooded the streets. The torrent tossed barrels, boxes, and everything else not anchored to the ground down the steep streets, now miniature waterfalls, coursing toward Shockoe Creek east of Capitol Square and then on toward the James River. By nightfall the creek had risen eighteen feet above its normal level. According to a witness said to be the oldest inhabitant, the creek had never in his lifetime reached that high. Cellars in the lower part of the town flooded, and then the water rose up to the second floors of many buildings.

The terrified cries of people in the night added to the din. Some families climbed onto their rooftops to escape drowning. Rescuers brought horses, ropes, and even washtubs to save residents from inundated houses. No one drowned, but the same could not be said of hundreds of goats, pigs, cows, and chickens swept away by the current. At the height of the storm, so much heavy debris had sluiced down the streets and battered the pontoon bridge that it broke loose from its moorings. Some walls of Lumpkin's former slave jail were washed away. Merchants who had been fortunate to survive the evacuation fire now lost everything. Even after such a deluge, when the sun came out the next morning, residents saw thin tendrils of smoke, like accusatory fingers, still rising from the ashes.[21]

5
Angry Passions Hushed

May to June 1865

In Alexandria, Virginia, just across the Potomac River from Washington, a nervous Francis Harrison Pierpont awaited the call of destiny as the final acts of war unfolded. A shrewd entrepreneur and attorney from the western part of the state, Pierpont had adamantly opposed secession in 1861. He earned the sobriquet "Father of West Virginia" for his part in separating the mountain counties from the Confederate east. After West Virginia achieved statehood, Pierpont became governor of that smattering of eastern Virginia counties in Union hands. His writ ran only to that part of the state occupied by the Union army—a few counties bordering Washington, the Eastern Shore, and the hinterlands around Norfolk.

On the day after Appomattox, Lincoln sent Pierpont a terse cable to come see him at once. At their meeting, Pierpont believed that Lincoln expressed full confidence in him and his loyal government of Virginia, recognized by the North as the only legitimate authority for the whole state. He would not have been pleased to know that at the next cabinet meeting, some of the president's advisers damned Pierpont's administration with faint praise. Yes, it was a legal government, and certainly a loyal one. But hardly any Virginians supported it. And yet Lincoln invested great hope in steadfast white southern unionists like Pierpont, a righteous remnant around whom a chastened South could be brought back into proper alignment with the nation. Pierpont, like Virginia, was Lincoln's most anomalous bequest to Andrew Johnson. The governor also inherited the wartime hatreds and irreconcilable differences

Francis Harrison Pierpont, the loyal unionist governor of Virginia, alienated both unionists and former Confederates. (Wikimedia Commons)

over race that Lincoln's idealism could not resolve. In the meantime, a minuscule core of unionists in Richmond eagerly awaited Pierpont's arrival. Their more numerous Confederate neighbors winced at the prospect, fearing the imminent advent of "Pierpont with his gang."[1]

The head of that "gang" possessed the strong constitution necessary to match his ambitions and the task before him. Of medium but powerful build, with thick, unruly brown hair and a full beard, Pierpont projected the image of a stolid workhorse inured to hardship and strain. His fashionable high wing collar and broad cravat, framing his square face, high forehead, and determined eyes, reinforced his appearance as a leader not to be trifled with. He was a true scion of the northwestern part of the state. He embraced the Whiggish dream of a commonwealth of middling farmers and workers and opposed the slave-owning Democrats who had dominated Virginia before the war and wrenched it out of the Union. It did nothing to soften his attitude toward these eastern elites that his wife, Julia, was the daughter of New York abolitionists. "I do not expect to have the love and sympathy of the Rebels," he vowed, "but . . . I mean to have their respect."[2]

Pierpont faced formidable obstacles, more than he anticipated when he left the nation's capital. The catastrophe of fire was daunting enough, but he could not have foreseen the intransigence he would meet when he set out with high hopes from Washington. If he had had the gift of prophecy, he might not have gone to Richmond.

The army settled into the routines of garrison duty, and residents scratched for a living in the shattered city. But no one as yet knew the shape of the new polity that would replace the old one. That would depend on the president. As a so-called War Democrat, governor of unionist Tennessee, and later as vice president, Andrew Johnson became famous for his harsh prescription for rebels. A short man with a furrowed brow, he viewed the world with a perennial scowl and projected the image of a more radical politician than Lincoln. With his booming voice and ferocious zeal on the stump, he flayed opponents without mercy. His favorite formula was straightforward: "treason must be made odious and traitors punished." Some radical Republicans thought he went too far. "One would have thought," wrote a bemused Carl Schurz, former German revolutionary and Union general, "that if this man ever came into power, the face of the country would soon bristle with gibbets."[3]

Johnson did not make known his plans for more than a month after Lincoln's assassination. Like Lincoln, he wanted a swift restoration of the wayward states, not a thoroughgoing restructuring of southern society. All he asked was acceptance that slavery was dead and a repudiation of secession and Confederate war debts. And he, not Congress, would determine the process, at least until the national legislature reconvened. Because the next session would not be until December, the president had free rein. But what was his plan for the southern elites whom he despised with such passion? As Johnson took his time formulating his ideas, the white South fretted, at times taking heart from hints that federal rule might be light and at other times worrying that the president would make good on his public utterances to the contrary.

Finally, in early May, Johnson appointed governors in the former Confederate states to reestablish their governments. Virginia was an aberration because it already had a regime-in-waiting in the person of Pierpont. The Virginian later complained he did not get enough guidance from Johnson. But for now, they saw eye to eye. The president after all was the font of his legitimacy. Like Lincoln's successor, Pierpont disdained Tidewater planters more than he cared for the people they had enslaved. On May 9 he received the imprimatur from Washington he had been waiting for, an order that pledged federal approval for him to extend his sway throughout the state.[4]

Two weeks later, an official reception committee mounted a line of horses and carriages in front of the stone Customs House, the only building below Capitol Square to survive the fire. This large assemblage included representation from the city council, the courts, the business establishment, the press, and the clergy. A battalion of the Eleventh US Regulars and bands of the Fourth Regulars and the Twenty-Fourth Massachusetts Volunteers lent martial polish to the procession. When the cavalcade reached the steamship dock at Rocketts Landing a short distance east of the city, however, it learned it had been misinformed. The ship that arrived did not carry Pierpont, only some of his staff. This "non-arrival of the Governor," in the infelicitous words of a reporter, caused great disappointment.[5]

Pierpont did arrive the next day but only after several false starts and, for the superstitious, at least one bad omen. His party set out from Alexandria on the former blockade-runner *Diamond* and included Pierpont's family and political officials. The ship made an unexpected stop at Point Lookout, Maryland, because the pilot took sick. Then it stopped again for the night at Fort Monroe at the tip of the Virginia Peninsula. The captain declined to run up the James River at night because of all those red flags marking the location of Confederate torpedoes. (Pierpont skipped the chance to see the fort's most recent resident, Jefferson Davis, who had been captured in Georgia two weeks earlier and was incarcerated at the fort.)

When the reception committee's marshal received another telegram from the landing that Pierpont had finally arrived, he gave the order for the cavalcade, reassembled once more at the Customs House, to move out. It took a full hour for the column to reach Rocketts. Charles Palmer, a prominent import-export merchant and chairman of the committee, went on board the *Diamond* and welcomed Pierpont with a short address that spoke of hope. "Let us all," he begged, "both people and rulers, in a spirit of mutual forgiveness and forbearance towards each other, wipe out the asperities of the past."[6]

The delay of a day proved unpropitious. A heavy rain had fallen and marred the proceedings. Then, as the line of carriages snaked up from the steamship landing to the governor's mansion, it suddenly halted. Anna, Pierpont's then seven-year-old daughter, later recalled her mother's fright. The governor's carriage was up ahead of theirs, and soldiers suddenly crowded around it. Had assassins attacked him? After a few anxious moments, an officer rode back from the front of the procession and reassured them: a wheel had come off Pierpont's carriage.

As the column threaded its way through sodden lanes cleared of debris, from which stubborn filaments of smoke still rose, a detachment of artillery below the capitol portico thundered a series of salutes. A northern journalist noted that few white residents came out to line the route, only African Americans and soldiers. Only at Capitol Square did a crowd gather. The governor's daughter remembered their sullen faces outside the iron fence. At the mansion a portrait of George Washington adorned the porch. Union flags hung in profusion in the parlors. Rain kept the ceremony inside the mansion, to the disappointment of onlookers who had gathered outside in the hope of hearing from Pierpont but were held back by a line of soldiers. When the rain let up a little, a sympathetic visiting abolitionist went to see the governor's arrival. The participants, she said, "were a wet, muddy & tired looking set. It was quite like a funeral procession!"[7]

Inside, after the gas chandeliers were lit to dispel the gloom, Francis Smith, soon to be appointed state treasurer, delivered a more elaborate welcome than Charles Palmer had offered on the *Diamond*. He apologized that the deluge had kept many women away and claimed with more hope than evidence that a conciliatory spirit was rising throughout Virginia. He asserted that in Richmond there had always been a righteous core of unionists, bowed but not beaten by Confederate despotism but now eager to welcome their deliverer. He asked the governor to take inspiration from the statue of Washington in the square outside. No one could forget the dreadful trials of the past four years, but, he said, "let us endeavor to forgive, that angry passions may be hushed into silence."[8]

"With a throbbing heart," Pierpont frankly replied, "I earnestly engaged in opposing this terrible rebellion." He asked his hearers if the charred ruins around them were not the fruit of secession. He praised the work of the army and private charities in giving succor to Richmond's citizens and asked rhetorically if the flag of their nation was worth defending. He concluded by pledging himself to the arduous task of reconstruction that lay before them.[9]

Only three days had passed since the Union army's grand victory parade in Washington. The trial of the Lincoln assassins still had weeks to run. The last Confederate forces under General Edmund Kirby Smith in the trans-Mississippi had not yet surrendered.

Before reaching the capital, Pierpont had issued an address to the people of Virginia that spelled out his priorities. He laid out in a clear-eyed fashion the lamentable state of affairs in the Old Dominion: Richmond's business district in ashes, banks defunct, public utilities damaged or destroyed, towns and villages devastated, farms desolated, homes and factories laid waste. Methodical and tireless in his wartime labors in West Virginia and Alexandria, the governor embraced the monumental task before him in Richmond with energy and resolve.

He soon learned that physical reconstruction was not the greatest task he faced. Four years of war had upended the social structure of Virginia, and its people were now groping for some as-yet undefined new system for ordering their community. Uncertainty hung over the city, then and long after. The hopeful band of unionists who crowded into the governor's parlor that first day would not be enough to ensure Pierpont's success. Nor would it be enough even if the governor included leading Confederates, many of whom attended the reception that he and his wife held three days later. Both gatherings, the welcoming event and the reception, omitted representatives of nearly half the city's population. Even as Pierpont exchanged hopeful predictions with his unionist and Confederate well-wishers, those excluded Richmonders were clamoring to be heard.

Pierpont could count on support from a handful of influential citizens in the former Confederate capital. The sentiments Charles Palmer expressed in his welcome speech were heartfelt. He had suffered imprisonment in a Confederate jail for disloyal statements, given aid to desperate unionist families, and supplied military intelligence to the spy network that kept Grant's army apprised of activity in Richmond. In bitter terms, he denounced Jefferson Davis (that "ungrateful Devil") for reducing Richmonders to beggary and repaying those who had supported the Confederacy with the destruction of their property.[10]

Palmer had lived above his office as a commission merchant and shipping agent at the corner of Cary and Virginia Streets, an unfortunate address at the epicenter of the Burnt District. Homeless, he moved in with his unregenerate Confederate son on West Franklin Street and began rebuilding his business. Within two weeks he became a partner in a new firm selling tobacco and within a month was director of the First National Bank. Shortly after Pierpont arrived, he appointed Palmer to a commission to assess the status of all banks. Before long, newspapers carried frequent notices of ships departing and arriving filled with cargoes owned by Palmer and his associates. He had worked and prayed for Union victory, lost everything, and meant to play a leading role in reviving his city.[11]

Franklin Stearns shared a spot on the reception committee with his friend Palmer. He had arrived in Richmond from Vermont at age eighteen with twenty-five cents in his pocket. Beginning as a day laborer on the James River and Kanawha Canal, he eventually made a fortune distilling whiskey and was counted as one of the city's richest men. He sent his older sons out of the country to avoid Confederate conscription. Like Palmer he aided the Union spy network and suffered imprisonment for unpopular opinions. Unlike Palmer, he watched the fire burn up to his threshold but not beyond. His children and his mother welcomed the Union army with garlands of flowers. When voters later elected him to the legislature, he donated his modest salary to the poor.

The most prominent political prisoner to share a Confederate jail with Palmer and Stearns was former Whig congressman John Minor Botts. A large man with a massive head, bushy eyebrows, and bombastic style of speaking and writing (his long public letters were "universally dreaded by printers," one of them lamented), Botts did not suffer fools and earned the nickname "Bison." After his release from prison, he maintained neutral isolation for the rest of the war at a Culpeper County farm he had won gambling. In the chaotic days after the fall of Richmond, a group of bushwhackers accosted him there for money. With a wave of his double-barreled shotgun, he told them to fire away because he had none. He seemed to relish a state of permanent choleric annoyance. Not a forgiving man, he told Palmer those who caused the evacuation fire deserved to hang. He was appalled to learn that Pierpont was consulting with former Confederates. When he was asked to confer with these same men about Virginia's future, he exploded with volcanic fury. "They and I," he fulminated in a letter to Palmer, scratching out his bile in a neat, regular hand, "can *never never never* be politically associated together."[12]

The most celebrated unionist of Richmond never darkened the doors of a Confederate prison. Elizabeth Van Lew spent her wealth on food for imprisoned northern soldiers and helped escapees make their way to Union lines. With even more daring, this slight, determined woman orchestrated a network of spies under the nose of the rebel provost marshal to send a stream of intelligence to the encircling Union army. Her espionage included placing Mary Richards Bowser, a formerly enslaved member of her household whom she educated in the North, in Jefferson Davis's residence. Confederate officials suspected Van Lew but could never catch her. As she watched Weitzel's soldiers pour into town below her Church Hill mansion on April 3, Van Lew exclaimed, "Oh, army of my country, how glorious was your welcome!" The army posted guards around her house, and a parade of senior officers came to pay their respects.[13]

She did not hesitate to berate the Union provost marshal, Marsena Patrick, when she thought he was being too cozy with Confederates. He was amused to see the expression on her face change when he disabused her of that notion. Given his conservative views, however,

Elizabeth Van Lew, a successful Union spymaster during the war who was never caught by the Confederate authorities. (National Park Service)

she may not have been entirely mistaken. After the assassination, she wrote a paean to the Union army for overthrowing "the most merciless, relentless, vindictive of despotisms." No Richmond newspaper would publish it.[14]

A few ordinary white Richmonders shared the unionist sentiments of these prominent citizens, though far fewer than Francis Smith had claimed when he welcomed the governor. One anonymous woman had better luck than Van Lew in persuading the papers to publish her praise of the Stars and Stripes. In words that echoed Van Lew's, she scorned the Confederacy for leaving the city's ruins as proof of its perfidy. "The air feels purer" now, she wrote. Another unnamed contributor to the paper called Confederate rule the most despotic since "darkness was changed into light."[15]

Two inconspicuous, workaday residents who agreed were Mary and Frank West. A native Virginian, Mary stood by her New Hampshire husband, a newspaper compositor, and his political leanings. She was the strong one in the marriage. She managed to get Frank released from the Confederate draft and sold her clothes and jewelry to buy food when he was without work. She declined her father's offer to take in her and her children because she believed her duty was to stay with Frank. Their prospects improved when he found a job setting type for the *Whig*, now transformed, if only temporarily, into a thoroughgoing unionist newspaper. For the first time in years, he began earning money to support his family and, she hoped, his frail self-respect. Grateful for the turn of events, Mary West wrote her sister that she could look out the window at the Stars and Stripes flying over her city again and hoped it would continue to do so "until time shall be no more."[16]

Unionists were in a tiny minority, and they knew it. For the moment, though, events had given them an outsized influence in the prostrate city. From the outset, Confederate sympathizers agonized over the triumph of their unionist neighbors and feared retribution. "Union men began to show themselves," groaned Judith McGuire, a clergyman's wife filled with bitterness and anger, "treason walked abroad." In turn, Burnham Wardwell, an ice merchant and Van Lew associate, disdained Confederates as base murderers. Dealing with these radically opposed sentiments would present the new governor with a puzzle that, in the end, he could not solve.[17]

Five days after the fire—and a day before Lee surrendered—some unnamed unionists, giddy with optimism and full of triumphalist disdain for the vanquished, proposed to raise a grand monument in the Burnt District. It would remind residents of "the infamy of those who sought to destroy, by treachery, a city they could not hold by force of arms." The journalist who reported this story said no such monument was necessary because the ruins themselves would be a sufficient reproach to the Confederacy for years to come. A northern observer made a contrary prediction a month later. He feared that Lee was so revered that Virginia would soon add a statue honoring him along with those of Thomas Jefferson and Patrick Henry around the base of Crawford's equestrian Washington on Capitol Square. The urge to continue the conflict through public statuary, already strong, would only increase as time passed. For the moment, it was unclear which side would prevail.[18]

Among the many visitors who called on Governor Pierpont in his buoyant first days at the governor's mansion was one who acquainted him with the racial complexities of the city. Julia Wilbur, the abolitionist who came to see the sites and dispense charity to the poor, went in the company of a Mrs. Jennings to visit Pierpont. Jennings had been enslaved and, in fact, was the half sister of the wealthy banker William Macfarland, who had just headed a delegation to see the governor. Their father had acknowledged her and sent her to Philadelphia to be educated. She now returned to teach newly freed children. When Wilbur introduced Jennings to Pierpont, she explained this family connection. The governor recognized the tie and engaged in a wide-ranging discussion about slavery and its consequences that pleased the two women. They did not know then how much Pierpont would eventually disappoint freedmen in their quest for equal treatment.[19]

After the exhilaration of being greeted by so many well-wishers, Pierpont turned to the mundane flood of paperwork that was the lifeblood of administration. Among the governor's papers, a document entitled "List of the Prominent Union Men of Richmond and Its Vicinity" stands out. It was dated eleven days after Pierpont's arrival and, though unsigned, was compiled by a committee appointed to vouch for citizens on whom the new government could rely. The fact that the first two names on the unalphabetized list were Charles Palmer and Franklin Stearns suggests who might have drawn it up. Some of the 132 names on the list later received appointment to office. Among them was John Van Lew, brother of Elizabeth, who found a role as a detective hired to sniff out disloyal activity. Others in her wartime spy networks secured similar employment. But were the 132 enough to create a loyal unionist Richmond?[20]

Clerks in county courthouses across the state wrote Pierpont about reestablishing local government. "We are here completely in the dark," worried the clerk in Middlesex County, northeast of Richmond. He wanted to know the procedure for filling the offices of the county, which had been declared vacant. Letters of introduction flooded in, some by mail and others by the hands of hopeful supplicants who lined up outside the governor's office. A torrent of letters sought appointments as tobacco inspector, notary public, customs agent, vaccination agent, commissioner of local elections, and a host of other minor posts that carried with them some form of compensation in a state starved for greenbacks. Others made more brazen requests for favor. "I have been a Refugee from Richmond," pleaded C. P. Carazo, who said he had never supported the Confederacy, was unemployed, and had a wife and seven small children. "I appeal to you for some appointment."[21]

Only three days after Pierpont arrived in Richmond, a decision announced in Washington addressed the overarching question that hung over the South since Andrew Johnson's accession to the presidency. That decision would roil Virginia politics for the rest of the year and beyond, complicate Pierpont's plans for restoration of the Old Dominion, and intensify hostility between North and South. After six weeks of uncertainty, on May 29 Johnson finally issued a proclamation spelling out his vision. It gave general amnesty and pardon to all who had supported the rebellion and restored their property, provided they signed the oath of allegiance to the national government and accepted emancipation. In Richmond, Confederate veterans and civilians had been signing the oath in great numbers in the first weeks. This blanket decree now allowed them to regain their citizenship and resume their peacetime lives.

The proclamation, however, specified a series of exceptions that included all high-ranking Confederate officials and all civilians worth more than twenty thousand dollars. These exclusions from the generosity of the general pardon sent a shiver down the collective spine of the southern ruling class. In the capital of the Confederacy, elite Richmonders had feared for their lives and their estates. Now that dread seemed to be justified, at least for property. Even the Union provost marshal, General Marsena Patrick, was appalled. As a conservative man, he feared the twenty-thousand-dollar clause put "a direct premium on meanness and rascality." Its effect, he feared, would be to deliver the civilian government that would eventually take over into the hands of the rabble. Governor Pierpont, too, feared that the prospect of reprisals, especially through confiscation of property, would undermine his principal goal of reviving the broken economy.[22]

For the next few anxious months, it was unclear how the federal government would apply the proclamation in practice. It appeared that President Johnson, the scourge of the landed slaveholding class and a drunken traitor in the eyes of Confederates, was determined by means of the exclusion clauses to confiscate their estates and bar them from returning to power. They clutched at the straw of hope offered by one provision in the decree. It stipulated that members of the excepted classes could individually apply for a special presidential pardon. But would Johnson endorse many such requests? It was not at all clear on May 29 that he would, and with each passing week tensions grew. All summer long uncertainty about pardons and fear about expropriation weighed on the minds of those in the excluded classes and thwarted efforts to revive the local economy.

Before the war, John Curtis Underwood had earned notoriety as one of the first, few, and certainly most vociferous Virginia supporters of Abraham Lincoln. A New York native, he had moved to northern Virginia in the 1850s, married a cousin of Thomas Jonathan Jackson before he became "Stonewall," and then been hounded out of the state for his strident Republican views. From his base in Alexandria, under the protection of Union guns, he plotted his revenge. Lincoln rewarded him with appointment as federal judge for the Eastern District of Virginia, despite his hazy grasp of the law and aversion to judicial impartiality. By the end of the war, Confederates had fair warning of his intentions toward them. By then he had publicly vowed to crush the slaveholding elite by confiscating their estates and dividing them up among loyal citizens, Black and white. And then, he warned, "what a signal display of retributive justice shall we see."[23]

Two days after Johnson's proclamation, Underwood made good on his threat. He sought indictments for treason against thirty-seven Confederate generals and civilian leaders in Virginia, including Robert E.

Lee and former governor Henry Wise. Underwood proceeded, with the president's blessing, and gave an inflammatory charge to his grand jurors "to present for trial the authors and conductors of the most gigantic, bloody and unprovoked crimes that ever cursed our world." There had been, he intoned grandiloquently, "nothing so terrible since the Crucifixion." The grand jury agreed and arraigned them all a week later.[24]

Lee worried that the indictment might supersede his Appomattox parole. Others under indictment had no such doubts and fled. Some left Virginia behind and sought their fortunes beyond the reach of federal law. Not Henry Wise. Ever a quixotic, protean figure, he made the transition to peacetime refusing to be intimidated by defeat. He would remain true to the memory of those who died for the South, as he wrote in a letter that summer to the family of Barksdale Warwick, killed days before Appomattox. After the war, he growled, "we ought not to wish such spirits [as Warwick's] still alive, to suffer the humiliation of submission." He proclaimed loudly and often that because he had done nothing wrong, he had no cause to apply for pardon or fear indictment. He would, he cheerfully said, "rather take arsenic than take the oath."[25]

Underwood, like Wise, was a man of striking contradiction. He worked tirelessly to achieve full civil rights for Black Virginians when few other white men would do so. With impolitic, intemperate language, he cast lightning bolts of vituperation from the bench, locked horns with Governor Pierpont, enraged his opponents, and embarrassed his friends.

With the indictments, Underwood brought down upon himself the almost universal loathing of white Virginians. He did not care. The local press fumed that he had dared to condemn Lee, "the latchets of whose shoes he is unworthy to loose." The apotheosis of Lee could not happen before he died, but the veneration shown him while he lived already approached idolatry. Any man who denigrated him earned a swift rebuke. One of the judge's enemies said he insulted the people of Virginia with his pronouncements, which, "for violence, blasphemy and unfounded aspersion of a brave and chivalrous people, beggars imagery and defied comparison." Beyond the thirty-seven indictments, Underwood was about to become the scourge of hundreds more. In doing so, he would secure his place as the most reviled figure in the pantheon of demons that tormented defeated Confederates. In the process, he focused special scorn on Richmond. He denounced the city and its people for, in his way of thinking, prolonging the rebellion and, when it was over, refusing to recant their treason or express the slightest sense of remorse. They in turn, repaid his derision with unremitting contempt. That bitter antipathy became the hallmark of tension between unconditional unionists and unrepentant Confederates.[26]

6

Our Quivering Flesh

May to June 1865

Two decades before the Civil War, an enslaved Virginian named Fields Cook wrote an autobiographical essay intended, he said, for his own benefit in the future. That introspection by itself set him apart from the vast majority, Black and white, enslaved and free. By that time, he had persuaded his owner in King William County to allow him to go to Richmond and hire himself out. It was an illegal but common practice for enslavers to permit their human property to find work in town and even arrange for their own room and board to generate income for both parties. Cook sensed that greater opportunity awaited him in the city.

Within a few years, he had saved enough of his wages to purchase his freedom and then that of his wife, Mary, and their children. He joined the First African Baptist Church and became a self-taught preacher. Literate, articulate, and gregarious, by war's end he was about forty-eight, a tall man with an agreeable personality, and a leader in his community. Though the sources are unclear, he also likely worked as a waiter and caterer with his brother Jim at the Ballard House Hotel.[1]

Cook would need all of his wits when he came up against the hostility of the US Army and, especially, of reinstated city officials. They were trying, he believed, to relegate freed people to a level no higher than that of free African Americans under the Confederacy, a status without civil rights and more akin to slavery than freedom. Barely two months into the uncharted sea of postwar Richmond, Black people were about to assert demands for rights equal to those enjoyed by their white neighbors. Their fears that they might be rebuffed cast a cloud over their joy. How could they be sure slavery was indeed dead?

On May 24, General Oliver Otis Howard joined President Johnson, General Ulysses S. Grant, and Secretary of War Edwin Stanton at the White House as a grand review of the victorious Union armies passed by. A slight, humorless officer with a shrill voice, the devoutly religious Howard had left an arm on the battlefield at Fair Oaks, Virginia. The president had just appointed the sad-eyed Maine native to be commissioner of the newly created Freedmen's Bureau. From its headquarters in a townhouse at I and Nineteenth Streets, confiscated from a secessionist congressman, he set out to oversee the nation's effort to usher four million people into the postemancipation age. The day after the grand review, for the first time he met his assistant commissioners, who would direct the Bureau's work in individual southern states.[2]

Howard chose Orlando Brown as assistant commissioner for Virginia. An army doctor, Brown had worked with freed people in Norfolk before the fall of Richmond. In that task, he won praise from his military superiors and African American leaders. The latter predicted that as assistant commissioner he would be "*the man to act* justly for our people." With those endorsements, Brown arrived in Richmond on the last day of May expecting army commanders to support the work the Bureau had been created to perform. Instead, they stunned him with their shabby treatment. They had provided him with neither staff nor offices. Worse, the army was vague about exactly when it might transfer freedmen's affairs from the provost marshal's jurisdiction to his, as Brown expected. "Everything has been as bad as it possibly could be," he lamented. Depressed at his reception, Brown left Richmond after only a few days to complain to Howard in person.[3]

The Johnson administration wanted military rule to be replaced by civilian authority in the South as quickly as possible. In the case of Richmond, the army's initial compliance with that directive increased the difficulties African Americans faced. After being in charge for nearly two months, the triumvirate of Generals Halleck, Ord, and Patrick believed it was putting the city back on track. They had fed the population, begun to clear the wreckage of war and fire, and encouraged first efforts at reopening businesses. But they were frustrated with the labor issue: how could the mass of freedmen be profitably employed? That they posed the question like that, however, suggests their lack of empathy for people they did not think to consult. The generals believed the quickest way to revive the city was to make the military presence palatable to the pro-Confederate majority, even at the cost of disappointing freed people. They reasoned that upsetting the traditional social order in pursuit of new rights for Black people would complicate their efforts to restart the battered economy.

The movement of Black men and women across Virginia, and especially the seemingly unending flow of plantation laborers into Richmond, alarmed the generals and convinced them they had to control the freed people and compel them to work. To them, it was so much idle wandering and vagrancy at a time when Virginia's devastated farmlands were in desperate need of attention. White people could see that the traditional norms that had kept African Americans subservient were dissolving. To them, the movement of those people was a foreboding development. Mobility and emancipation went hand in hand. It gave to the newly freed a mastery over themselves they had never enjoyed before. And it increasingly troubled both former enslavers and the city's new military overlords.[4]

General Halleck was concerned that the demographic turmoil he could see every day as more rural residents filtered into town would disrupt spring planting. That would without doubt lead to shortages and even famine in the following winter. "The planting season is so nearly over," he worried, "that I fear the colored population will not settle down to quiet and labor in time to raise grain enough for the coming year."[5]

In early May, the generals began a systematic attempt to thwart rural Black people leaving their farms for Richmond. Halleck reinforced this effort by telling his officers to encourage planters and workers to reach equitable contracts for terms of labor. For their part, the planters complained that their former workers resisted such contracts. The landowners therefore banded together in associations across the outlying counties to impose agreements at low levels of wages. The generals approved of the planters' combinations and urged Black workers to accept these unfavorable terms. Not only did the army make a concerted effort to prevent rural African Americans from moving to the capital, but it also expelled many who had already relocated into town since the fire.

To enforce restrictions on freedom of movement and labor, Provost Marshal General Patrick decreed in late May that all Black people must carry a pass signed by a white person vouching for their employment. The police began strict enforcement, "molesting the blissful security of every negro who was found sunning himself on the street corner," sneered a white observer. Patrick also instituted a curfew that applied only to African Americans. The curfew and pass system pleased white Richmonders and sparked consternation among African Americans. "When will it end?" asked a northern abolitionist visiting the city.[6]

The most alarming development for Black residents came with the reinstatement of Joseph Mayo as mayor on June 5. He was, one of their ministers said, "a man without a heart." A balding disciplinarian with protuberant eyes and an unfashionably clean-shaven chin, Joseph Carrington Mayo had presided for many years over his Mayor's Court. He was notorious for dispensing harsh punishment to Black men and women for trivial infractions. He routinely sent those who fell afoul of his personal interpretation of the law to the whipping post and jail. African Americans complained that "his administration has been marked by cruelty and injustice to us." William Jackson, formerly coachman to Varina and Jefferson Davis, said Mayo was a greater villain than the Confederate president. Jackson said people called Mayo "Black Joe" because he once supposedly had fallen down drunk and given himself a black eye. The pass and curfew policies gave him carte blanche to renew his stern rule. A northern journalist believed the restoration of Mayo, two scant months after he surrendered the city, seemed "to have let loose all evil passions." Now that he was back in charge with the same racist police officers as before, he quite literally wielded the whip hand.[7]

Newspaperman Thomas Chester had stayed on in Richmond after the army sent the United States Colored Troops (USCT) regiments to the Rio Grande because he suspected there would be more stories

Black journalist Thomas Morris Chester marched into Richmond the day of the fire with regiments of United States Colored Troops. (New York Public Library)

to come out of the former Confederate capital. His hunch was borne out when a protest over the passes and other abusive treatment boiled over. The son of Pennsylvania abolitionists, Chester had decided as a youth that America held no future for Black people and emigrated to Liberia. He made frequent trips back home, however, and was in the North when war broke out. He became the first African American to receive a commission in the Pennsylvania state militia and the only one to serve as a reporter for a major newspaper. In a postwar photograph, his close-cropped hair, full beard, and penetrating gaze suggest the fierce independence that shines through in his reporting. Chester's blunt, sometimes inelegant, but forceful prose in the *Philadelphia Press* gave the most detailed insight that survives into the condition of Black people in the early days of postwar Richmond.

As Chester and others reported, African Americans quickly organized to protest the pass and curfew system. On May 24, the *Richmond Times* dismissed their grievances and refused to publish a notice from them outlining the injustices they alleged. The paper airily denied their objections because, it said, the pass system was necessary "to let no idle negroes loaf around the city, but to put them to work, and to make them earn their own living." With unconcealed glee, another newspaper reported that before 2:00 p.m. on June 7 the police had arrested more than 250 men who could not show a pass. The authorities set them to work cleaning rubbish from streets and alleys. Nancy Carter, a Black landlady, said her tenants were discouraged by this turn of events and called Union soldiers "rebels disguised in Federal uniform."[8]

Escalating abusive treatment and the reinstatement of Mayo prompted African Americans to take stronger action. On June 7 they sent a letter to the *New York Tribune* to air their grievances on a national stage. "All that is needed to restore Slavery in full," it asserted, "is the auction-block." Their fears of a return to grim servitude were palpable. The next day another group appointed Fields Cook chairman of a committee to take statements from those who had been badly treated by either the army's provost guard or the city police. They took their findings to the assistant commissioner of the Freedmen's Bureau. Orlando Brown, just returned from Washington but as yet given no office or staff, expressed sympathy. He said he would address the abuses as soon as the army gave him jurisdiction over African Americans. It was a lame statement, and it galled the proud army doctor to admit he was impotent without that authorization. He was about to get what he wanted, but not until the Black protest bore fruit.[9]

The depositions that Cook's committee collected described a range of petty harassment, verbal and physical abuse, and horrific instances of outright brutality, mostly at the hands of Mayo's police but also by Union soldiers. Entrepreneur Albert Brooks had revived his thriving taxi and livery business only to discover that the pass system, with policemen stopping his drivers on nearly every street corner, "make it nearly impossible for me to carry on my business." He was arrested and thrown into jail despite his protest. William Ferguson, proprietor of a barbershop at the Exchange Hotel, intervened in a fight between a drunken white man and a Black youth. Ferguson got the young man released from jail after police arrested him. But a short time later soldiers assaulted the barber while he was talking in the street with a Union army chaplain.[10]

Similarly, John Oliver, who came to Richmond from Boston, ran afoul of a provost guard who accosted him in the street, used abusive language, and arrested him. At the provost marshal's office, he was told his identity papers signed by the secretary of the Commonwealth of Massachusetts were invalid. Oliver's colleague, another African American from the North, fared worse. When he denied being insolent to the guard, that officer got off his horse and beat him.[11]

Thomas Chester had found his next story. Indeed, he became a part of it when he went to the steamboat landing to send off dispatches to his Philadelphia newspaper. While there, a provost guard assaulted him. When he sought help from the lieutenant on duty, that officer told the soldier to strike Chester again with the butt of his musket. Later, when Chester protested a witness's version of the altercation, another officer said he "must not contradict a *white* man in his presence." Chester was a muscular man of thirty-five who did not shrink from a fight. He had fought with a paroled Confederate officer in the state capitol the day after the fire and given his opponent a black eye. But he knew not to dispute armed men.[12]

Jinny Scott's story was the worst. She testified that she and her husband were walking down Main Street with another couple, Richard Adams and Jane Minor, when two Confederate veterans approached them and sneered that they "were not agoing to get out of the way for damned niggers." The Black couples moved aside, but one of the soldiers struck Jinny Scott as they passed. Her husband and her assailant traded insults, and then, she testified, the soldiers called her "bad names and threw rocks at me." She ran off home and so missed seeing what Adams reported later: Union soldiers came upon the scene and joined in insulting Scott and then beat him. The next day the provost marshal ordered his men to subject Scott to the traditional military punishment of bucking and gagging. Trussed and bound, he endured more verbal and physical abuse. The soldiers cut him loose, only to tie his hands and feet again and put him in an open coffin. They set the coffin upright and smeared his face with molasses to attract flies.[13]

A letter to Orlando Brown summed up the pass regime: "The power given the police & guard to inspect the passes of colored men has been the past two days, sadly abused. A further continuance is to place a class of our citizens in a state of anarchy and conduce more than any other measure to injure the cause of freedom and Union." As he forwarded these complaints to General Howard, Brown said they may seem incredible, "but I fear they must be believed."[14]

Fields Cook and the others called a meeting at First African Baptist Church to present their depositions. The large redbrick church barely accommodated the three thousand–plus residents who responded to the call. C. Thurston Chase of the American Union Commission, one of the northern relief agencies, had almost convinced the gathering to go through the Freedmen's Bureau in seeking redress when Thomas Chester objected. He said going through channels would take too long. Instead, he said, they should take their protest directly to President Johnson. Electrified by this suggestion, the assembled freedmen agreed.[15]

The meeting appointed Chester and men from each of the six Black churches, with Fields Cook as chairman, to call upon the president. It added to the delegation a white journalist named Van Vleet, the *New York Tribune*'s Richmond reporter. Perhaps they thought it prudent to have a white man introduce a committee of African Americans at the White House. Certainly there was scant precedent for such an extraordinary deputation.

It is not known how they traveled to Washington. Because the rail lines north had not yet been fully restored, they likely went by steamer down the James and up the Chesapeake Bay to the Potomac. It must have been a heady moment for them, knowing that they were the among the first Black men to speak for their people directly to the president of the United States. Cook, who had purchased his freedom before the war, must have marveled at the trajectory of his life. Chester, who had never been enslaved, could take satisfaction in his leadership role within a community he had known only for two months. Before leaving Richmond, they called on Governor Pierpont to give him their evidence of abuse. Although he did not make the freed people's cause his special concern, and would soon provoke their anger over his policies, on this occasion the governor showed sympathy for their grievances. To their surprise, he removed Mayor Mayo from office. That decision gave a lift to their spirits as they embarked on their mission.

On June 17, they went to the White House, where Van Vleet introduced them to President Johnson and read their memorial of complaints. It alleged that life in Richmond was now worse than under slavery. Then they at least could count on slave owners having a financial interest in their physical well-being, but now those same white people had become their enemies. They protested the pass system and claimed that the army's provost guards took them out of their homes and places of work without warning simply because they had no pass. They objected to the continuation of the rule that their ministers must be white and their church property held by white trustees.

The delegates made a heartrending appeal on behalf of husbands and wives who had been separated under slavery and had come back to Richmond searching for their missing partners, only to be thrown into jail for lack of a pass. Their most bitter grievance concerned Mayo, the authoritarian scourge in city hall who had ordered them bound to the whipping post and whose restored police were the same men who had applied the lash to "our quivering flesh." They demanded all the legal and civil rights accorded white citizens.[16]

The president endorsed the depositions of maltreatment and told the delegation to take them to the Freedmen's Bureau commissioner, General Howard. He asked why they had not spoken to General Halleck in Richmond. Cook coolly answered that they had tried to see Halleck several times but could not gain an interview. Further, when they approached Provost Marshal Patrick, he dismissed them out of hand, saying he would not be dictated to by anyone.[17]

If Van Vleet had satisfied racial etiquette by introducing the men, it was Cook and Chester, not the white journalist, who forcefully answered Johnson's queries. The president listened to their complaints and said everything that could be done would be done. But he ended dishearteningly, saying, "While you are in this state of transition, there are many things which we might prefer to be different . . . that yet must be submitted to till they can be remedied."[18]

Earlier in the war, before a crowd of African Americans in Nashville, Tennessee, Johnson had famously invoked the biblical story of Moses standing up for his people before the pharaoh in Egypt. With false humility, he said if another leader could not be found, "I will indeed be your Moses, and lead you through the Red Sea." Did he think of that paternalistic self-image during this extraordinary audience with Black petitioners from Richmond? Whether or not he did, at least one African American journal later invoked that comment in a way Johnson would not have liked. He was, it said, nearer to being pharaoh than Moses.[19]

At the same time Richmond's Black leaders took their grievances to the White House, Secretary of War Edwin Stanton completed the replacement of the trio of generals that had been part of their complaints. Provost Marshal Patrick resigned, disgusted with his work. Halleck, equally disgruntled with what he called the disagreeable job of trying to reconcile Black and white residents to a new social order, got the transfer to California that he desired. Ord went to an Oregon command.

As commander in Virginia, Stanton chose Major General Alfred Terry, a tall, energetic Connecticut lawyer with pensive eyes and an extensive combat record. He had commanded Black soldiers and dealt with freed people more fairly, and he learned quickly that returning authority to civilian control was not in the best interests of Black Richmonders. As much was plain in his order that "people of color will henceforth enjoy the same personal liberty which other citizens and inhabitants enjoy." Now, unlike under the previous commanders, the divergence between civilian and military authority became highly pronounced. Soon after Terry arrived, he ended the hated pass system and made clear his intent to work with Orlando Brown and the Freedmen's Bureau. Confederate Richmond came to detest Terry, and he warmly reciprocated, later calling the city one of the most troublesome places he knew. Though better remembered as commander of the punitive expedition against the Sioux in the Little Big Horn a decade later, Terry would arguably make a greater mark during a crucial chapter of postwar Virginia.[20]

Major General Alfred Terry took over the Richmond command in June 1865 and repeatedly locked horns with former Confederate citizens. (Library of Congress)

As his chief subordinate for that troublesome place, he chose the like-minded General John Wesley Turner. At only thirty-two, the New York native and West Point graduate had seen action throughout the war, most notably in the Petersburg and Appomattox campaigns. Like his commanding officer, after a few weeks the plainspoken soldier came to believe the majority of white Richmonders hated the United States. He thought they meekly accepted the army's presence at first but became more assertively disloyal as time went on. The sight of Confederate uniforms on the streets, and how warmly they were greeted, especially in contrast to the cold disdain people showed for blue uniforms, infuriated him. He even privately confessed that he began to wonder what he had been fighting for. He would not have to serve in the post long before he felt the need to take action to curtail that perceived disloyalty. In response to Black protest, the new generals set up a new police force drawn from the army in place of Mayo's men. A provost court for minor offenses and a military commission for serious crime gave African Americans greater protections than before. This new arrangement heightened the tension between civil and military authority that would characterize Richmond for the rest of the year and beyond.[21]

On leaving his Richmond command, General Halleck, who could not write a short report, sent a lengthy assessment to Secretary of War Stanton. On his arrival in April, he said, the city was burdened with thousands of Confederate and Union soldiers, yet little violence ensued. It was physically devastated, but the army had cleared away much of the wreckage and encouraged the locals to restart business. With staggering understatement, he said sudden emancipation "produced no little excitement, both among the freemen themselves and their former owners." He worried that Black Richmonders would fall into bad habits if they did not better heed the obligations of marriage. Halleck made the optimistic prediction that the South would without too much difficulty build a proper system agreeable to both capital and labor. But he did not reckon with the unwillingness of Black Richmonders to accept the subordinate role he imagined for them or with the resistance of former Confederates to change.[22]

After they returned home, the men who had spoken to the president reported on their achievement at another crowded gathering at First African Baptist Church. It was cause for celebration. The governor had deposed Mayor Mayo even before they had gone to Washington, and the former army commanders were on their way out of Richmond even as the delegation entered the White House. Even so, it felt like their bold action had accelerated this dramatic turnabout. Fields Cook's lengthy report reviewed the events leading up to the meeting with Johnson. When he reached the climax—Black men speaking directly and forcefully to the president of the United States—his audience responded with thunderous applause. Richard Wells, pastor of the Manchester African Baptist Church, said he regretted that so many of their white neighbors still wanted to oppress them. But he ended on a high note. In short order, he reminded the gathering, they had reached the point "where they could whisper into the President's ear." Their success in Washington and the encouragement they took from General Terry's actions buoyed the community in its quest to assert the rights of citizens.[23]

Richmond newspapers put a different slant on the events of early June. They were appalled. They praised the pass system as a beneficial innovation to control indolent African Americans, especially those who came into town from the surrounding countryside. It angered the editors that freedmen presumed the right to take their grievances directly to the president. The *Whig* reported the bare facts of the White House meeting and disputed each of the complaints. It thought the government gullible for believing them. It mischaracterized the delegation as coming from the criminal dregs of society when in fact it represented the elite of Richmond's African American community. The press disparaged the abilities of Fields Cook and the others and claimed that the white journalist Van Vleet had written the address, not any Black man.[24]

After two months, white Richmonders had begun to hope that the new dispensation might be milder than they expected when the Union army arrived amid smoke and flames. Now, they complained, a few disaffected Black men who did not know their proper place in the natural order threatened to bring down on Richmond the tyrannical rule from the North they had originally feared. After working there for a half year, the Freedmen's Bureau's Orlando Brown testified before a congressional committee that white residents had not given up their belief in a right to enslave people. If that sounded exaggerated, it should be kept in mind that when Fields Cook's contingent returned from Washington, many enslaved people across the rural South had still not heard about emancipation. It was not until later that month that the army announced to people in Texas that slavery had ended, an event marked today by the national holiday Juneteenth. That state of ignorance in the far reaches of the former Confederacy did not apply to Black people in Richmond. They had known since the dramatic April 3, if not long before, about the freedom that was promised to them. But it was a precarious promise that had not yet been realized or, for that matter, even fully defined. The old issue of control would not release its grip on the imaginations of much of white Richmond. In June 1865 that frame of mind presaged a future of conflict with the determination of Black men and women to embrace freedom.[25]

Out in Amelia County southwest of Richmond, a famous Virginian from earlier days observed the events in the capital from afar. He saw no reason to recant his dire prophecies. Edmund Ruffin, wild-eyed agricultural reformer, apostle of secession, hater of all things northern, brooded over every scrap of news from Richmond. He agonized over the future of the South. To this long-haired seer of doom, who had fired the signal gun opening the bombardment of Fort Sumter in 1861, Governor Pierpont represented "the most bare-faced usurpation." Ruffin thought a celebration organized by northern teachers at newly opened schools for Black children served only to incite hatred toward white people.[26]

In declining health, Ruffin had long ruminated on suicide to avoid becoming a burden to his son. With his money all invested in Confederate bonds, now so much scrap paper, and his health unexpectedly improving, the worry became acute. He admitted that the prospect of ending it all had obsessed him ever since the fall of Richmond. And yet he remained transfixed by each newspaper account of the fruits of northern victory and especially of emancipation in the former Confederate capital. They horrified him. He did not live long enough to comment on the success in Washington of Fields Cook and the others or to applaud the sneers of the white press. He had read enough. In his final diary entry, he declared his "unmitigated hatred to Yankee rule" and despaired that deliverance would not come until far in the future "for the now ruined, subjugated, & enslaved Southern States!" With that last bilious malediction, on June 17 he put a musket to his open mouth and with a forked stick depressed the trigger.[27]

7
Correction of Every Evil

June to July 1865

Richmond's first postwar Fourth of July, coming only three months after the fire, was always going to be an uncertain milestone for Governor Pierpont and the local army command. However the government chose to celebrate, former Confederates were going to feel aggrieved at this reminder of their defeat. The meaning of the Fourth had changed, especially the meaning of independence and freedom for Virginians newly released from bondage.

In early July rumors of a Black insurrection made the rounds, and the army took the precaution of doubling its guard. Nervous shopkeeper George Bagby worried about "frequent assaults and burglaries by armed Negroes in & around this city" and confessed to a growing dread that serious violence lay ahead. Gossip about rural African Americans being unwilling to work because they expected plantations to be divided up among them found a ready believer in Bagby and others like him. He noted with bitter scorn that the Fourth would be celebrated by soldiers responsible for killing southern boys whose bones were bleaching in the sun on battlefields across Virginia.[1]

The Freedmen's Bureau assistant commissioner for Virginia, Orlando Brown, chose the Fourth of July to issue an address reminding Black people of their duty as new citizens. He told them what they already knew, that they must work hard to secure that citizenship ("be industrious and frugal," "education is of the highest importance," "become independent of charity and of government aid," "be quiet, peaceable, and law-abiding citizens"). His approach was patronizing, but he also vowed that the entire federal government stood ready to defend them against anyone who would deny them equal rights—a hopeful promise, if he could keep it.[2]

A crowd, mostly African American, gathered on the morning of the Fourth at the west front of the capitol facing Crawford's statue of Washington. The first buoyant days of their liberation had passed, and the mundane demands of getting and spending to keep body and soul together defined daily existence. Uncertainty about the practical meaning of freedom still prevailed, however, about whether their white neighbors accepted equality among all Richmonders. But this Fourth would be their first opportunity to participate in the great civic ritual that had previously excluded them, and they did not want to miss out. The war had given a hopeful answer to Frederick Douglass's famous antebellum address "What to the Slave Is the Fourth of July?"

The American Union Commission planted its headquarters tent at the center of the square, where it doled out food, garden seeds, and religious tracts to poor Black and white people. Artillery salutes resounded, and an army band played the "Star Spangled Banner," the first time many Richmonders had heard the tune in four years. A few days before, word circulated that Dr. Mary Walker would read the Declaration of Independence. At thirty years old, she was a minor celebrity, being among the first women to earn a medical degree in her native New York. Her cachet, though, attached less to that pioneering status than to her campaign for women's rights in general and in particular to reforming women's fashion. She often provoked ridicule for her various combinations of skirts worn over men's trousers. As a surgeon to an Ohio regiment, she was captured behind southern lines attending the wounded. The Confederates imprisoned her because they thought she was a spy. She returned to Richmond briefly after the war. When this strangely attired young woman, with an open, round face and hair pulled back and tied in a bun, walked down the city streets, she invariably attracted attention.

A southern journalist sneered at Walker for appearing at the Fourth of July ceremony "dressed in her usual jaunty hermaphrodite style," this time adorned with a federal major's gold braid. It pained him to see the Fourth monopolized by his conquerors. It aggrieved him more to hear the Declaration read by a woman, especially one

Pioneering woman physician Dr. Mary Walker read the Declaration of Independence at the first postwar Fourth of July celebration on Capitol Square. (National Institutes of Health)

of such avant-garde views. Walker—proud to be the first woman awarded the Medal of Honor—later said, "I have got to die before people will know who I am and what I have done." In the end, her appearance was anticlimactic: a disappointed northern visitor reported that Walker's voice was too weak to carry much beyond the speaker's platform.[3]

Afterward, the local press warned that remarks by two northern chaplains who followed Walker served only to "tear open the wounds of the past." That evening, a few drunken Confederate veterans got into fights with soldiers in blue. Fireworks lit up General Terry's headquarters, the house formerly occupied by Jefferson Davis. From the point of view of Confederates, the day was a sad commentary on the suspect Pierpont regime and the military administration that propped it up.[4]

Governor Pierpont was already in trouble before Dr. Walker's declamation on Capitol Square. The danger was brewing, in fact, before Fields Cook's delegation returned in fleeting glory from its meeting with President Johnson two weeks earlier. The governor had planted the seeds of his betrayal, as unionists saw it, during his first week in Richmond. They might forgive him for the presence of Confederates among the crowd who elbowed their way into the governor's mansion at his first reception there three days after arriving. But they blamed him for the shocking remarks he made the following morning.

It happened on May 30, when Pierpont received a delegation of county leaders from north of town. They came to offer their cooperation in restoring Virginia to its former prosperity. The spokesman declared their readiness to help Pierpont reestablish civilian government. He welcomed their sentiments and responded with like-minded platitudes that invoked the example of the Virginia founders. References to Crawford's nearby statue of Washington and to Houdon's smaller figure of the first president inside the capitol had by now become de rigueur for Pierpont.

With the conventional aside beloved of Upper South unionists, he ascribed the blame for war to South Carolina hotheads. He said he wished the last four years could be buried and forgotten but knew that was not possible. It was the task of all Virginians to heal the wounds. It was not, he said with a curious metaphor, "to your interest nor mine, when we meet on the street, to be snarling, and biting, and ready to tear out each other's vitals" but to foster goodwill to build the state anew. He concluded with the standard pieties of elected officials everywhere promising prosperity and happiness.[5]

He then uttered words that sent a frisson of horror down the spines of unionists who read them in their newspapers the following day. "The Constitution under which we are now acting was, you all know, a provisional one," he began. "It was made in time of war, and you all understand the fury of war legislation. Fortunately, it has within itself the correction of every evil it contains." Here was the loyalist governor of Virginia, who had kept the flame of Union burning throughout the rebellion, now planning to overturn the provisions of the 1864 Alexandria constitution, a document crafted expressly to protect the minority unionists from being submerged in a sea of rebels. The unfortunate phrase "every evil it contains" referred to the clause denying the franchise to those who supported the Confederacy, a clause Pierpont now seemed willing to jettison.[6]

As the governor saw it, his chief role was to help stitch together the frayed sinews of government so that Virginia could revive its broken economy. He came to believe he could not restore the state if it excluded from voting and officeholding the great majority of the white male electorate who had supported the South. There just were not enough unionists in Virginia to rely on them alone to populate the offices of local and state government.

On June 19, two days after Fields Cook and his compatriots stood before Andrew Johnson in the White House, the governor convened the Lilliputian legislature that had followed him from Alexandria to Richmond. They easily fit into his parlor because there were only three senators and thirteen delegates representing the few counties under Union rule for most of the war. For the past several years they and their Confederate counterparts in Richmond had spat venom across the contested hundred miles that separated the two warring capitals. Pierpont had participated in that vituperation, but now times had changed. He convinced the legislators to revise Virginia's constitution and restore the vote to most supporters of the Confederacy. All that would be required of them was to take the oath of allegiance as defined in President Johnson's May 29 amnesty proclamation. At his urging, they fixed a date in October for electing congressmen and a new state legislature. At the same time, a referendum would decide whether to extend the same rights not only to ordinary supporters of the Confederacy but also to those who had held office under it.

The result, alarmed unionists warned, would lead in a short time to former Confederates dominating state and local offices. Before June was over, unionists began to denounce Pierpont's betrayal. Some asked the federal government to replace him with direct military rule. Their opponents dismissed these charges as "bigotted cavillings" of insane men. But a more prescient observer predicted that as soon as Pierpont finished selling himself out, the Confederates would "kick him to the dogs."[7]

It troubled the governor that he could not persuade his unionist base of support that it should accept the aid of former Confederates to rebuild the state. He offended them and their opponents equally. He would not learn the full extent of his blunder until the fall elections for Congress and the state legislature. In the meantime, his efforts to revive Richmond's municipal government moved forward, starting by appointing former city council president David Saunders as provisional city manager. Saunders, a grocer and banker, was responsible for keeping the water and gas works running and collecting taxes. The governor declared all local offices vacant in the capital and other cities. He chose July 25 for a citywide election for mayor, city council, and other offices so that, according to the *Whig*'s stilted syntax, "the semi-chaotic state of affairs in our cities—Richmond especially—may continue but a short time longer." The city's prominence as the former Confederate capital meant that the election there would have broad significance as an early gauge of postwar southern opinion. For that reason, the North was watching the outcome too.[8]

Joseph Mayo had not learned his own lesson from the Black protest in June. The great-grandson of one of Richmond's founders, he was as out of style in his waistcoat and blue, brass-buttoned coat as in his outmoded political views. A die-hard Confederate, he was oblivious to the angry mood of the North, where the trial of the Booth conspirators transfixed the nation. The week before the assassins hanged, he blustered that he would stand for mayor once more "in spite of the government of the United States, so help me God. I defy them all." When General Turner, the local commander, told him bluntly the army would not stand for his candidacy, Mayo prudently recanted, but he did not intend to stay silent for long.[9]

Because there were no political parties, voters looked to the character of the candidates and their standing in the community to make their decisions. Where those candidates stood during the war was crucial. James Wesley Lewellen's *Republic* was the only even mildly Republican newspaper in town. He urged voters to select only candidates who were unobjectionable to the US Army. If they voted for men who failed that test, they would prolong military rule and might provoke widespread confiscation of property. The conservative press scoffed. It dismissed as ridiculous any thought that the election would pit secessionist candidates against Union men.[10]

Long-serving mayor Joseph Carrington Mayo repeatedly clashed with Black citizens striving for equal rights. (Collections of the Confederate Memorial Literary Society, Virginia Museum of History and Culture)

With Mayo out of the running, two candidates bid to occupy his chair. Nathaniel Sturdivant, a Virginia native, had unsuccessfully sought the office before and during the war served as a Confederate major. By early June he was advertising his law practice in the papers. His opponent, William Taylor, a New York–born merchant who had married a Richmond woman, had prospered in the capital for more than thirty years and was known for his wartime charitable work. He publicly proclaimed himself an unconditional Union man and hinted that his opponent was not. Incensed, Sturdivant asserted he was a loyal American, too. He denounced as mischievous lies the rumors that the election would be between a Union man and a secessionist. Like most Confederates, he said he accepted defeat and emancipation. That being the case, he could not imagine why anyone would expect more of him or think him disloyal.[11]

The election passed with only minor discord. Soldiers had to break up a fistfight among drunks at one polling station. Guards arrested a citizen for trying to vote three times. And one formerly enslaved man,

Robert Bolling, tried to vote but was turned away, to the merriment of bystanders who laughed at his impudence for thinking he could cast a ballot. If they had been paying attention, they would have known that African Americans were already agitating for equal rights, including the vote.

Generals Terry and Turner thought the temporary closing of one newspaper for disloyal statements and the jailing of another's imprudent editor would convince voters not to elect former rebels. They were wrong. It became clear from the sentiment of the crowds around the polling stations on election day that the winners would be those candidates who could boast of Confederate service. That meant Sturdivant won handily by almost a two-to-one margin, as did most city councilmen who had served in that role before and during the war. The press congratulated the citizenry for a peaceful election. Shopkeeper George Bagby conceded slyly that the victory of Sturdivant and other Confederates "may have been to some extent the result of their service in the field" but tried to argue that they won solely because they were better qualified.[12]

A day after the election, the winners and other officials assembled in city hall to organize the new municipal government, not just mayor and councilors but prosecutor, sheriff, superintendent of the gas and water works, and two dozen other minor offices. A congenial crowd of idlers bantered and swapped tales while they waited for the swearing in to begin. Just as the successful candidates were about to take their seats, an army officer strode into the room. He read a statement from General Turner that voided the election. After this bombshell, the uninaugurated councilors called on Governor Pierpont, but he would not overturn the army's decision.

The generals—and Pierpont too—had assumed that frequent protestations of loyalty by residents meant they would repudiate any rebels running for office. Sturdivant's landslide on the backs of voters who had served in the Confederate army confounded them. They failed to place themselves in the shoes of southern veterans who naturally supported men who had served with them. Terry later admitted his error privately to Judge Underwood. The election, he wrote, demonstrated that widespread sentiments of disloyalty still prevailed. He devoutly hoped the federal government would "be firm with these people" and pledged himself to that end. It was naïve of him to think that those Confederate sentiments, annealed by fire, death, and shared privation, could so quickly be shed by a community that had suffered through four years of war.[13]

It was another example of miscalculation, of one side misinterpreting the other's intentions, of failing to accept that they held strikingly different views on what loyalty meant. It would not be the last misapprehension as the different factions of citizens, the army, and the governor groped toward reconstructing the city. The tension between civil and military authority, which had been heightened with the appointment of Generals Terry and Turner in June, was even more pointedly brought to the fore with the dispute over the July election. The generals saw more clearly afterward that a too-hasty return to civilian control would not be in their interest or those of Black residents.

After the vote, the army knew, if it did not before, how much its notion of loyalty diverged from that of most white residents. The latter would not accept that their professed allegiance to the national government was insufficient for restitution of their rights. Some of them claimed there had been no division between Confederate and Union candidates at all but that they were all good citizens of the reunited nation. Others admitted that the mayoral race, at least, did give voters a choice between a red-blooded Confederate and a unionist, and they rejoiced in that clear-cut option. Some even went so far as to say, provocatively, that the army should praise them for holding their heads up and not cravenly turning their backs on "opinions which their kith and kin have died for." Black residents watching from the side knew the election results boded ill for their enjoyment of freedom. A Black newspaper said it enabled the whole country to see how former Confederates would act if left to their own devices. The result would be slavery "in more than its pristine vigor, although, perchance, its name may be changed." The promise of emancipation once more seemed in question. White unionists argued that the election proved their contention that their Confederate neighbors could not yet be trusted to hold public office. What could be expected from them, the *Republic* asked, these "silent rats who dodge around corners, boasting in the dark that they have never taken the oath of allegiance"? Those rebel neighbors, though, would not be shamed by such talk. Who was a loyal American citizen was a question that would be hotly contested for years to come.[14]

8

Stern Exactions

Summer 1865

Like other propertied men, Gustavus Adolphus Myers fell under the exclusion clause of the May 29 amnesty. A successful lawyer of sixty-four, Myers was a widely respected advocate, witty and well-read. He made his home, on Governor Street opposite Capitol Square, the center of a literary salon. A tall, lean figure with deep-blue eyes, curly brown hair, and high forehead, he had become a genial elder of charm and erudition with an equable temperament. He married the daughter of a governor; was a long-serving member of city council; board member of two Jewish congregations, Beth Shalome and Beth Ahabah; director of the Mutual Assurance Society and of Hollywood Cemetery; and leader of the Virginia Historical Society.

His house survived the inferno, but he had placed some of the historical society's manuscripts in a bank vault for safekeeping, where they met their fiery doom on April 3. Myers met Lincoln on his visit to the city. He told him the army had won the gratitude of residents for its conciliatory approach and hoped it would not require an oath of allegiance. That was all ancient history now. Since then, Myers had taken the oath to resume his legal practice.

With the end of the war, he renewed correspondence with a fellow attorney, the scholarly Conway Robinson, who had moved to Washington, DC, before Virginia seceded. The two old friends reveled in their revived contact. When Robinson asked Myers about the fate of libraries in Richmond, he could report that most had survived intact, though the state library had suffered terribly from carelessness and misuse. Myers also disabused Robinson of any thought that the two friends might retrieve a cent from the funds they had invested in Richmond banks.

In the face of the city's plight, Myers believed it his duty to submit humbly to the will of providence. He said it was in his nature to make the best of whatever befell him. That was false modesty. It is true that the equanimity with which he faced his altered circumstances shines through in his letters. And he may have taken consolation for his losses, as he told Robinson, by contemplating the stoicism of ancient Romans such as Cicero and Seneca. But with his property now under imminent threat of expropriation, this scion of one of the city's most prominent families was in no way passive and bent every nerve and sinew to secure it.

All during the summer of 1865, Richmond elites obsessed over the same topics as Myers. How would the granting or withholding of amnesty and the threat of confiscation unfold? The anxiety generated by uncertainty over these issues agitated them even more, for the moment, than what rights should be accorded to African Americans. They no longer feared for their lives as they had done in the early weeks, but expropriation threatened nearly every landowner, merchant, and lawyer worth more than twenty thousand dollars. As the perceived threat of physical violence receded, white Richmonders in the excluded class agitated more forcefully to safeguard their property. They made the case that confiscation would prevent them from aiding the rebuilding of the city. Uncertainty about enforcement of the law, they said, was "the chief cause of the paralys[i]s which has thus far kept the best portion of our city a mass of ruins."[1]

As Edmund Ruffin predicted before he stepped off the stage for good, that uncertainty made owners indifferent to improving their land or buildings. Pardon brokers began a controversial exchange that exploited the hopes of supplicants to have their requests expedited. It appalled Gustavus Myers to learn that the flour-milling Haxall brothers had to pay at least three thousand dollars. Richard Barton Haxall could not understand why they had been singled out, showing that he too had not fully appreciated his predicament. Myers called the whole pardon process a fraudulent swindle. He revealed his own naivete when he expressed hope that abuses in the system would be brought to the president's attention, as if Johnson had no clue. The flood of applications threatened to overwhelm the pardon clerks in the attorney general's office in Washington. The stack of paperwork from Virginia was more than ten feet high, higher than that of any other state, and contained more than three thousand petitions.[2]

On June 28 a group of citizens, worried that few applicants for pardon were winning President Johnson's approval, met at city hall and drafted a memorial describing the disasters that had befallen Richmond. Four years of war, the great fire, and the collapse of the currency had left people prostrate and despondent. At first northern money began to flow to aid the rebuilding. But just as quickly, that capital dried up when the attorney general declared that taking the oath of allegiance was not enough to secure a pardon. The twenty-thousand-dollar exclusion clause had a ruinous effect. Those encumbered by it were considered uncreditworthy. It therefore made title to property insecure. No sales were possible, and no money could be raised by taking out mortgages. "Industry is paralyzed," appealed the petitioners, "work is discouraged, energy is annihilated."[3]

They pleaded their case by emphasizing what this state of affairs meant for ordinary working people. They argued that "The poor tradesman or mechanic, the woman who earns her bread with her needle, the freedman seeking honest employment, all are discouraged and dejected." It was, said banker-lawyer William Macfarland, with thunderous understatement, "a serious embarrassment." The delegation that took the petition to Washington believed they had misjudged the president earlier. They were relieved when it seemed their fears about his intentions were in error, and, they said, they hoped the South would not be penalized further.[4]

When the president received the three-man delegation, however, he spurned their pleas. They emphasized the main point of the memorial—that the twenty-thousand-dollar exclusion prevented capital from being deployed to rebuild the city and employ workers. They appealed to the president's sense of fair play. Johnson replied in his usual sarcastic manner. If they were so concerned about indigent laborers, he asked, why did they not give the poor their wealth in excess of twenty thousand dollars? That would put them below the excluded level and aid the underprivileged at the same time. The conservative Johnson might not be allied to the radical Republican minority in Congress—vilified day and night in the Richmond press as "those pestilent marplots"—but like them, he still could not abide the arrogance of the moneyed classes of the South.[5]

In Richmond those wealthy individuals worried about a wartime precedent established not far away in the Virginia Tidewater, where the Union army had been dominant since 1862 and where freed people occupied abandoned plantations. One such estate, Rolleston, belonged to a former governor, Henry Wise. It was an irony not lost on him that, when he returned after the war, he found Rolleston possessed by formerly enslaved workers learning to read and write. One of their northern teachers allegedly was the daughter of the man Wise had hanged at Harpers Ferry, John Brown. Owners of great plantations in the Piedmont region around Richmond dreaded the same fate for their property.

At the Freedmen's Bureau in Washington, General Howard worried too but for different reasons. He correctly feared that as the prospect of a few exemplary hangings receded, white southerners would be emboldened. They might convince Johnson to approve their individual petitions for amnesty even if he did not rescind the twenty-thousand-dollar clause wholesale. In either case, that would mean the return of their property from the government. That included all those acres the Bureau was already using as farms and camps for freedmen and the even greater expanses of land Howard had his eyes on. He ordered his assistant commissioners across the South to make a quick record of all the abandoned and confiscated lands they possessed to expedite the process of expropriation. Orlando Brown, his man in Richmond, needed no such encouragement. He was already on record favoring comprehensive confiscation for the benefit of freed people. Brown urged his boss to accelerate the process before the former owners could reclaim their property.[6]

Because the legal process of confiscation was novel and uncertain of success, pessimistic unionists despaired. Some of them, like Alexander Rives, feared Confederate property owners would wriggle from under the threat. An eccentric conservative jurist who had bitterly opposed secession, the scholarly, bespectacled Rives had denounced the Confederacy and sat out the war as a neutral. Reactionaries later burned him in effigy. He warned the president against pardoning too many Confederates. He suggested that, instead of confiscation, punitive fines in proportion to means and guilt would at least extract some penalty, even if the owners eventually recovered their property.[7]

The move to seize the holdings of wealthy Richmonders, only theoretical until then, began in earnest in mid-July. Judge Underwood had enraged white Virginians in June by seeking the indictment of prominent Confederates for treason. Now he earned double damnation by going to Richmond and libeling, or marking for confiscation proceedings, more than one hundred properties of residents covered by the twenty-thousand-dollar clause. Two days after Mary Walker read the Declaration of Independence on Capitol Square, the US marshal set up shop to serve writs the judge had drawn. The properties included the Spotswood Hotel, owned by Joseph Crenshaw, and the Tredegar Iron Works, owned by Joseph Reid Anderson. The *Whig* denounced confiscation as revolting, cowardly, and despicably unjust. For those intemperate words, General Terry shut it down for two weeks.[8]

Some confiscation had been anticipated after the failure of the delegation to persuade the president, but the scope of planned expropriation astonished citizens. They had expected the blow to fall only on Confederate officers above the rank of colonel, but now it appeared that rich civilians were liable to have their property seized too. The *New York Times* reporter in town observed that the writs "caused such consternation among the moneyed men of the city as nothing else." They fumed with incandescent rage as they read the lists of dozens of individuals whose property was libeled. More would follow.[9]

While Judge Underwood's writs of confiscation rattled them, they also learned the troubling news that President Johnson himself had been behind the military action to void the July city elections. In regard to southern elections in general, Johnson said that whenever people showed a continuing spirit of rebellion, they should not be surprised if the government punished them. He singled out the Richmond mayoral contest as an example of bad behavior he would not tolerate. It was, he said emphatically, "with his sanction that the military authorities had set aside the election."[10]

The city's leaders decided they needed to make a more forceful assertion of their loyalty to the Union, and they called for a mass meeting on Capitol Square on August 29. The *Republic,* which had warned against electing Confederates, said that voters had been misled into thinking they could choose Sturdivant and other southern veterans without offending the people of the North. The meeting on the square would allow them to demonstrate that they supported the president's policies. The meeting's organizers agreed with the *Republic* about Johnson's policies, but most had no intention of repudiating their support of the Confederacy. That much could be inferred from a glowing account published the day of the meeting about a proposed gift from English supporters of the South—a statue honoring Stonewall Jackson. It would be the first of many such monuments that white Richmond would deploy to interpret the city's past through Confederate eyes.[11]

The organizers of the meeting intended it to be a grand affair. They turned to architect Henry Exall, an English native who had built many houses during the city's prosperous prewar years. He had seen his commissions go up in smoke on April 3 but offered his services to those bold and optimistic enough to rebuild. Although Exall had failed more than once in his real estate speculations and was considered a bad credit risk, the planners asked him to design a large platform against the eastern side of the capitol capable of seating a hundred people. It would need to be that large to accommodate all the dignitaries, speakers, secretaries, and musicians.[12]

Exall ran ropes from an upper window of the capitol across the speaker's stand to a tree on the grounds and hung an American flag and a state flag. The Virginia banner had flown from the capitol on many occasions, but on the day of the evacuation, relic hunters had torn out the state seal in the center. They left only the state's motto,

"Sic Semper Tyrannis," which had acquired an unfortunate notoriety as Booth's departing shout when he jumped to the stage of Ford's Theatre four months earlier. The organizers had to borrow the Stars and Stripes from the army.[13]

At 5:00 p.m. a crowd gathered, with white people to the left of the speaker's stand and Black people to the right. All around them they could see the ashen fruits of secession. The presiding officer chosen for the event, the young judge of the Hustings Court, William Lyons, gave the principal address. Lyons may have lacked an elegant speaking style, but he commanded widespread respect for his probity and for working with the Union army to reestablish the city's court system. He made the usual protestation that Virginians had not started the war but entered it with reluctance. They did, however, submit to the military outcome and, he vowed, accepted that secession and slavery were both dead. Further, Lyons said, they had taken the oath of allegiance in good faith. But now it appeared to him that many northern editors and politicians still did not believe Virginians could be trusted and must be subjected to martial law. Therefore, it was necessary to call this public meeting to express their devotion to the Constitution.

The speakers following Judge Lyons were all prominent former Confederates. They included city attorney Raleigh Daniel and banker William Macfarland. The latter made some opaque remarks about "the stern exactions of adversity" and urged his fellow citizens to do their civic duty. Daniel, like Macfarland, grudgingly accepted the war's outcome but denounced accusations that Richmond was still a hotbed of disloyalty. In particular, he faulted the North for misinterpreting the recently voided municipal elections. They did not, he asserted, demonstrate lingering secessionist sentiment. He came closer than other speakers to a fair assessment of the nation's woes when he admitted to "the general ignorance of both sections as regards each other."[14]

Even more provocative remarks came from a third speaker, the wealthy lawyer James Lyons, father of the meeting's presiding officer, personal friend of Jefferson Davis, and a former member of the Confederate Congress. Before the end of the war, he had vowed to wade through northern blood up to his armpits before allowing the Union army into town. Judge Underwood had indicted him, and his property was threatened with expropriation. Among other impolitic remarks, he said, "The North having relieved us [of] our slaves, he wished to God it would relieve us of their presence as freedmen." When he said that, he was well aware that half of his audience was Black.[15]

The meeting passed resolutions expressing the indignation of Richmonders at the efforts of some northerners "to brand the people of the South with perfidy and insincerity." They did pledge to accept the abolition of slavery and the defeat of secession, the standard concessions of white southerners who could not understand that any more was required of them. They would never admit that some feeling of penitence for plunging the nation into fratricide might be appropriate. The resolutions pledged to support President Johnson's Reconstruction policy. This, the audience was pointedly reminded, meant a restoration of the rights of all states, including the power of each to regulate suffrage. If that was not clear enough, the resolution denounced those who sought to give Black men the vote. That declaration showed the limitation to the meeting's understanding of what the end of slavery meant.[16]

A concluding resolution gave florid support for Johnson. It designated three citizens to take a copy to him with an invitation to visit Richmond. If he came, attorney Gustavus Myers privately noted, he would "see for himself how wretchedly we are slandered." The three were Macfarland, banker and former Confederate congressman; Robert Ridgway, the former editor of the *Whig* who had opposed secession but also the prosecution of Confederates; and one steadfast unionist, Charles Palmer.[17]

The small size of the crowd, estimated at no more than six hundred in addition to the dignitaries on the platform, must have disappointed the organizers. The self-pitying defiance of Lyons's address and the seconding speeches hardly constituted ringing endorsements of loyalty to the Union. The northern press declared the meeting a failure because it demonstrated that, even if the power of secession in Richmond was broken, "the spirit and wish to do evil still remain."[18]

Richmond elites and their northern antagonists continued to speak at cross purposes about what constituted devotion to the Union. The former believed the conditional unionists of 1861 who only reluctantly bowed to secession should be considered unionists in 1865. For the

North, only those persecuted few who never recanted their support of the Union throughout the war could be considered loyal. Both parties were just talking past one another in the summer of 1865. They would continue to do so for years to come.

A week after the meeting on Capitol Square, the *Republic* ran a supplement that illustrated the high stakes for rebuilding the city. In it, page after page of nearly identical one-paragraph announcements, boxed by black lines that mimicked death notices, spelled out financial doom for more than 250 well-to-do Richmond families. Here were Judge Underwood's dreaded writs to confiscate their property, prefaced by the ominous salutation from the federal district court, "to all whom it may concern, greetings." Some of the writs had been known to the owners starting in mid-July, but seeing them all together in print in early September sent a renewed collective thrill of horror through most of the city's leading households. The notices all ended with the same warning giving the date of the trial at which all interested parties should present themselves and show cause why their property should not be condemned. Some of them seized physical properties; some confiscated shares of companies. One of them targeted the luxurious Spotswood Hotel, the renovated watering hole for wealthy visitors since before the war. Alarmed by the announcement, the managers posted a notice denying the hotel was closed. Not so, they said, the Spotswood remained open for business. But was Richmond?[19]

9

Phoenix Arising

Summer to Fall 1865

Francis Pierpont had arrived in Richmond with the traditional distaste of western Virginians for wealthy easterners. But he consulted with citizens of every political stripe—steadfast unionists, old-line Whigs who had given only tepid support to the Confederacy or none at all, southern-rights Democrats grudgingly resigned to defeat, and even die-hard rebels who had denounced him during the war and after as a usurper and a traitor to the Old Dominion. There is no evidence he sought out Black leaders for their opinions, however. Before long, he began to appreciate the proprietors of Virginia's railroads, mills, and factories, who came to advise him. He knew he would need their help reviving the state's shattered economy. He accepted their protestations of loyalty at face value and assumed they would repudiate the secessionist extremists who had precipitated the war. And he thought they would treat the freed population with reasonable fairness, even if neither he nor they believed African Americans merited social equality or the vote.

By the end of summer, Pierpont's attempt to be evenhanded had widened the gap between himself and other white unionists without winning over those who had supported the South. More and more, he found himself caught between disappointed unionists and assertive former Confederates. He was certain of one thing—the destructive effect of Judge Underwood's expropriation of property on his attempt to stimulate economic revival. He lobbied the US attorney general to get the confiscations stopped. At the same time, he began endorsing and passing along to Washington most individual requests for pardon.

These decisions would have been of little consequence, though, if the president had not made a shocking reversal in his attitude toward the defeated South. That stunning volte-face threatened to dash the hopes of freed people and embolden former Confederates. It profoundly altered the course of reconstructing southern society and politics. It set Andrew Johnson on a collision course with the Republican Congress. In Washington, it would seem, the fortunes of the Richmond establishment were about to undergo a dramatic turn for the better.

As early as June, Johnson began receiving reports like that from his longtime friend Harvey Watterson, a newspaperman and former Democratic congressman from Tennessee, who showed little sympathy for the freedmen. He had toured Virginia and concluded that Richmond "is as quiet as before the Rebellion." In a stunning misreading of silence, Watterson told the president that submission to Union victory was absolute and sincere. Such reports merely confirmed Johnson in his astonishing change of opinion. In contrast to his outraged scorn for Confederates only months before, he now appeared willing to grant them absolution. It seemed that no forest of gibbets would be needed after all. In turn, southern whites began to mute their loathing of the president. By the end of summer, they had transformed him into their paladin. He would, they now fervently hoped, save them from radical Republicans in Congress, restore their power, and, crucially, reaffirm their control over Black southerners.[1]

There were plenty of false signals. Not least were Johnson's acceptance of the grievances presented by Fields Cook's delegation to the White House in June, his snide dismissal of the Richmond merchants who pleaded in early July for lifting the twenty-thousand-dollar exclusion, and his voiding of the city election later that month. His reasons for jettisoning his earlier vow to bar a return to power by the antebellum elites are obscure. But by late summer he was rapidly signing individual pardons for wealthy southerners, many dozens a day. Nothing did more to brighten the prospects of landowners and to dismay the Freedmen's Bureau and its clients. The president now reckoned that he needed an alliance with the upper classes of the South in his bid for reelection. The quickest way to cement that tie was to give them amnesty. He and they both believed the South should remain a white man's country. In Johnson's political calculus, disappointing the freed population and the Bureau would do him no harm.[2]

The reversal of fortune for Richmond's traditional power brokers was not instantaneous, but it was undeniable, and it had profound consequences. Over the course of little more than a single month, a seesaw pattern of press reports began to reveal the tectonic shift in the president's policy. On August 29, the mass meeting on Capitol Square entreated the president to abandon confiscation. A week later public notices detailed the drastic reach of expropriation, extending to most of the better-off white families of Richmond. But then, on September 11, unionist Charles Palmer returned from the White House with good news for his Confederate neighbors who were fearful of losing their property. He was right: two weeks later Johnson suspended the issuance of any new writs of confiscation. Four days after that, General Howard announced that rumors the government would give freedmen parcels of land at Christmas were false. On October 9, it was reported that Johnson had signed 2,658 pardons, three-fifths of them in the previous ten days.[3]

As he pressed his own case, Gustavus Myers could sense the change, and it buoyed his spirits. He good-naturedly wrote a friend that by the time Judge Underwood convened his court in October to expropriate estates, "I hope I shall be a 'pardoned traitor.'" That flippant attitude soured when he finally was able to register his pardon at the federal marshal's office. It appalled him to see how eagerly officials there were to collect the requisite, and in his eyes, exorbitant fees. Even so, the change in pardon policy heralded better times to come for people like him. The people who had wielded economic and political power in the Confederate capital looked set to do so again.[4]

The most prominent Richmond beneficiary of Johnson's reversal was Joseph Reid Anderson, principal owner of the city's largest employer.

Former Confederate general Joseph Reid Anderson built his Tredegar Iron Works into a leading industry in the postwar city. (Library of Congress)

The massive Tredegar Iron Works occupied a vast complex of buildings along the river just beyond the western edge of the Burnt District. Before the war Anderson had built Tredegar into the fourth-largest such manufactory in America. He employed eight hundred skilled men, some of them enslaved. His personal wealth exceeded three-quarters of a million dollars. His foundry survived, in part because the fire did not reach it and because he had armed his workers to deter looters on the night of evacuation. His quest for pardon began before Richmond's ashes cooled, when he met Lincoln on the president's visit to the city. But he failed to prevent federal agents from filing suit in July to confiscate his business assets, those of his associates, and even their private homes.

Over the summer Anderson pressed his case. In the petition he sent to Washington requesting a pardon, crafted by lawyer-banker William Macfarland, he failed to mention his secessionist views in 1861 and minimized the size of his Confederate contracts. Governor Pierpont was willing to overlook that history and made a compelling personal plea to Johnson for the iron maker. He argued that the government should not pursue a policy to "strike down men of great energy like Anderson," whose force of character and talents were essential to hastening economic recovery. With this endorsement, Anderson went to the White House and spoke to the president in person four times. His timing was excellent: he arrived just as Johnson began to soften his animus toward Confederates. The South's leading industrialist left the president's office on September 21 cheered by the coveted slip of paper in his hand granting him pardon.[5]

As amnesties flowed from Johnson's pen and the threat of confiscation faded, business leaders could focus on rebuilding. Like Anderson, hatmaker John Dooley was energized by his pardon. By summer he hired a contracting firm to build a new factory in a prime location on Main Street. He decided he needed better quarters for his retail shop and moved to rented space on the ground floor of the Spotswood Hotel. As public-spirited as before the war, Dooley served on William Munford's committee for poor relief. He was well on his way to reclaiming his place as a community leader, throwing himself into Irish and Catholic charity work and becoming a director of the Farmer's National Bank.[6]

After lawyers like Gustavus Myers received their pardons and civilian courts reopened, the once-vibrant legal culture of the Virginia capital resumed. One of their number, Robert Ould, had been the Confederate head of prisoner exchanges. An outspoken irreverence and taste for gambling imparted a raffish air to the confident, urbane Ould. His relationship with his Union counterparts in the exchange earned him early release from jail after the city fell. Within days he was dining with them at the Spotswood Hotel. Ould attracted unwelcome attention during the trial of Henry Wirz, commandant of the notorious Andersonville prison camp. The northern press was aghast when testimony surfaced quoting a wartime letter from Ould touting the prisoner exchanges as a way of getting rid of "miserable wretches." The flap blew over quickly, though, and failed to derail Ould's pardon or his return to a lucrative civilian practice.[7]

Richmond had been a center for milling wheat and the leading exporter of it before the war. A handful of giant enterprises, using enslaved as well as free labor, intensive capital inputs, and the latest technology, dominated the export market in high-quality flour between Rio de Janeiro and Richmond. The largest of these, the colossal Gallego Mills, located on the rapids to take advantage of the city's superb source of water power, had towered physically and financially over its competitors. For a time it was the largest such mill in the world. Then the Warwick and Barksdale families who operated Gallego watched their giant building collapse in a shower of sparks during the evacuation fire. Undeterred, Abraham Warwick announced plans in June to rebuild on an even grander scale on the same site, an undertaking that would take many months.[8]

More than iron and milling, Richmond's economy hinged on tobacco. Great fortunes had arisen as the snuff and pipe tobacco of colonial times yielded to a mania for chewing in the early nineteenth century. In dozens of factories, hundreds of enslaved workers deveined the leaves, soaked them in a viscous syrup of sugar and licorice, sometimes adding a sprinkling of rum and spices, and then molded and pressed them into plugs or twists. By midcentury, cigar smoking was beginning to rival chewing, but the habit of the plug and the twist continued to enjoy wide acceptance, ingrained at all levels of society. Foreign visitors remarked on the ubiquity of spittoons and the sight of men spewing tobacco-infused spittle, with, as a visiting Charles Dickens remarked in disgust, "yellow streams from half-chewed tobacco trickling down their chins." Repellent or not, the chaw was golden.[9]

The prince of tobacco manufacturers before the war had been James Thomas Jr., a pious but aggressive entrepreneur who dominated the production of chewing tobacco. He was one of the richest men in town, employing more than three hundred African American men, who chanted and sang to relieve the monotony as they stemmed, lumped, and pressed the tobacco that was the source of his fortune. His stylish Italianate house escaped the fire, as did his main factory at Cary and Seventh Streets, though he lost much other property in the Burnt District. An associate told him he was lucky: "Your losses though immense are not as great as many others, as they lost all."[10]

With his bald pate and clean-shaven chin, Thomas looks almost cherubic as he stares out from a prewar daguerreotype proudly grasping the font of his wealth—a golden sheaf of dried leaves in one hand

James Thomas Jr., one of the city's richest men before and after the war, employed hundreds of African Americans in his tobacco factories. (Virginia Baptist Historical Society)

and a great plug of chewing tobacco in the other. Despite his benign appearance, he was known for sharp business practices. When the crisis of 1861 paralyzed domestic trade, he shrewdly rushed great quantities of product to his British factor on the eve of Virginia's secession and kept the profits there. Like Tredegar's Anderson, who also had a substantial sterling account in London, he thus ensured the survival of much of his wealth whoever won the war. While competitors were starved for capital in 1865, Thomas possessed ample funds to restart his business and rehired large numbers of workers. Despite being plagued by debilitating nervous complaints, with his pardon firmly in hand on August 20, he too began to rebuild.[11]

The army returned ownership of railroads to their stockholders over the course of the summer. By then the roads had repaired their lines well beyond the meager distances in service at war's end. By September, the Richmond, Fredericksburg & Potomac could carry passengers to Washington in eight and a half hours, twice daily. Baltimore was eleven hours away, Philadelphia sixteen and a half, and New York twenty-one.[12]

In September the Richmond & Danville line, which had spirited Jefferson Davis away on the night of April 2–3, held a stockholders meeting. The election of a new president to replace Lewis Harvie, one of the original secessionists of 1861, illustrated how blind some Richmonders were to the changed political landscape. The favorite candidate among individual stockholders was Confederate general Joseph E. Johnston. Many speakers extoled his virtues, but Charles Palmer, the unionist ally of Governor Pierpont and holder of the state's proxies, branded such a move impolitic. On hearing this, John Harmer Gilmer, a meddlesome conservative lawyer, got the meeting adjourned for a day because he was sure he could persuade General Terry to allow Johnston to become the railroad's president. He failed. The next day the meeting reconvened and chose an alternative candidate. An overwhelming majority of individual shareholders still stubbornly voted for Johnston, but Palmer cast all the state's proxies for the alterative and thus decided the outcome.[13]

Waterborne passenger service with the outside world expanded to the point that the Powhatan Steamboat Company announced a triweekly service between Richmond and Baltimore. The Old Bay Line and the New York and Virginia Steamboat Company offered spirited competition. Commerce on the river was still hazardous, however. In September, after loading a cargo of flour for Rio, the *Aquidneck* struck a Confederate mine and had to be towed to Baltimore for repairs to its copper bottom.[14]

A slow but steady uptick in the local economy was apparent by autumn. Gustavus Myers noted approvingly a burst of activity in the Burnt District. A wave of public notices, full of hope, announced shareholders meetings, the formation of new partnerships, and the resumption of businesses closed by war or fire. Skilled and unskilled workers in the building trades found employment as more businesses needed quarters to resume operation. Dozens of little machine shops began churning out the elements necessary for rebuilding—doors, sash windows, blinds, and a myriad of other iron and wooden fittings and fixtures. Blacksmiths resumed hammering out countless varieties of kitchen and farm implements. Stores offered up every variety of paint, glass, hardware, masonry, and other building supplies. A local Freedmen's Bureau official, Halstead Merrell, optimistically believed the city was quickly being rebuilt. Another report in a similar vein said, "The burnt district has been made musical by the clear ring of the carpenter's hammer."[15]

The aroma of progress once more suffused the air—a pungent mixture of wood and bituminous coal smoke, curing sweet-scented tobacco, horse manure, and the reek of Shockoe Bottom tanneries. But amid the too-sanguine stories about revival and rosy predictions for the future, it was obvious that Richmond was still a city more of potential than actual prosperity. The cornucopia of goods and services offered in city shops belied the nagging stagnation that held back the local economy, still starved of capital. New buildings were slowly rising in the fields of ash, but rubble still predominated. New construction was surrounded by wretched streets and worse sidewalks. No one had collected rubbish from the malodorous alleys during the war or after. People still dumped the carcasses of dead horses in Shockoe Creek. Appeals to enforce city ordinances against dumping went unheeded. Residents accepted the stench of outdoor privies and open sewers as an unavoidable cost of urban living.

Signs of the war and its consequences abounded a year and more after the fire. Life went on, but no one could avoid being reminded of the human cost the conflict had wrought in the city. Dr. W. M. Maclure offered to help. He announced he had obtained complete lists of those who had died in military hospitals and prisons and was willing to "disinter, disinfect and send home at a low cost" such remains. In sad juxtaposition, the advertising sections of newspapers ran frequent notices for two products in great demand in Richmond: prosthetic limbs and fireproof safes.[16]

The differing perspectives between white southerners and northerners were nowhere starker than on the issue of labor. For the former, no problem loomed so large as how to regulate Black labor in the postwar economy. Most white people believed they had to supervise African Americans in freedom just as they did under slavery, and that perspective was the measure of their inability to imagine Black men and women as fellow Virginians. "The Negro is in no condition," wrote a Richmond merchant to a sympathetic northern cousin, "to be trusted with his entire freedom." White people believed that they had the best interests of the freedmen at heart. This was a mantra repeated over and over. White Richmonders told themselves that, left alone, they would treat Black people with kindness and generosity. They thought they understood African Americans and northerners did not. According to them, freedmen were indolent and only worked when they pleased or were compelled. In the words of one observer, "A more worthless and unproductive set of laborers cannot be found at present in any part of the civilized world." People like him thought the teachers who came down from the North in the guise of aiding freed people were intent only on sowing discord between the races. As a result of these interlopers, southern whites believed, they "will be made to suffer by negro cupidity, partisan calumny and fanatical tyranny."[17]

For their part, northern observers of the prostrate city believed former Confederates could not be trusted with the well-being of African Americans. "As soon as pardoned," one outsider despaired, "they put on their old airs, and crack their whips over Union and colored men."[18]

Black Richmonders had no doubt they were better off out from under the control of the former system. That fall a visiting journalist asked a worker in the Burnt District if it was true what the writer had been told, that Black people preferred slavery to the uncertainties of freedom. The young man was quick to correct him. "Oh, no, sir!" he replied with alacrity. "We're men now, but when our masters had us we was only change in their pockets." They knew that the economic distress afflicting all of Richmond fell hardest on them and were eager to disprove the canard that African Americans were predisposed to be lazy. They knew widespread worries about the harvest meant a hard winter was coming. The wheat crop across the South had failed that year, and the corn crop, though promising, had not been planted as extensively as before. Starvation loomed for city residents if they did not find employment. The city's African Americans denied charges that they would steal for food or die of starvation from sloth. "We can say for ourselves," a group of tobacco workers declared, "we had rather work for a living, give us a Chance."[19]

The complete overturning of the southern system of labor that emancipation wrought caused immense anxiety. Because white Virginians thought they could not rely on freed people, they cast about for an alternative source of labor. Despite abundant evidence that Black men and women were working hard to make a life amid the ruins, whites clung to the belief that they were naturally lazy. With freedom, one wrote, they had "become idle, vicious in their habits, vagabond and vagrant." It drove former slave owners to distraction because they thought northerners had no idea of the problems the South faced. They founded organizations to attract workers from the North or from Europe, any source of white labor they could imagine. As early as June, Governor Pierpont lent his name to the masthead of one such effort. Another, the Virginia Central Immigration Society, sought to dispatch an agent to England and Scotland to recruit agricultural workers. Others cropped up over the next few years. They all failed miserably.[20]

The chimera of importing white labor fed, in part, on a bizarre prediction that rapidly gained currency: the concept of "the vanishing Negro." This notion appealed to many white Americans, North as well as South. They thought African Americans, once cut adrift from the supposed benevolent paternalism of the peculiar institution, could not care for themselves. The day before Lee surrendered, Christopher Tompkins, a planter to the west of town, observed the exodus of his former slaves toward the capital. He doubted they would find paradise there, believing they would "be exterminated like the Indians." Susan Hoge, the minister's wife who gave African Americans credit for good behavior in the first postwar weeks, nevertheless bought into this fantasy. "Poor creatures!" she asserted with scant charity, "their doom is sealed in a few generations." Journalist Francis Dawson claimed without evidence that freedmen were dying in droves from starvation and sickness. They could not care for themselves, he exclaimed, "I can only hope . . . that the whole negro race will soon become extinct."[21]

Misguided hope for white immigration was not the only *ignis fatuus* to beguile city residents. The gold that left on the night of the evacuation haunted them, especially bankers desperate for capital. In addition to what belonged to the Confederate treasury, Richmond banks had entrusted their bullion and coins to the fleeing southern government. Although most of the Confederate specie was paid out for expenses as Davis's party fled south, the portion owned by Richmond institutions made it safely to a bank vault in Georgia.

With federal blessing, William Macfarland's Farmer's Bank of Virginia and others sent agents under Union army escort to retrieve their money. They succeeded and began the return to Richmond in five wagons. Bad luck dogged their path as robbers, likely Union deserters, relieved them of most of their assets. In a mad scramble across Georgia, the agents managed to recover $100,000 in gold, but then Union general Edward Augustus Wild intervened. The flamboyant abolitionist claimed the funds belonged to the Freedmen's Bureau because they were captured or abandoned property. As a result, the treasure ended up being taken to Washington until the contested ownership could be sorted out.

That tale explained why Macfarland went to Washington in September to seek an audience with the president. He was in the federal capital as part of the delegation to plead Richmond's loyalty but used the chance to make the case for his fellow bankers. Not until 1893, after lawyers wrangled for decades, did a small portion of the gold—only $16,987.88—return to Richmond banks.[22]

The president's changed opinion about pardons heartened white Richmonders who had expected the North to impose a draconian peace. It also gave Governor Pierpont hope that he could enlist the support of well-to-do residents to rebuild the city. But he learned that becoming more charitable toward these former Confederates and supporting their pardon applications did not mean they would become his friends. To them, he was still their wartime foe. He could not please every side and ended up satisfying no one.

Residents of the Virginia capital had begun to spar with their occupiers as soon as the US Army arrived. Tensions ratcheted up in tandem with Johnson's softening stance toward southern elites and with the army's demobilization. At first, Confederates saw hopeful signs that the army might not be as demanding as feared and might even favor restoration in some fashion of the prewar status quo. Their hopes were dashed in June when Generals Terry and Turner replaced their more conservative predecessors. For more than a year, from that point forward the tension between civil and military authority was the hallmark of municipal affairs.

The antagonism flared when General Turner, as commander in the city, annulled the municipal election and periodically shut down newspapers for disloyal comments. As the fear of expropriation diminished, white people began to reassert themselves in a determined effort to re-create as much of the old order as possible. Turner's superior, General Terry, was convinced that the proprietors of the city's newspapers "hate us as thoroughly now as they did during the height of the rebellion." He watched with dismay as they adroitly praised President Johnson's policies. Under the cover of that allegiance, he believed, they continued their treasonous ways. Terry privately lamented that he could not very well punish editors for writing articles that praised Washington's course. As a serving officer, he knew his power was derivative: he could not be seen to oppose government policy. He might nominally wield great power in Richmond, but he was increasingly constrained by the common cause former Confederates were beginning to make with the Johnson administration.[23]

Rapid demobilization progressively reduced the number of soldiers at Terry's and Turner's disposal. By autumn, the drawdown began to overstretch the army and impede the Freedmen's Bureau, which relied on the military for staffing. At the same time, the generals retained power to intervene in local affairs, and martial law remained in effect for the rest of 1865 and beyond. Nearly four hundred army posts across the South, even as demobilization of the large armies continued, let white southerners know the power of the federal government was more than a theory. To them, historic fear of a standing army became a present threat. Resentment festered on both sides. Former Confederates fumed at being subject to the military presence, and army officers ground their teeth at the resistance of white residents. Both sides learned that a defeated people were not without power. Few of them imagined the crooked road their path would follow to give Richmond's people a sense of normalcy in their relations with Washington and with each other.[24]

Among the first regiments into the city on April 3 was Colonel William Kreutzer's Ninety-Eighth New York. A tall, erect officer with close-set eyes and a Van Dyke beard, Kreutzer had seen the evacuation fire at its hottest and witnessed frightened citizens huddling that night inside the capitol and on the lawn below. Later he denounced relic hunters for their gruesome harvest from the battlefields around the city. He remained for five months as district provost marshal and adjudicated every species of infraction between civilians and soldiers. He once sent a detachment to break up a drunken crowd of Union soldiers who were harassing African Americans at the steamboat landing. But it was Kreutzer's own men who bound Jinny Scott's husband in a coffin and smeared molasses on his face to attract flies.[25]

In the summer the wealthy unionist distiller Franklin Stearns gave a dinner for Governor Pierpont, Colonel Brown of the Freedmen's Bureau, and local unionists. Kreutzer, a scholarly officer who had taught college courses before the war, was asked to give a speech on the future of Virginia. He argued for breaking up large estates and embracing the potential of free labor to make the Old Dominion prosperous again. He raised eyebrows when he said, "Out and down with your foolish aristocratic ideas." Further, he instructed them, it was modern civilization and free labor, not simply superior numbers, that had won the war. Kreutzer confessed that a few lame attempts to cheer his remarks failed to rouse the audience. Later Stearns privately told him he agreed but dared not openly endorse such an opinion.[26]

As demobilization gathered steam in late summer, Kreutzer's regiment looked longingly toward its departure for home. In a round of farewell visits, the colonel reminisced with the local lawyers and journalists he had come to think of as friends. A group of real estate agents invited him to share his ideas on how to induce discharged northern soldiers to settle in Virginia. He reprised his ideas from the Stearns dinner about dismantling sprawling estates but found no takers. The night before he sailed home, he and his comrades visited the offices of the *Republic* for a farewell dinner. The editors praised his work as provost marshal. They even intimated that he planned to return to practice law and make the city he had helped conquer his home. It never happened. He went back to Lyons, New York, raised a family, and became the proverbial pillar of his community. As his impolitic remarks at the Stearns dinner revealed, he never really understood the people of Richmond, Black or white.[27]

10
An Equal Chance

Summer to Fall 1865

Edmonia Lewis was a sensation. The first female sculptor of color to achieve wide success, she enchanted Boston abolition circles with her portrait busts of John Brown and Robert Gould Shaw, colonel of the celebrated all-Black Fifty-Fourth Massachusetts Regiment. The shrewd daughter of an African American father and a Native American mother, she encouraged the press to emphasize her exotic background to further her ambitions. She allowed people to think of her as an untamed child of the wilderness. In fact, she grew up in New Jersey and attended Oberlin College, thanks to a rich half brother. She later joined a fabled circle of expatriate women sculptors in Rome, returned briefly to acclaim in America, and then disappeared from public view in London. In 1865, however, international success still lay in the future for this driven self-promoter, only twenty-one years old. In July she put her promising career on hold to teach in the burgeoning network of schools for the newly freed children of Richmond.

When she arrived, the spontaneous creation of schools had enjoyed several months of energizing success. They became a magnet for northern teachers keen to bring literacy to the first generation freed from bondage. The June change in military command to the more sympathetic Generals Terry and Turner gave heart to Richmond's African Americans and to teachers like Lewis. As time went on, however, former Confederates shed their fear of reprisals and with growing force tried to reassert control over Black residents. At a meeting at Second African Baptist Church, parishioners and others complained about robberies,

The sculptor Edmonia Lewis briefly came to Richmond to help teach the first generation of emancipated children. (National Portrait Gallery)

assaults, and "the seeming inability of the provost-marshals to accord us justice." Lewis fell victim to that abuse. A month into her teaching stint, she and her companion from Boston returned to their boardinghouse one day and found that their trunk had been stolen, taken to a vacant lot, and rifled. The two young women were left with little more than the clothes they wore. The next month Lewis sailed for Rome. She later said, "The land of liberty had no room for a colored sculptor."[1]

After she left, freed people publicly proclaimed their demands for political equality. They successfully took control of their churches. They welcomed the Freedmen's Bureau's relaunch after its false start in May. They enjoyed a measure of progress with their schools and justice through the Bureau's court. But they did not achieve what they wanted because Virginia, like other former Confederates states, ignored their pleas for equal rights.[2]

A few weeks after Lincoln's assassination, the Rev. Peter Randolph, forty years old, arrived in Richmond from Boston. He was met by

Fields Cook at the Rocketts steamboat landing below the city. It is not apparent how they knew one another, but both men were Baptist ministers. One was already a leader in the local community, and the other soon became one. Like Cook, Randolph had been born into slavery in rural Virginia. Unlike Cook, who earned enough to buy his own freedom, he was emancipated by his owner's will along with more than sixty others. The executor, however, illegally kept them in bondage until Randolph, who was literate, had read the will and worked with a lawyer to gain their freedom after three years of litigation. They received a joyful welcome in Boston, where he became a minister and engaged in antislavery work.

Like many other northern African Americans, Randolph wanted to see for himself what was happening in Richmond after emancipation. Shortly after arriving, he began preaching at Ebenezer Baptist Church, which soon asked him to be its interim pastor. A charismatic preacher, during his four years there he increased the church's membership and its role in the community. He once had a conversation with Robert Ryland, the white former pastor of First African Baptist Church, that reveals the chasm separating their views of slavery. At the time, Ryland did not know his interlocutor was Virginia-born and tried to tell him how mild bondage had been in the Old Dominion. Randolph remembered that he replied with a sigh, "If Hell was any worse than slavery in Virginia, I did not want to go there."[3]

Randolph typified the first generation of postemancipation leaders, a large portion of whom were, like him, literate, politically moderate, and of mixed Black and white ancestry. He was a man of steely purpose. He involved himself in politics from his first days in Richmond and had a hand in the meetings that sent Fields Cook and others to the White House in June. He also became the spokesman for Black Baptists negotiating to reclaim their church property from white trustees. In those discussions, he asked that they "meet us as Christian brethren, and not as slaves." That proved to be too much to ask, and after three rounds of talks, the stalemated negotiators went their separate ways. The Freedmen's Bureau's Orlando Brown joined the effort of Black Methodist parishioners to gain control over their buildings. He was especially concerned because southern Methodists, and in particular their white trustees in Richmond, were staunch Confederates. It took more months of negotiation, but by early 1866, African Americans achieved their goal and replaced white church trustees with their own.[4]

At the same time that thieves were tossing Edmonia Lewis's steamer trunk, a remarkable meeting that heightened white concern over rising Black political consciousness took place one hundred miles north of Richmond in Alexandria's Lyceum Hall. A convention of African American men gathered there to demand equal rights as free citizens of the commonwealth. The Colored State Convention feared that the promise of emancipation would be negated and the oppression of the past reinstituted. In addition to fifty certified delegates, hundreds of spectators, both men and women, and even a few curious former Confederate officers, observed the proceedings. Prominent in the Richmond delegation was Fields Cook, whose leadership during the June protests led to his appointment as one of the convention's vice presidents. Other Richmonders included R. C. Hobson, Robert W. Johnson, and N. H. Anderson. Manchester, the suburb directly across the James River from Richmond, sent R. T. Edwards and Jordan Smith.[5]

Some delegates reported that hostile parties had tried to prevent the assembly, some by bribing men to stay away, others by more sinister threats. At the end of the four-day meeting, Cook electrified attendees when he read a letter he had received. It read, in part, "Beware! beware! Fields Cook, you and other negroes will die before the autumn leaves fall upon the unavenged graves of the many Southerners who are buried through our land." Cook assured the gathering that such threats did not scare him.[6]

Among the resolutions the convention endorsed was an appeal written by Cook. It expressed the heartfelt desire of emancipated Virginians to live in peace and friendship with their neighbors. But it warned that there were those "who despise us simply because we are black." And it declared that freedom could only be secured by the franchise and the bayonets of the US Army. The appeal denounced Governor Pierpont for selling out the freedmen and siding with disloyal Virginians before he had been in Richmond a month. He had been seduced by the Richmond elite, it said: "Behold the potency of wine and fine dinners!" Looking to the fall elections, it implored Congress not to seat representatives from Virginia until Black people received all the rights of white citizens. The burning desire of the delegates for respect from their white neighbors as equals suffused the appeal. But it was more than a desire; they would accept nothing less than equality as the just outcome of freedom. "All we ask," they demanded, "is an equal chance with the white traitors varnished and japanned with the oath of amnesty."[7]

Across the South, African Americans held conventions like the one in Alexandria, but the state governments set up by President Johnson ignored them. In Richmond, white residents professed to believe the city's Black residents did not support the sentiments of Cook's appeal. But that expression of assertiveness gave fair notice that the formerly enslaved would not settle for second-class status. It illustrated their fears that the oppression of slavery might not be past after all. It was a warning shot in an unequal seesaw contest that would persist for years.[8]

The one thing on which there was no disagreement among white Richmonders was that the vote belonged exclusively to white men. Nor, in the summer of 1865, did many northern Republicans dissent. It did not occur to many in either camp that Black men might think they deserved the franchise. More broadly, white people could not imagine conceding the equal chance that Fields Cook and the Alexandria meeting demanded. The first stirrings of such sentiment in Virginia began in Norfolk, which had been occupied early in the war. Richmond did not lag far behind. On May 9, hardly a month after the fire, a group met expectantly at the house of shoemaker Robert Johnson to form the Colored Men's Equal Rights League. Their constitution asserted their claim to the same respect and dignity accorded other men and appealed for recognition of their rights as citizens. Even though Black Richmonders could not yet vote, the July election campaign for city offices was still of keen interest to them. They had suffered the mailed fist of local power under Joseph Mayo and did not want to experience it again.[9]

The struggle for the vote still lay in the future. More immediately, as important to them that summer was seeing whether the Freedmen's Bureau would gain traction after its inauspicious start in June. The Bureau's assistant commissioner for Virginia, Colonel Brown, had been frustrated by the previous army commanders, and the Bureau got off to a slow start. But Brown knew the change of command heralded a new departure. It was a heady moment for him when he was able formally to request of General Turner on June 12 that the army turn over to him the management of African American affairs in Richmond and the surrounding Henrico County. He immediately began corralling whatever resources he could glean for his cash-poor organization, starting with surplus army tents, boats, hospital beds, and cooking implements.

A six-foot Connecticut native with blue eyes, a full beard, and thick, unruly hair, Brown was graduated from Yale Medical School and enlisted as a surgeon in the Eighteenth Massachusetts Regiment. For two years he served as superintendent of Black affairs in the area of Virginia below the James River occupied by the Union army. He knew that, because of its importance to the Confederacy and because of its proximity to Washington, Virginia would showcase the Bureau's work more than any other state. Brown had the trust of his superior, General O. O. Howard, and developed close ties with General Terry, a fellow Connecticut native who had a more sympathetic view of the freed people than the Halleck-Ord-Patrick triumvirate.

It energized Brown to think of teaching African Americans how to fit into the postwar world. He could be condescending toward them and never considered them his social equals. But he worked hard in their behalf and believed they should enjoy the same civil rights as white Virginians. He naively thought that all it would take was a good dose of Yankee thrift and determination for them to succeed as free workers. General Terry sent Brown a few army officers to staff his operation but never enough. Lack of manpower in Richmond, and even more so in outlying counties, remained a chronic problem for the assistant commissioner.[10]

Brown divided Virginia into eight districts and appointed a New York quartermaster lieutenant, Halstead Merrell, as superintendent of freedmen for the Third District, consisting of Richmond and the bordering Henrico County. Merrell, twenty-five, had an irascible disposition that often put him at odds with his colleagues. It did not improve his humor when his workload expanded to include neighboring Chesterfield and Hanover Counties. He may have been guilty of some financial self-dealing. But he did do some service for the freedmen in pressing their claims for aid, and they publicly praised him on his retirement from the Bureau.

The assistant commissioner told Merrell his first task was to conduct a census of African Americans to gain a sense of the scope of his territory. He rattled off a daunting series of orders to his subordinate. Merrell should protect the rights of Black people, see to it that former enslavers did not oppress them, help them find employment, and advise them in making advantageous contracts for their labor. He should not issue rations to those who could work. Those who refused should be considered vagrants and turned over to labor under military guard without pay until they saw the light. He should consider freed people to be under the same common laws as free laborers in the North. If that was not enough, Brown told his subordinate to instruct freed people that no proclamation could make them entirely free. Only through frugality and economy, he said, could they stand on their own without charity or government support.

Brown was eager to acquire property to use as homes for destitute freedmen and as housing for their schools and teachers. He envisioned one such home in each county and directed his staff to begin taking possession of the properties they chose for these purposes. He identified private buildings whose owners were not covered by the general amnesty and wrote General Howard to ask if he could occupy them for the Bureau's purposes. Howard disabused him of that plan. He said the Bureau could not short-circuit the formal process of confiscating abandoned property. The assistant commissioner would be frustrated again and again in his efforts to acquire private real estate to achieve the Bureau's objectives. At least in Richmond, he had the benefit of buildings seized from the Confederate government and army, most notably the Chimborazo military hospital, whose eighty barracks became a bustling camp for more than a thousand people.

The assistant commissioner took a special interest in helping reunite families. They, in turn, learned they could count on him for transportation to rejoin scattered relatives. He instructed his staff to seek favorable rates from railroad companies for this purpose. He thought the Bureau could appeal to the railroads with the argument that bringing families back together would reduce the number who would be a burden on the government. The Bureau took over from the army the task of distributing food relief. It gave free rations to far fewer Black men and women than the army gave to poor white people, even though the population was divided roughly in half between the two groups.[11]

With mixed results, the Bureau tried to coordinate the scattered efforts in support of educating Black children, which had begun with such hope and energy. Northern philanthropic agencies could not agree on a common plan of action. It did not help that northern missionary societies and local Black churches failed to cooperate. As a result, there was confusion when the schools reopened at the end of the summer. The fall term began with schools in four Black Baptist churches and two African Methodist churches, in addition to one at the Chimborazo freedmen's camp. The one thing the parties could agree on was that they needed the Bureau's help, even if Brown could offer few buildings and no money.

Ralza Manly, a Methodist minister from Vermont, served as chaplain of the First US Colored Cavalry before becoming superintendent of schools for the Freedmen's Bureau in November 1865. It was a disappointment not to be able to use confiscated private property, but he found space in hospitals, church basements, and former barracks. By the end of 1865, the Bureau operated twenty-six schools in the city. Manly's greatest innovation was establishing the Richmond Normal and High School to train African American teachers. Like many white northerners, however, he condescended to them and doubted they could run their own schools without significant white tutelage. He therefore resisted placing graduates of the normal school in sole charge of schools of their own.[12]

William Harris, one of three African American brothers from Cleveland, Ohio, who came south to teach, became pastor of the Third Street African Methodist Church in August 1865. Concurrently with his pastorate, he served as representative of the American Missionary Association. He was as keen on education as on religious instruction and taught at the night school he set up in his church after being in town only a few weeks. He worked with Manly, but they held markedly different views on the capacity of African Americans to apply their education.

When white Richmonders saw the explosive growth of schools in Black churches, they marveled that these formerly enslaved people could organize so quickly. By the fall, many of them increasingly resented the northern teachers who came to help. In part they were indignant that African Americans sought assistance from outsiders. Even more, they accused northern teachers of filling the students' heads with an alien ideology, which is to say, ideas of equality. Whites invoked the law to minimize outside influence on Black education. When Orlando Brown asked state senator and lawyer John Gilmer if northern organizations could hold property for educational purposes, he was told emphatically that doing so would violate state law.[13]

Resentment of northern teachers also thwarted efforts to provide schooling for poor white children. General Turner had appropriated the former Confederate naval laboratory for a school where 250 white pupils were taught. But an effort to cooperate with white citizens to enlarge such free schools failed. A northern minister who visited the laboratory school thought he saw the reason for failure in Richmond's pride. Confederate Richmonders were humiliated by their loss but not humbled.[14]

In the fall, Brown had better success when the Bureau established the Freedmen's Court. It proved to be the Bureau's most notable institutional creation and gave people cheap access to legal representation and a generally fair hearing for adjudicating grievances. The court consisted of three judges, one to represent the Bureau, one to represent the Black community, and one to represent white residents. Brown's assistant in the Richmond district, Halstead Merrell, sat for the Bureau. The Black community could not decide at the outset on its representative. The Bureau suggested they pick a moderate white man rather than a Black man or a radical white, either of whom would offend the larger white community and undercut the court's legitimacy.

They finally chose T. P. A. Bibb, a white Kentuckian who favored equal rights for African Americans. From its beginning, the court enjoyed considerable success, wide acceptance by the freedmen, and even tentative approval by the local press.[15]

The choice of George Fitzhugh to represent the white community on the court, however, was a troubling premonition for the future of race relations. Before the war the combative attorney wrote journal articles and two books, *Sociology for the South* and *Cannibals All!* In them he vehemently argued that free labor was more oppressive than slavery, and he reveled in the outrage his writing provoked among abolitionists.

After a year serving on the court and living beside the freedmen's community at a camp just outside of town, Fitzhugh published a scathing critique of the Bureau project, repellent in its grotesque racist tropes. He likened it to a "Negro nursery," a symbol of dependency that proved African Americans were ignorant and incapable of self-support. He claimed the Bureau stole the idea from former enslavers because their paternalistic care for their human property supposedly was all that separated Black people from a life of crime and poverty. He infantilized them as grown-up children who needed guardians, proof that they were unfit for political rights.[16]

In its first six months of operation, the Freedmen's Bureau gave important support to the newly emancipated people of Richmond. It provided rations, clothing, medicine, housing in camps, legal protection through the Freedmen's Court, some aid though no funding for schools, and assistance from Bureau officers in dealing with white employers, especially in negotiating labor contracts. Colonel Brown and his assistants could be pleased with these achievements. But their operation was hamstrung from the outset, even after the appointment of the sympathetic Generals Terry and Turner. Despite its modest accomplishments, its failure to secure confiscated land stifled the Bureau's larger plans for giving Black Virginians the start it intended. Understaffed, underfunded, and under constant threat of dissolution, Brown and his men learned to work in straitened circumstances.

To these hindrances was added the increasing hostility of the white community as the year drew to a close. The press echoed George Fitzhugh in what would become its dominant theme of race relations: the childlike freed people needed protectors and patrons with more influence and intelligence than they could ever muster. It was native whites, the papers argued, not the Freedmen's Bureau, who knew best how to treat them, just as they had done before emancipation.

When Orlando Brown's year-end report to General Howard appeared in print, it provoked white animosity. Swayed by tradition and habit, the assistant commissioner wrote, most white Virginians "only sullenly acquiesced in the freedom of their former slaves." Many wanted them removed from the state or bound with labor contracts that gave them little more freedom than they had before. Uncertainty about whether such views would prevail hung over the city. It was no wonder that Fields Cook and his colleagues to the Alexandria convention worried about the precarious state of their emancipation. Brown's assessment could not have been more at variance from the attitude of the former enslavers. It was, they believed, a gross calumny of the kindly feelings they had always shown toward the freed people: "The people of this State know the negro better than any other—they know his capacity and his wants, and can now take care of him better" than anyone else, especially northerners "who are making him . . . the everlasting cause of accusation and vituperation of the people of the South." This intransigence augured ill for the future.[17]

Brown stuck with his work for nearly four years, despite his frustration with lack of funds, lack of staff, lack of property, and lack of support from the white community. He vacillated between optimism about the prospects for making a difference in the lives of freed people and depression over the obstacles in his way. Hostility toward the Bureau and toward Brown personally grew as the months lengthened beyond the fall of the city. A photograph of him in later years captures him looking into the distance with a sad dignity that perhaps reflected the mixed results of his time in the former Confederate capital.

In the half year since the fire, Richmond's Black people had shaken off the bonds of slavery. They struggled with poverty, squalid housing, and limited employment. But despite lacking resources, they built a community. They created schools, expanded their prewar churches and social organizations, reconnected many of their scattered families, and in large part made the adjustment to a free labor economy. They accomplished all of this with the help of the Freedmen's Bureau, northern teachers, and the army, but they did it mostly on their own. They also began to assert themselves in the political realm. The *Christian Recorder*, a Black newspaper in Philadelphia, avidly followed events in the former Confederate capital. When the General Assembly convened at the end of the year, the paper's reporter in town expressed more hope than circumstances warranted that legislators would rise above prejudice "and give to every man equal rights before the law, irrespective of color."[18]

As night drew on in the chill evening of November 1, an emotional event took place at the railroad station in Lynchburg, 130 miles west of Richmond. One hundred and fifty African Americans prepared to entrain for Baltimore to take passage to Liberia. Hundreds more crowded around to say their farewells. They sang and prayed and cried. Ministers blessed these hardy travelers, who had decided to leave the land of their birth and make a new start across the ocean in a strange country they did not know. Could it really offer better prospects than Virginia? All of them, those who left and those who remained, doubted they would ever see one another again. That realization made the scene at the station poignant beyond words.[19]

This last gasp of the American Colonization Society (ACS) never got off the ground beyond the group headed to Baltimore that evening and a few others. The prewar ACS had sought to remove free African Americans from the country in the belief that Black and white people could not live together in a free society. The intended beneficiaries had largely opposed the effort from the beginning, and the postwar attempt to revive it failed. At the same time, another effort to entice emigrants abroad commenced as Matthew Fontaine Maury tried to lure other Virginians to his tenuous colony in Mexico. The rebel naval commander would not accept the war's outcome as final. He fervently believed he could create "New Virginia" below the Rio Grande to resurrect the Old South. Few Black people would join the Lynchburg voyagers, and few Confederates would cast their lots with Maury.

The journalist Thomas Chester was one of the few African Americans who had been to Liberia but returned to his native land. He had been present at the fall of Richmond and hoped that emancipation would give Black people a better future in the South. He agreed about little else with Robert E. Lee, but on the matter of emigration the two men thought alike, at least about the best course for their own people. Each believed that the emigration of his own race offered no solution to the challenge of rebuilding the Old Dominion. Lee would just as soon see Black Virginians leave the state—as he would tell a congressional committee the following year—but he opposed leaving for the veterans of his army. For better or worse, Virginia would be the setting in which the people who emerged from slavery and those who survived defeat in war would build their uncertain futures.

11

Extricate Us from All Our Troubles

Late 1865

In 1861 John Brown Baldwin of Staunton, an eloquent debater with a command of the law beyond his thirty-seven years, represented his hometown at the Richmond convention debating the momentous issues facing the nation. As a leader of the unionist faction, he both opposed secession and defended slavery. For him, slavery was a good thing, but he believed it could best be protected within the federal Union, not by seceding and joining the misbegotten slave republic forming in the Deep South. Virginia, he argued, was a lighthouse founded upon rock, able to withstand both "Northern fanaticism" and "Southern violence."[1]

Just before Fort Sumter, Baldwin met with Lincoln in a failed secret attempt to avert war. That controversial meeting would be disputed for years to come. But at the time, his gravest challenge was a public one on the floor of the convention in opposition to Henry Wise. By sheer force of incendiary rhetoric, the former governor had molded the rapidly growing secessionist sentiment in the hall. He browbeat Baldwin with hateful taunts and accused him of the unforgiveable sin of disloyalty to Virginia. The normally ramrod-straight, forceful Baldwin could not match his opponent's oratorical savagery, and he slumped in defeat. He sorrowfully warned the convention that the future looked dark and foreboding. He failed to prevent secession, and like so many of his conditional unionist colleagues, he served the Confederacy, in his case both as a regimental colonel and member of its Congress.

Four years later, in autumn 1865, all had changed. Now it was Henry Wise who was the broken symbol of the past, railing in impotence against southern defeat. Baldwin was the man of the present and, he hoped, the future. He had met with Governor Pierpont the day after the latter's arrival in Richmond and staked his claim to helping restore Virginia. In the following months, Baldwin gave voice to the Old Dominion's antebellum establishment, hoping to grasp power again and intent on re-creating as much of the old order as it could. That prospect, and the real possibility that resurgent southern conservatives might join hands with northern Democrats to wrest power at the national level filled Republicans with foreboding.

The end of 1865 witnessed change at all levels of the city and state—a heightened antagonism with Congress, election of a new General Assembly, and changes in municipal authority. Political change proceeded alongside a quickening of rebuilding in the Burnt District and revival of the city's influential newspapers. December brought reflection on all sides about the tumultuous year past and renewed fears for the future as uncertainty about the shape of Reconstruction persisted.

When Governor Pierpont had called the special session of the General Assembly in June, he set in motion the political juggernaut that soon marginalized his own position. Those legislators had constituted the loyalist Restored government of Virginia domiciled in Alexandria under the guns of the Union army. They warily acceded to Pierpont's request that they call congressional and legislative elections for October 12. With no change in the electorate, as before, all white male residents could vote. The large number of Confederate veterans chosen in county and city elections that took place earlier, in July, reflected the sentiments of those voters. No thought was given to admitting Black men to that privilege, though they had begun to agitate for it in earnest.

As with those local elections, there were no organized political parties in the contest for Congress. Voters looked at the reputation of their neighbors who put themselves forward for office. A central issue emerged: could the candidates take an ironclad oath that they had never fought against the United States or otherwise supported the

Confederacy? Governor Pierpont warned that those who could not take the oath would give the state "the appearance of persistent and continued rebellion." The former Whig congressman John Minor Botts, whose unbending unionist principles had landed him in a Confederate jail, would have no truck with former rebels, reluctant or otherwise. He said it was better to elect ignorant men who could comply with the oath rather than educated ones who could not. In August a conservative editor confessed that he had earlier scorned politicians who had opposed secession and only reluctantly endorsed it later, but he admitted Virginia needed them now. They were "the very men who at this time can extricate us from all our troubles." He had in mind men like Baldwin but not Botts.[2]

The northern press was watching too. One writer predicted it would fill Congress with disgust and loathing if the South sent "members so leprous with secession that they cannot take the oath." Despite the importance of the election, far fewer voted than in the last prewar contest. Apathy seemed to be the predominant sentiment among both the small number of Republicans in the state and the conservative majority. The outcome set Virginia apart from the rest of the South, which elected many who had served the Confederacy and could not take the ironclad oath. None of the Virginia congressional winners had been states' rights Democrats or secessionists. Most had been old-line Whigs who had been skeptical of the Confederate experiment. All but two could pass the oath test. Even so, Virginia's winners, like those elected farther south, failed to display the contrition that the victors demanded. They might not have been violent secessionists in 1861, but they still had been part of the antebellum establishment, and most had acquiesced to Confederate rule. Their election filled northern congressmen with dread.[3]

When it convened in December, Congress refused to seat any southern congressman, however spotless his unionist credentials. It set up the Joint Committee on Reconstruction to assert its power in determining how the wayward states could be made whole within the Union again. The committee announced it would hold hearings early in the new year. These highlighted the growing and ultimately irreconcilable gulf between Andrew Johnson and the Republican majority in Congress, both radicals and moderates. The hearings demonstrated Congress's continuing fears that the South had still not accepted the outcome of the war. Virginia's establishment leaders denounced Congress for denying seats to their duly elected representatives but were oddly passive. Even though there was not now a clear path for Virginia to be readmitted to the national legislature, that setback seemed to them less important than reasserting dominance at the local and state level.

There was nothing passive about the way the Old Dominion created a new state legislature. At the same October election for Congress, Virginians voted for a new General Assembly representing the whole state to replace the truncated wartime legislature that Governor Pierpont had brought from Alexandria. The contest for the Richmond seat in the Virginia Senate revealed the sentiment of voters in the capital. Standing for that seat was Charles Palmer, the import-export merchant who had graced a Confederate jail for his unionist opinions and welcomed Governor Pierpont to town. He embraced the opportunity to run for office but warned that "we are not yet entirely delivered from the hatred, and malice and deep-rooted prejudices, under the influence of which we can never prosper." Although sixty-six years old, he promised to bring the energy and resolution needed to rebuild the ruined city, "a modern Pompeii" brought low by the Confederacy.[4]

John Harmer Gilmer opposed Palmer. It did not faze him when he heard it said that he should decline to run because his election would be distasteful to the US Army. Hearing this unwelcome rumor, he rushed to speak to General Terry. The general probably later regretted saying he harbored no objection to Gilmer's candidacy.[5]

Palmer was a respected member of the business community. He had been chosen for the three-man delegation to visit the White House in September and invite President Johnson to visit the city. But he was still suspect because of his unionist opinions. Because Confederate sentiments animated most white Richmonders, it was the conservative Gilmer, not Palmer, who stood on the portico of city hall on October 12 to thank voters for his election. He asked them to support Virginia "in this dread hour of her trials!" He lost little time in writing to the president to dispute the allegation that his election demonstrated continued disloyalty in the capital city. The new senator promised to be a recurring irritant to General Terry and Republicans in general.[6]

The General Assembly elected by the voters consisted largely of moderate men, overwhelmingly former Whigs rather than Democrats. No Republicans were elected, but no one who had been a secessionist won either. In one sense this should have been the ideal legislature to deal with issues of returning to normal relations with the North, but even these moderate former Whigs did not accept how much had changed since the antebellum era. They could not grasp how much even moderate northerners—men like themselves—would require of them to atone for the Confederacy.

John Brown Baldwin now came into his own when the House of Delegates elected him Speaker. A tall, erect figure with a high forehead, thin lips, and a neatly trimmed salt-and-pepper beard, he possessed the intellect and quick wit necessary to dominate the House. His speaking ability, mastery of parliamentary rules, experience in the Confederate Congress, and wide network of acquaintances underpinned his dominance of what became known as the Baldwin legislature. He reflected the views of a majority of white Virginians. He hinted at future discord between the races when he said white people were "deeply apprehensive of the future with a people who have received their freedom without 'preparation for its duties or responsibilities.'" That sentiment was at odds with the desire of newly freed Virginians for equal rights.[7]

Under Baldwin's guidance, the legislature enacted a series of laws that looked backward to antebellum days, despite the entreaties of Colonel Brown and Governor Pierpont. The governor's faith in the former Confederate leaders of Virginia was misplaced. They accepted military defeat because they had to, but they would not express any regret for what they saw as the honorable defense of their state. And they were not prepared to endorse the extension of rights promised by emancipation. That obstinacy made Republicans fear that the antebellum order might yet be restored.

At the same time, the army gradually turned over the operation of Richmond's government to civilian authority. In August it had invested

John Brown Baldwin, Speaker of the House of Delegates in the postwar General Assembly, led the effort to reestablish traditional rule in the legislature. (Wikimedia Commons)

the provisional city manager, David Saunders, with the powers of the city council. Then, at the end of October, General Turner offered a compromise. He would relent if Nathaniel Sturdivant, the Confederate officer who had won election as mayor in July, and two other officials would disavow their claim to office. If they did, he would permit all the city councilors elected in July formally to take their seats, no matter that they represented the prewar regime. Sturdivant and the others quickly agreed, and the army handed over control of city hall. Turner made the compromise in the first instance because he needed officials in place to conduct the fall election for the legislature. But he also wanted the city to create a gendarmerie to replace his own men. And he wanted the city to reduce its reliance on army rations for the hungry. He achieved neither of these latter two objectives as soon as he would have liked. After months of foot-dragging, the city finally put in place a civilian police force at the end of the year. Turner would have preferred to wait longer before allowing Confederates to take part in the city's governance. But with the reestablishment of civilian courts and municipal government, he lost the wide jurisdiction he had had in the summer and fall. In the end, he was profoundly frustrated by his assignment, describing himself as "trying the best I know how to govern these people."[8]

The renewed confidence that business leaders began to feel after reasserting their authority in city hall and the state legislature manifested itself in accelerated construction in the Burnt District. The efforts of the past nine months were a source of satisfaction for a people who had lost so much. Merchant William Maury, a cousin of the Confederate naval commander, exulted that the city was being rapidly rebuilt. He boasted to a New York associate that in two years nothing would be left of the ruins. He perhaps exaggerated, but by the end of the year the evidence he cited was obvious. Most antebellum businesses had been no more than three or four stories tall with pitched roofs. They were replaced with structures that rose higher above the streets, with flat modern roofs and sheer fronts, frequently made of iron, which allowed for a greater area of window display at street level. They began to give the business quarter a contemporary look akin to that of northern cities. They were purpose-built for commerce, unlike the prewar buildings, which had originally been residences, then converted to stores, with the owners living above the shops.[9]

On Cary Street alone, with sixty-seven vacant lots, seventeen new buildings were in the works and fifteen were completed or nearly so. The foundation was complete for the mammoth new Gallego Mills. When finished, it would dwarf the burned structure it replaced, a huge building whose haunting ruins featured in many photographs of the destruction. Five more hotels joined the Spotswood, the first to reopen after the fire. By December, 120 new buildings were under construction or complete. Despite this progress, much remained to be done, considering that as many as one thousand structures had burned.[10]

It was not enough to repair physical destruction; economic revival needed a boost in commerce to justify all those new buildings. That meant at the outset the need to reconstruct the paper records dealt such a cruel blow during the turmoil of April 2–3. The Richmond & York River Railroad was not alone in suffering from this fragility when it told holders of its stocks and bonds that it needed to reregister those documents. In the frenzy of evacuation, the firm's records, like those of many others, had been burned or scattered to the winds by looters.

Richmond did not just produce flour, iron, and tobacco. It also produced opinions. Newspapers had always wielded an outsized influence in the city, the state, and the wider South. Most of the printing presses burned on April 3, but over the course of the summer, the old titles reappeared and new ones emerged. By late 1865 they gave voice to the increasing confidence felt by Richmond's traditional power brokers, finally assured that their property no longer faced confiscation and certain of conservative control of the General Assembly.

The first newspaper to resume publication was the *Whig*. It survived the fire and printed a single broadsheet one day after the Union army arrived. Its proprietor, William Ira Smith, expressed Union sentiments at first, but the *Whig* later assumed the conservative coloration of the other papers. The *Commercial Bulletin* consistently hewed to a conservative line but folded before the end of the year. The *Enquirer* burned in April but resumed publication in the fall. The prewar *Dispatch* burned but reappeared in December, soon to become the dominant Richmond paper, unapologetic for its Confederate past and proud to be the mouthpiece of the city's business elite. It restarted publication, in the cocky words of its owner, James Cowardin, "endowed with the Promethean fire, and speaks to its readers as though it never lost its breath."[11]

The *Republic*, edited by James Wesley Lewellen, was the only newspaper to endorse even the moderate republicanism of Governor Pierpont. Lewellen lost everything to the fire. He had worked at the *Dispatch* during the war but vowed that "my skirts are clean" of helping precipitate it. Penniless, he attempted in his journal to hew to a middle course between radical Republicanism and the Confederate slant of the other papers. Behind the scenes, General Terry urged Judge Underwood to support Lewellen's paper and said he would ask the postmaster to send it advertising. But the *Republic,* in Terry's regretful words, was "swimming against the tide." It would not survive long into the new year.[12]

Federal officers in Richmond periodically censored the newspapers when they thought their editorials stepped over the line. They closed the *Whig* for two weeks for denouncing federal policy, shut the *Commercial Bulletin* for disloyal content, and warned the *Times* against intemperate language from one of its editors. It grated on Terry that he could not do more. In the case of the *Bulletin,* he had to permit it to resume publication because of instructions that came directly from the president.[13]

The most flamboyant editors—strident in their advocacy of southern rights and violent in their personal lives—were two brothers, Edward Alfred Pollard, thirty-three, and Henry Rives Pollard, thirty-two. Edward had rocketed to national attention with his antebellum defense of slavery, *Black Diamonds.* He scorned the culture of the North as debased and vulgar and dismissed its "coarse ostentatious aristocracy that smelt of trade." Both brothers had honed their journalistic style at John Moncure Daniel's angry secessionist *Examiner* during the war. (Daniel bequeathed his dueling pistols to Henry.) From him they learned to despise lukewarm Confederates as much as Yankees and to denounce them all in sneering, slashing, sarcastic prose. The army jailed them briefly, but Henry revived the *Times* by the end of April. Edward kept his head down for the moment, hard at work collecting material for a book on the war.[14]

Disputes, both physical and epistolary, kept the brothers in the public eye. People often confused the two because of their combative personalities, their penchant for the code duello, and their insouciance at airing their sordid personal affairs in public. By fall, Henry had fallen out with the co-owner of the *Times* and resurrected the *Examiner* to give his bad-tempered style greater scope. Edward could not stay quiet long and began to flay former Confederate leaders who, in his acidulous words, kowtowed to Washington and "eat the most dirt." He poured particular scorn on Richmonders: "what new absurdities of humiliation" would they think of next in abasing themselves before the North?[15]

Also that fall, Edward announced that his forthcoming book would give a definitive account of the war, exonerate the Confederacy, and spell out chapter and verse the manifold iniquities of the North. He gave it a title that would lend its name to the attitudes that soon animated the white South. *The Lost Cause* did not appear until mid-1866, but advance publicity already linked its title and bellicose author to the standard of southern defiance. Both brothers would have more to say and in the coming months would engage in violence, or the threat of it, to defend their views.

The end of the year had always held a double-edged meaning for enslaved people—a time of holiday rest from their labors but also the prelude to contracts for the new year that often broke up families. It had been impossible to enjoy Christmas when what some called "heart-break day" arrived. A correspondent for the African American journal *Christian Recorder* who visited the city at the end of 1865 remarked how different that holiday season was from earlier times. He recalled that he had spent the last days of the previous year with others "huddled together here in small filthy offices, to be hired out to the highest bidder." That unhappy memory was now a thing of the past, and he could celebrate Christmas 1865 with unalloyed joy.[16]

If year's end no longer threatened African American families as before, it troubled white Richmonders for a different reason. At the end of the year, they linked the hesitation of Black people to sign new labor contracts to hopes they would receive land from the government. To counter the rumors, General Terry issued a circular directing his officers to meet with freedmen and disabuse them of any thought that they were going to be given land at Christmas.

Even more worrying to white people was the recurrence of an old fear. Rumors spread that Black people would revolt at the end of the year and seize land by violence. To many white people, every sharp household implement now looked like a potential murder weapon. Similar paranoia fed by memories of Nat Turner had periodically disturbed them before the war. Now that they feared they could no longer control freedmen the way they had in the past, new variations on an old terror arose. That African Americans could now legally own firearms gave added weight to these worries. Rumors became so rife that General O. O. Howard asked Orlando Brown to investigate. He, in turn, asked Halstead Merrell, his agent in charge of the Richmond region, to examine the allegations. Merrell found no evidence of any insurrectionary plot. Brown thought it was a case of rumormongering by disarmed whites to agitate for permission to reestablish some kind of military force to control Black people.[17]

Parishioners convened a meeting at the First African Baptist Church to allay the fears that agitated their white neighbors. They denied holding secret conclaves to plot insurrection. They admitted that they had created clandestine organizations under slavery that met in secret because they were illegal then. But since the war, these societies could meet openly. They should not alarm anyone because their purposes were entirely benign, being designed to care for sick, infirm, aged members and to give them proper Christian burials. They denounced those who spread the rumor and promised they wanted racial harmony. But, they warned, that would only be possible if they could enjoy equality before the law, and that was something that had not yet been achieved.[18]

By mid-December, the *Richmond Dispatch,* ever the optimistic booster of the local economy, began directing readers' attention to the bountiful stock of potential Christmas presents in the city's shops. The paper blithely dismissed the hardships of the times and baldly claimed there was never a better selection of goods available. That comment likely triggered some angry letters. A day later, the paper admitted more realistically that there were many homes "in which no stockings can be hung up, no Christmas trees planted." It would, the editor admitted, be heartless to wish its readers a Merry Christmas. Poverty in the place of plenty, dark clouds hanging over the future, and the "iron foot-prints of war, with half a million of their best and bravest sleeping in bloody graves," had reduced seasonal jollity to bad taste. But the editors implored their readers not to despair and to take heart from the perennial Christmas message of goodwill, hope, and peace.[19]

Despite the straitened times, and perhaps because of them, churches made a special effort to decorate. Cedar wreaths and braids of greenery transformed their sanctuaries, reminding white parishioners of past Christmases in happier times. At the first Christmas of freedom, Black churches were especially joyful. The Third Street African Methodist Episcopal Church was decorated with evergreens and holly as bountifully as its white neighbors, with the addition of the Stars and Stripes hanging above the pulpit. It was, a visiting minister rhapsodized, "soon to be the emblem of what it was intended to symbolize—equal rights for all." The word "soon" indicated how precarious the status of those rights remained.[20]

In the end, Christmas was uneventful. The worst that happened was a garbled rumor that inflated a minor disturbance into a full-blown race riot in the suburb of Manchester. It turned out to be only a street brawl between a few Black and white drunks. The day was to have been the "tocsin of negro uprisings, insurrections and murders," the *New York Times* scoffed, but it passed in remarkable quiet.[21]

If white Richmonders were relieved that no racial violence flared during the long holiday, their Black neighbors were overjoyed that the "day of horror and distress" was no more. They enjoyed Christmas as never before, without fear that their families would be broken up on New Year's Day. They could celebrate a new year of freedom and openly honor Lincoln on the anniversary of the Emancipation Proclamation.

Coming at the end of a year like no other, the holidays invariably prompted reflection on the recent past. Though people focused on private affairs, public events could not help but intrude into hearth and home, where there were so many empty chairs at family Christmas dinners, in both Black and white households. The city's traditional leadership had weathered the threat of treason trials and expropriation. It had reasserted its authority over local and state government, even if it had been denied representation in Washington. Governor Pierpont had established his administration in the capital city but was increasingly frustrated at being spurned by his former unionist allies and distrusted by former Confederates. The Freedmen's Bureau had assisted with food relief, schools, and a measure of justice under law, but it failed to deliver on the earlier promise of confiscated land. Colonel Brown stated the problems that the Bureau faced in blunt terms. How could it, he wondered, "provide for the protection, elevation and government of nearly half a million of people suddenly freed from the bonds of a rigorous control, acquainted with no law but that of force."[22]

This precarious state of affairs was nowhere more apparent than in the fact that the Thirteenth Amendment abolishing slavery was not ratified until December 18, 1865. Even then, the exemption for criminal conviction that allowed for involuntary servitude provided an ominous loophole that some southern governments exploited. Further, though the amendment was indispensable, it was not sufficient to define or safeguard the rights of formerly enslaved people.[23]

Black Richmonders had made strides in building a community after emancipation, in reuniting families, and in educating their children. Most importantly for the future, they began to assert their claim to political rights. But signs of an ineluctable flow of power away from their protectors in the Bureau and the army abounded. The new leaders of the city council and the General Assembly were often the same leaders as before the war, men who valued and defined order as they had done in the past. The lack of any sense of having been in the wrong among former Confederates signaled trouble to come. They believed the great majority supported them in their determination to resist concessions to the North or, as one wrote on Christmas Day, echoing Edward Pollard, "to eat no more dirt."[24]

The tensions apparent in the first months after the fire continued to aggravate postwar Richmond. No longer able to rely on the legal prop of slavery, white people tried to forge new ways of controlling their emancipated neighbors who just as determinedly strove to be left alone to build their own lives. The other main antagonism in the city—that between civil and military authorities—grew more acrimonious as increasingly assertive residents pushed against the power of the federal government, manifested locally in the Freedmen's Bureau and the army. The new buildings going up in the Burnt District added the latest layer to the palimpsest of Richmond, as contending interests among the residents—Black and white, Union and Confederate, civil and military—sparred around them.

When Christmas arrived, the large Maury family had scattered to the winds. The patriarch, Confederate naval commander Matthew Fontaine Maury, had reached Mexico at the beginning of his star-crossed effort to establish a new Virginia there. In Richmond, the commander's niece, twenty-three-year-old Isabel Maury, kept a flame brightly lit in the tabernacle of Confederate devotion. She had grown up a block from the house Jefferson Davis occupied and with trepidation witnessed the entry of federal troops into the city. A slight figure known as "Miss Belle," she never married but made it her life's work to serve a museum dedicated to the southern cause. She tried to describe for a cousin in English exile what it was like to celebrate the first Christmas in the occupied capital of lost hopes. Her letter alternated between cheery tidbits about family and bitter laments about being reduced to "this slavery." As for the real formerly enslaved, she accused northerners of failing to help them as much as they promised: "The poor servants too, how they must suffer." She delighted in describing how haughty Richmonders shunned the company of the northern army officers quartered in their midst.

Like many other Confederates, she turned inward, away from public gaze, and focused on family. The Christmas tree she decorated for the children of the household displayed her fierce allegiance. She proudly topped the tree, not with an angel or a star, but with two Confederate flags. Directly below them she hung an image of the new icon for Confederates keeping hope alive. "Bless his soul," she wrote reverently. It was a picture of Robert E. Lee.[25]

12

The Box of Pandora Is Opened

Early 1866

Three years earlier, on December 31, 1862, African Americans waited for what Frederick Douglass called "the glorious morning of liberty about to dawn upon us." Black Richmonders could not openly celebrate the Emancipation Proclamation that year, or the next two. But on January 1, 1866, they gathered by the thousands at First African Baptist Church. So many streamed in that by midday they spilled outside into the surrounding yard. The band of the Twenty-Fourth Massachusetts Regiment serenaded the crowd with patriotic music while they assembled. Parishioners had decorated the church with evergreens, yellow and blue tissue paper, and a forest of American flags. The local press could not resist noting with disdain the presence of visiting clergymen, radical newspaper correspondents, and philanthropically inclined women from the North.[1]

Robert Johnson, a free shoemaker before the war in whose house the Colored Men's Equal Rights League had been organized the previous May, opened the meeting. He compared the experience of emancipation with religious conversion. Fields Cook, who had led the delegation to the White House in June, was naturally upbeat, and the present moment finely suited his temperament. He predicted that in a decade "white people who fought for slavery would celebrate the anniversary of freedom with them." One day, he promised, "white and black children would grow up together in harmony."[2]

Peter Randolph, the pastor of Ebenezer Baptist Church, praised the martyred Lincoln. He urged his listeners to prove to their white neighbors "that freedom is not a failure." John Oliver, who came from Boston to see Richmond the previous summer and served as a notary with the Freedmen's Court, read the text of the proclamation. He declared that African Americans wanted justice and protection under the same laws that governed white society. After four hours of speeches, interspersed with music and prayers of thanksgiving, the jubilant assembly filed out of the church to the Black-owned Walker Hotel for a celebratory feast. Uncertainty about the provision for that equal justice still cast a shadow, however. The new year brought increasing hostility by the legislature and municipality toward that goal, more strident Confederate sentiment openly expressed, and the convening of the congressional Joint Committee on Reconstruction to investigate conditions in the South.[3]

Richmond's city councilors and state legislators did not entertain the same expectations African Americans expressed in their celebration of the Emancipation Proclamation. When the General Assembly reconvened after the Christmas holidays, it eliminated the antebellum slave code from the statutes, but it refused to accept Black service on juries or the right to testify against white people. It emphatically rejected giving Black men the right to vote. Most controversially, it passed a law that gave magistrates the right to arrest anyone they deemed vagrant and hire them out to employers. Although the statute did not contain racial language, everyone knew its purpose. General Terry intervened to disallow the law because, he said, it restored slavery in all but name. That was a refrain that had been repeated frequently since the past April by Black people and by army and Freedmen's Bureau officers alike. Even at the beginning of the new year, the fear still troubled them, and the law confirmed them in their alarm.[4] John Gilmer, the state senator for Richmond, argued for amending the criminal code to remove racial language, but not because he wanted equal rights for Black people. He did not. Rather, he thought doing so would help convince them that white people had their best interests at heart. More importantly, he said bluntly, it would enable the former ruling class to "keep the proper moral and legal control" over African Americans. They, he fervently believed, should be kept in a subordinate position in society. The quest for control, and resistance to it, suffused all aspects of politics.[5]

The reconstituted city council had already removed race-specific language from its statute book, more at the urging of the army than from any solicitude for Black citizens. Out of stinginess or antipathy, it refused to take over from the army any provision for poor Black people, as General Terry had asked.

While the General Assembly impeded the aspirations of Black Virginians, like those expressed by Fields Cook, Peter Randolph, and John Oliver on New Year's Day, it also bared its teeth to Governor Pierpont. The legislators spitefully revoked Virginia's acquiescence in the creation of West Virginia, without hope that it would have any effect. It not only failed to advance the reforms the governor advocated at the end of 1865 but also began replacing his key appointees with men of its own choosing. (John Minor Botts later denounced the assembly's "keen-whetted knife of the political guillotine.") It did not matter that Charles Lewis, Pierpont's secretary of the commonwealth, opposed giving Black men the vote. He was a unionist and therefore deserved to be ousted in favor of a southern rights man.[6] The opposition of the General Assembly gave Pierpont fair warning that his dream of a middle way was a frail creature, unlikely to survive. Between President Johnson and conservatives on the one hand and radical Republicans on the other, there was little scope for the pragmatism Pierpont advocated. The sole Richmond paper to support him worried that the governor might not be able to retain power after the legislature rejected appointees like Lewis. The situation was, the *Republic*'s editor regretted, "a melancholy piece of work. The box of Pandora is opened."[7]

As the new year began, signs of increasing assertiveness by former Confederates about the state of affairs in the city abounded. Henry Rives Pollard, the turbulent editor known for his vicious temperament and penchant for fighting, put his hair-trigger tetchiness on display in January. He had hard, dark eyes, a dark complexion, a long black beard, and a sneering curl to his lip that matched his style of writing.

He always went about armed, "a sort of walking arsenal," in the words of one observer. Described by his friend and fellow journalist Francis Dawson as "a queer character: not without ability, but lazy, vain and dissolute," Pollard picked two public fights that month with other journalists. In the first, he took exception to comments printed in the rival *Enquirer* and stalked its contributors, Nathaniel Tyler and W. D. Coleman, at the state capitol while the House of Delegates was in session. All three men carried revolvers. Pollard first attempted to thrash Tyler with his walking stick. Each man fired his gun around Jean-Antoine Houdon's statue of Washington in the capitol rotunda. The only casualty was the marble tassel on the statue's staff.[8]

Undaunted by the uproar this contretemps caused, a week later Pollard assaulted the Richmond reporter of the *New York Times* at the Spotswood Hotel. "You d——d Yankee," he screamed at E. P. Brooks, "I'll teach you how to come down here to insult Southern gentlemen." Pollard beat him with a cowhide whip and pushed his head through a glass partition. Pollard's friend Dawson brandished his pistol to keep others from interfering until the fight had ended, but not until the northern journalist had pulled a hank of hair from Pollard's beard.[9]

The altercation briefly made Pollard a national news story. Dawson recalled that when he recounted the fight to a parlor of genteel Richmond women, they "clapped their hands with joy." They might not receive the disreputable Pollard in their homes, but they displayed the same devotion to the Confederacy and animosity to their conquerors as the *Examiner*'s truculent standard-bearer. They soon had cause to take his side again when Pollard incurred the wrath of the nation's general-in-chief.[10]

Ulysses S. Grant had revised his earlier, benign opinion of Confederate sincerity about returning to the Union fold. He had not wanted to ride through Richmond on the way back from Appomattox to Washington out of a desire not to be seen as lording it over his defeated foes. The southern press praised him for that sensitivity. On a tour of the South in November 1865, however, he finally went to Richmond, and his report to the president gave a more balanced perspective. Now he began to stress the need for justice for freedmen as well as conciliation of defeated whites. By the end of the year, he believed it was too soon to withdraw the army in the face of disturbing reports of violence against Black people across the South.[11]

It grated on Grant when unrepentant Confederate editors repeatedly spewed hostility toward the army. More than politicians, he groused, the press kept alive "the spirit of hatred between the two sections." Henry Rives Pollard triggered the general's rage with a seemingly trivial disparagement of a dance sponsored by General Terry's officers at the Spotswood Hotel. In his newspaper, Pollard ridiculed any local woman who attended the event as a flower that "thrives most when trampled on." "Poor, bleeding rose! Your garments are dyed in the blood of the slain." He named some of the Union women there, including Elizabeth Van Lew's niece, John Minor Botts's daughters, and "others too numerous and too insignificant to notice."[12]

Furious when shown the *Examiner* article, Grant ordered the newspaper shut down. He sent a blistering cable to Terry demanding that he "Send me copies of Richmond papers tabooing ladies for attending partys with Union Officers." Pollard raced to Washington to plead his case in person. Grant was unmoved. But the editor went over his head to the president, who countermanded the closure in exchange for Pollard's promise to support him and the Constitution. Grant was chagrined at being overruled and sullenly ordered Terry to comply. The incident, trivial as it was, helped convince Grant that he and the president had different hopes for the postwar South. Unlike Johnson, Grant now doubted there would be a rapid return to normalcy there. He did not trust the traditional southern elites, with whom the president had now reconciled himself.[13]

The next month an unchastened Pollard offended the Richmond commanders again with an article entitled "A General of the U.S.A. in Love," apparently a reference to Terry's Richmond subordinate, General John Turner. Terry demanded authorization to punish this "malicious or malignant slander," otherwise he and Turner could not honorably continue in their posts. Turner stormed into Pollard's office and received an apology, but the damage was done. The army was made to appear ridiculous once more.[14]

Pollard's writing highlighted anew the antagonism between army officers and white citizens. If in the early postwar months Confederates had accepted the army as a bulwark against anarchy, that appreciation did not last long. As much was apparent in Richmonder Anna Sherrard's arch comment that the "blue coats preserved the peace by their hateful presence." The same was true of relations with others from the North. Locals had always scorned northern teachers coming south to instruct freedmen—mocking them as "white cravatted gentlemen from Andover, with a nasal twang, and pretty Yankee girls." Isabel Maury, who decorated her Christmas tree with a portrait of Lee, shared that disdain. "The Yankees are convinced they cannot get into Society here: no one notices them," she gloated. "They have rented fine houses in good neighbourhoods, but no one disturbs them."[15]

The same held true for the governor. Frosty social relations dogged the Pierponts their entire time in Richmond and let them know where they stood with the residents. The handful of white citizens who had remained loyal to the Union and befriended the governor constituted a vanishingly small number. When Julia, his wife, wanted to have a party, she knew she could rely on army officers stationed in town but would not be able to attract many local women. She sought to resolve her problem by importing friends from Washington. Even then, there were some awkward moments, and she did not repeat the experiment.[16]

At the end of 1865, Congress set up the Joint Committee on Reconstruction. It consisted of six senators and nine representatives to gather evidence on conditions in the former Confederate states. The legislators were deeply skeptical that white southerners had forsaken their secessionist aspirations. In retrospect, this was an unwarranted fear. But at the time, unsettled conditions in the South, including rising violence against Black people and increasing numbers of former Confederates elected to office, made it seem plausible. Moderate Republicans, not the smaller radical faction, remained in charge of Congress. But they, too, were troubled by conditions in the South. In Virginia's case, the General Assembly avoided overtly racist language in the statutes it passed. But it was apparent that legislators still aimed to control the Black population as much they had done before. The latter recognized that intent, which heightened their uncertainty about the promise of freedom.

Senator Jacob Howard of Michigan, fifty years old, led the subcommittee tasked with collecting information on the Old Dominion. A large, clean-shaven lawyer with hooded eyes, he had helped draft the Thirteenth Amendment freeing the enslaved and was about to play a crucial role in passing the far-reaching Fourteenth Amendment. It would enshrine birthright citizenship in the Constitution, beyond the reach of state law to contravene. And it would be a bitter source of contention in the South for a year and more. A stylish dresser with an educated but ponderous manner of speaking, Howard was often the sole interrogator of the witnesses. His subcommittee interviewed forty-nine Virginians, mostly unionist but some conservatives and moderates.[17]

The first witness the committee called to testify was General Turner, the army commander in Richmond. In blunt words, he described how unwelcome the citizens made him feel. He said he was constantly reminded of their hostility, "a deep-abiding hate." He had never been invited into any of their homes, and not a day passed without being the recipient of some slight, some gesture by both men and women, who turned their noses up at him, or turned their backs to him, or crossed the street to avoid him. He often was forced to bite his tongue and suppress his indignation at rude treatment. Richmond was not a happy posting for a United States Army officer.[18]

It saddened Turner to see how downcast the small unionist remnant had become. He said the secessionist majority would tear down the American flag if they thought they could get away with it. He believed white people, knowing their need to employ African Americans, were disposed to get along with them, but they would never view them as equals or grant them basic civil rights unless compelled. Demobilization had gradually drawn down his force to the point where he only had about five hundred soldiers remaining in the Richmond area. He warned that there had been a marked increase in disloyal speeches and newspaper articles in direct proportion to the army's diminished presence. Even more alarming were his comments when asked by the committee about the prospects for a renewed attempt at secession. Turner claimed that if given the chance, southerners would try to separate themselves socially and commercially from the North, even if they could no longer effect secession by military force.

In charge of the whole state was General Terry, whose command consisted of between 2,600 and 2,700 men scattered in one- and two-company posts in twelve Virginia towns. Terry reinforced the opinions of his Richmond subordinate. He believed that since taking over in June, the evidence of disloyalty had increased. In reply to a question about the state of white unionists and African Americans if the army were withdrawn, he said they would be in "a lamentable condition." He thought white opinion toward Union men was as hostile as it had ever been. The goal of former Confederates, in his view, was the "desire to make treason honorable and loyalty infamous." Words like "contempt" and "bitter hostility" peppered his testimony.[19]

Echoing Turner, Terry allowed that many white people treated freedmen kindly and endeavored to accommodate themselves to postwar realities. But he believed a far greater number treated them unjustly. When asked if African Americans might be goaded by mistreatment to resort to violence, he said frankly that they "would commit those acts which an oppressed people sooner or later commit against their oppressors." Still smarting from Pollard's ridicule two weeks earlier, the general bristled when questioned about that affair, and his responses became terse. He, like Grant, had not been pleased that the president allowed Pollard to publish his newspaper again.[20]

Judge John Underwood had outraged white Richmond the previous summer with his indictments of leading Confederates for treason and his writs of confiscation targeting wealthy civilians. He told Senator Howard that, sooner than raise the freedmen to political equality, white Virginians "would prefer their total annihilation." When he was holding court in Richmond, a prominent citizen told him the turning point of war had been when Black men enlisted in the US Army. That was the heaviest blow to the rebellion, he asserted, and the cause of the present bitterness against formerly enslaved people. The judge declared that Andrew Johnson's liberal pardon policy had encouraged Confederates to think they might eventually take over the federal government. That could happen, Underwood suggested, if they returned to Congress and allied with northern Democrats against the Republican Party.[21]

Almost as an afterthought, seven Black Virginians appeared briefly before the committee. It heard their testimony in one day and accorded them collectively less time than it gave single prominent white witnesses. Surprisingly, the committee did not hear from any current Black residents of Richmond, and the omission must have troubled them. Dr. Daniel Norton, a physician in Yorktown, said, "The spirit of the whites against the Blacks is much worse than it was before the war." Madison Newby, a former free Black man of Surry County, complained that white patrols went around at night dragging people from their homes and beating them. Richard Hill, formerly of Richmond, was asked if there was danger of intermarriage. "I do not think there is any more danger of that now than there was when slavery existed," he caustically observed. "At that time there was a good deal of amalgamation." He also said it was a prevalent idea among white Virginians that if they ever got their representation back in Congress, they would oppress the freed people. Thomas Bayne, a dentist from Norfolk, echoed the common belief among freedmen that the army was the only institution on which they could rely. "The only hope the colored people have," he concluded, "is in Uncle Sam's bayonets." All of their comments suggest an abiding fear that they might still be subjected to a condition of bondage akin to slavery. Indeed, nearly a year after emancipation, they feared that slavery might not be dead.[22]

Former congressman John Minor Botts seconded Underwood's opinion that the president's liberal pardon policy had made Confederates bold and defiant. The social isolation of army officers and the small core of white unionist families was marked, as the contretemps over the Spotswood Hotel dance illustrated. Although Botts said his own daughters attended such events, others did not out of fear of the scorn that people like Pollard would heap on them in print. He quoted a unionist's letter railing against the growing fear that they had won the war, only to have victory stolen from them by resurgent, unrepentant rebels.[23]

Botts said the majority of members of the legislature in Richmond, though respectable and intelligent, had no experience of government and were easily led by a few "designing politicians." He had in mind the Speaker of the House of Delegates, John Brown Baldwin, with whom he had conducted a running feud ever since the secession crisis of 1861. As an indication of the extent of disloyal sentiment, he alluded to the incident in the House of Delegates when Baldwin said he hoped General Lee would soon be Virginia's governor. That admission, Botts claimed, "was received with great applause, both in the galleries and on the floor."[24]

A series of other white unionists paraded before the committee to give their views. They were chiefly concerned with making the case that Johnson's lenient pardon policy had put the state at risk and let former Confederates take power at the local and state level. They were outraged at Governor Pierpont for letting this happen. James Hunnicutt, a brash, outspoken Baptist minister, made a brief appearance. He echoed the comments of other unionists that Johnson's policy gave former Confederates renewed hope when they had none after Appomattox. Hunnicutt said there were seven newspapers in Richmond, all of them disloyal except for the moribund *Republic*. But, he said, he was getting ready to move there to publish a true Union paper. He made it clear to the committee that he would be heard from again.[25]

The testimony that the Joint Committee most anticipated came on February 17, when Robert E. Lee appeared. The last time he had been in Washington, he had gone in full-dress uniform with his brother officers to the East Room of the White House to shake hands with their new commander in chief, Abraham Lincoln. The summons to appear before the committee five momentous years later alarmed him. The Confederate chieftain, however, appeared calm and courtly throughout, resolute and wary in his answers rather than bitter. He claimed that he had supported gradual emancipation, that white southerners treated freedmen well, and that whites were willing for Black people to be educated. But he exhibited the condescension of most white southerners. "They like their ease and comfort," he said of freed people, "and, I think, look more to their present than to their future condition." If they were given the vote, "it would excite unfriendly feelings between the two races." He continued, "At this time, they cannot vote intelligently." Asked if he thought it better if the Old Dominion's African Americans left the state, he replied, "I think it would be better for Virginia if she could get rid of them." In its final report, the Joint Committee held up his testimony as proof that Johnson's policies had failed:

white southerners remained hostile to the federal government, would not relinquish their devotion to the Confederacy, and envisioned a subordinate role for Black Virginians.[26]

John Brown Baldwin, the Speaker of the House of Delegates, made the most forceful presentation before the committee. When asked by Senator Howard about giving Black citizens the right to vote, the adroit, supremely confident Baldwin reacted with horror. If that happened, he said, "we would have advocates of suffrage of women, of minors, and foreigners." Baldwin said no one loved Virginia more than he did, but he would flee the state as he would from the plague if Black men ever gained the vote.[27]

Baldwin said the General Assembly was going through all Virginia statutes and striking those with racial language. He claimed African Americans had all the rights of free men, but change must come slowly. He patronized his interlocutor with weary contempt: "You, gentlemen of the north, who have not a mass of 300,000 or 400,000 suddenly emancipated negroes in your midst, can hardly appreciate the caution which we feel to be necessary." Therefore, "we must let the public feeling of the white people mature." He made clear his belief that Black people would never have the persistence of purpose or energy or intellectual vigor of whites. If he had his way, their lot would forever be that of inferiors and servants, the biblical hewers of wood and drawers of water. He voiced the prevailing assumption among white southerners that they knew Black people best and deserved to control them.[28]

Another member of the legislature from Richmond, Peachy Grattan, bluntly seconded Baldwin's testimony. He said the worst thing that could happen to African Americans would be to give them political power. Enfranchising them would ineluctably lead to racial violence and could only result in their eventual extermination. He claimed most whites felt only kindness and sympathy for them. He showed a stubborn blindness to the evidence all around him of Black energy and thirst for schooling in the Virginia capital. Grattan claimed to the contrary that African Americans could not educate themselves, care for themselves, or be counted on to improve their lot in life. White people, he said, would view giving votes to Black men with "the same sort of repugnance which a man feels to a snake."[29]

The testimony of Black men, white unionists, and army and Freedmen's Bureau officers predictably outraged the Richmond press. It made a fair point of saying that the latter group had a vested interest in maintaining their organization's continuing existence. But that did not mean, as it alleged, that Orlando Brown made up out of whole cloth the stories of mistreatment of Black men and women. Nor was it the case that the Bureau and the army were engaged in an effort to foment ill-will between African Americans and white people. The *Dispatch* called the committee's work a mockery of investigation. The *Whig* said General Terry's comments did great injustice to Virginians. The editors' outrage demonstrated how far apart North and South remained.[30]

The previous April, when news flashed across the telegraph wires that Richmond had fallen, a boisterous crowd gathered in Washington to celebrate. When they learned that Union soldiers were helping put out the fire, they roared, "Let it burn, let it burn." The sentiments expressed by Confederates in Richmond a year later rekindled those emotions among many in the North. With publication of the testimony before the Joint Committee, the stark differences between the white South and Congress were out in the open for all to see.

The contrast between Lee and Baldwin, on the one hand, and the other witnesses, on the other hand, demonstrated the chief problem that Congress saw with the postwar South. According to its perspective, the president's policies had failed to reconcile former Confederates to the war's outcome and were therefore fatally flawed. There was no sign of regret for the disaster that secession caused, no admission of any wrongdoing. The evidence it collected convinced the committee that the South could not be trusted to manage its affairs without northern guidance. Without it, Black men and women had no chance for equal rights or opportunity, and the secessionist impulse remained alive.

The purpose of the Joint Committee was not just to collect information on conditions in the South through interviews. It was also responsible for drafting a far-reaching constitutional amendment that Congress approved in June and sent to the states for ratification. The Fourteenth Amendment defined birthright citizenship and guaranteed due process and equal protection under the law for all citizens. It did not directly enfranchise Black men, but it did mandate a loss of congressional representation for any state that prevented them from voting. The amendment shocked white southerners and engendered bitter contention in national politics and in affairs closer to home, that year and far beyond.

When Colonel Orlando Brown testified before Congress on February 15, he had led the Freedmen's Bureau in Virginia for more than eight months. In his comments, he put his finger on the fundamental issue: white people still wanted to control Black men and women. They thought the freed people could not care for themselves and, therefore, needed the same supervision they had required under slavery. As evidence of disloyal sentiment, he repeated a rumor that when the army shut down Henry Rives Pollard's *Examiner* on General Grant's orders, three hundred armed men were preparing to attack the guard at the paper's office and reopen it by force. It was nothing more than a rumor, but the fact that it was believed by some suggested to Brown the extent of the rebellious spirit still extant in Richmond. He said he was constantly receiving reports of violence against the freedmen. If the Bureau withdrew from Virginia, he was certain they would be even more severely oppressed.

Brown's remarks at the Joint Committee hearings treated serious issues of life and death for the freedmen. But near the beginning of his testimony, he was visibly bemused by a question that showed how little Congress understood conditions in the former Confederate capital. Asked if there was much ill-will toward freedmen in Richmond, Brown replied with the sardonic answer that white people were not inclined "to forgive the negro for being free."[31]

13
Winter into Spring

Early 1866

While the city council and the General Assembly reasserted their customary authority in Richmond, and while Congress grew increasingly dubious of that effort, citizens in the slowly reviving city were more focused on making a living. Poverty, crime, and underemployment continued to put their marks on the city. Gradually, though, industry and business revived, as did professional and cultural activity.

The poor especially faced daunting challenges keeping body and soul together. The evacuation fire had reduced the already cramped housing stock, and the resulting high rents led to repeated angry protest meetings during the winter of 1865 66. The siege works around Richmond in the last year of the war had stripped bare whole forests of hardwood and pine, making it difficult to find firewood to ward off the cold. In a bitterly frigid January, as color drained from the winter landscape, the canal froze over. Ice impeded traffic on the river below the city. The first grain harvest of peacetime had been mediocre. The deprivations of wartime had never entirely abated, and they intensified in winter as hunger once again stalked poorer neighborhoods of the capital.

In early 1866 Martha Chace visited poor Black families in Richmond for the New England Freedmen's Aid Society. She reported great privation during the cold months. The government had stopped giving food and firewood to African Americans who were sick, aged, or unemployed. She found the greatest need in the crowded tenements and dank basement apartments that clustered in low-lying precincts just outside the Burnt District. Chace said people were grateful for the food and wood vouchers she dispensed, but they asked for work more than charity. "Give me work," one of them begged her, "for which I can get money to pay my rent and buy bread for my children, and I'll *scuffle* along without help from Government."[1]

Indigent white residents suffered during the winter months as well. William Munford, head of the city's relief committee, had worked throughout the war to aid needy families of soldiers and refugees. In the final months of the conflict, he made repeated appeals for contributions. "Those who do not trouble themselves with the sorrows of the poor," he wrote, "have no idea of the suffering around them." And so it continued in peacetime. In the early postwar days, Munford served on the civilian commission created by the army to distribute government rations to destitute residents. At the start of 1866, he tried to encourage more efficient coordination between benevolent societies and the overseers of the poor. The modest turnout at a meeting at city hall on January 6 disappointed him. But he forged ahead because, he said, there was great suffering in the city. Loeb Brothers, a firm that employed several hundred manufacturing ready-made clothing, promised Munford it would hire only people recommended by the relief committee. It was a welcome offer but not enough to satisfy the need. Munford's charity continued to struggle with lack of funds and lack of interest among the citizenry.[2]

Crime, and the perception of it, did not take a holiday in Richmond. The widespread notion that disorder and turmoil still plagued society long after the chaos of April subsided remained firmly ensconced. Rightly or wrongly, the postwar capital developed a reputation of harboring more crime than cities farther south. One observer claimed other southern cities were overridden with desperate characters, but Richmond was the worst for general lawlessness.[3]

Thieves and footpads haunted the fringes of the Burnt District at night. Sensational beatings, knifings, and other forms of bodily harm garnered the most attention, but workaday burglaries and petty larcenies predominated among the cases brought before the Mayor's Court.

A nighttime break-in at Frank Lentz's store on Cary Street in January was typical, being distinctive only because of the ingenuity involved. Using a pair of pincers to turn the key left in the lock, the thieves stole a cash box and forty-six pairs of boots and shoes. To prevent being discovered, the culprits dosed Lentz and his assistant with chloroform. Later that year the press castigated Governor Pierpont for giving executive clemency to too many criminals. They, the editors complained, returned to all manner of villainy as soon as they left the penitentiary, located on a prominent hill to the west of town overlooking the ironworks at Tredegar.[4]

On the positive side, locals pointed with pride to the success of the new civilian police force in keeping in check the burglars, horse thieves, and garroters who bedeviled the city. The fact that residents subscribed to a fund to buy uniforms for the officers lends credence to that opinion. Touting the efficacy of the police, however, may have been a backhanded way of criticizing the army for failing to suppress crime before the city belatedly created the force. Similarly, an incendiary account of an interracial dance in January that degenerated into a brawling knife fight was a way to condemn gatherings that transgressed racial barriers rather than just to praise the police for preserving good order.[5]

Newspaper editors presented the evidence of crime and disorder in a way to guide the reader's interpretation, sometimes deploring, sometimes pitying, and often ridiculing the people involved. They were meant to stigmatize perpetrators—and sometimes victims, too—as living squalid lives outside respectable society. Josephine Dudley, a Black woman, could not set bail and therefore went to jail for using obscene and abusive language to a white woman. Peter Scott, a Black man, was convicted of assaulting his wife, Margaret, told to give security, and mockingly admonished "not to beat her again for twelve months and a day." Black residents were not alone in being subject to press ridicule and caricature. Pat Grogan and his wife, Lucy, were brought before the court for fighting in the street. Their comments to the judge were rendered in stage Irish dialect to encourage readers to dismiss them as disreputable people.[6]

In March an affray in the freedmen's village at the former Confederate hospital at Chimborazo, east of the capitol, pitted a group of

Chimborazo, the largest Confederate military hospital complex in the South, became a Freedmen's Bureau village for African American families after the war. (Library of Congress)

armed rioters in a shootout with police and soldiers. When a dozen African Americans were brought before a magistrate's court, however, it became apparent that others had started the disturbance. Even the *Dispatch,* no friend of freedmen, conceded that a gang of white men was to blame. They were "treating free negroes in a manner which would not have been permitted toward slaves." The fact that the paper was still using an outmoded term illustrated its failure to shed old categories and old ways of thinking. Before long it would revert to its more frequently negative view of Chimborazo as an unmerited luxury for idle Black families. In fact, the village represented one of the few refuges for homeless poor people in a city lacking in adequate shelter for all classes.[7]

The nexus of poverty, dislocation, and crime gave an especially pitiless cast to childhood for the many whom war had deprived of families. Unattached orphans of Confederate soldiers and parentless children from formerly enslaved families formed a mass of vulnerable young people, who were often sucked into the criminal demimonde in

Shockoe Bottom. Gangs of pickpockets, mostly children, roamed the streets. Bands of delinquent youths fought with stones and slingshots. The press complained of wild children living rough, preyed upon by unscrupulous adults. It alternated between worries over how to control them and proposing ways to care for them. This concern gave added poignancy to the general anxiety over social disorder. Most unattached children did not end up in orphanages but drifted between the city Alms House, relatives, and the street. Binding them out as apprentices might solve the problem of children without adults, but the system, and those enmeshed in it, suffered from abuse, especially Black apprentices. The previous summer visiting abolitionist Julia Wilbur thought children bound out from the poorhouse to work away from their mothers were already at risk of becoming "to all intents & purposes little slaves again."[8]

Economic activity since April might have seemed erratic to locals, but the evidence of revival was also there to see. Outside observers said all it took to disprove laments by residents about the scarcity of money was a walk through the Burnt District to see the rash of new construction going up. Someone must be supplying a great deal of capital to produce so much construction.

The trajectory of the Davenport family traced the course of commerce from antebellum to postwar Richmond. Isaac Davenport Sr. arrived from Maine in the 1820s and built a thriving mercantile firm. He later sent for his nephew to join him. The younger man, Isaac Davenport Jr., always retained that suffix to his name to honor his uncle. Davenport Sr. succeeded so well that when leading citizens formed the Hollywood Cemetery company, they chose him as its first president. His nephew struck out on his own in a wholesale grocery partnership. That effort languished, but it led directly to a more ambitious and wildly successful enterprise: shipping flour to South America and importing sugar and coffee on the return voyage. In the middle of the war, the nephew partnered with Charles Wortham to found a banking, investment, and insurance firm. On the last, chaotic day of Confederate Richmond, Davenport Sr. had the misfortune to walk past a brick wall as it collapsed, killing him outright. On the same day, the Davenport office went up in smoke. These personal and financial losses did not deter Isaac Jr. from rebuilding his firm. By the next year he was president of a new bank and then a second one, two years later, all the while building Davenport & Company.[9]

War and fire had reduced Albert Brooks's thriving livery stable from ten taxis and twenty-two horses to three wagons and a single horse. He had overcome adversity before, having purchased his own freedom and that of his family and created a prosperous company within the narrow space allowed to free Black people. Now, from a stable on Franklin Street near the Exchange Hotel, the forty-eight-year-old entrepreneur did the same again and in the wider scope that emancipation created. An acknowledged leader in the African American community and deacon at First African Baptist Church, he applied his optimism and talent to the nascent Republican Party. He supported his wife, Lucy Goode Brooks, in the charity she helped found that would later become the Friends' Asylum for Colored Orphans. Before the war she had lost a child to slave traders, and, following the end to slavery, she took a special interest in the fate of the many parentless and homeless children.[10]

The forges of Tredegar furnished a larger and more visible sign of recovery than the Davenport or Brooks firms. In 1866 the foundry could melt twice as much iron per day as before secession, thanks to wartime Confederate investment. But if the forges had escaped the fire, heavy wartime use had degraded the plant and equipment. Machines needed retooling and furnaces needed new firebrick linings. Luckily for Joseph Reid Anderson, the sterling account he maintained in London was intact, and the firm realized a handsome profit on cotton it owned. The first big infusion of northern cash came when Anderson sold his Dover coal mines to the west of town to a syndicate of New York money men. Southern bridge builders and railroads soon benefited as they had before the war from iron produced by Tredegar. By the time winter was over, the foundry was "now in full blast, with the red-forked flames belching forth from the tall chimneys night and day, and nearly a thousand workmen engaged in them."[11]

Directly across the river from this iron-producing behemoth, the Manchester Cotton Mills resumed operation. The Warwick &

Barksdale firm's rebuilt Gallego Mills was rapidly taking shape in early 1866. By spring, a horde of masons laid twenty thousand bricks a day. The press gushed about the millions of board feet of lumber that construction of the mill consumed but admitted it would not be complete until the wheat crop of 1867 had been harvested. Then, the writer boasted, Gallego would "exert a magic power in the restoration of Richmond to prosperity and fame."[12]

With the tobacco harvest of 1865 in, the sweet scent of curing leaves once more wafted from the downtown warehouses that survived. James Thomas Jr. was not content with using the money he had presciently parked in London during the war. Even two years later, he was still hectoring Washington to recover tobacco that he claimed it seized in 1861 before formal imposition of the blockade. Worth more than a half million dollars before the war, Thomas recovered nearly that much again within two years of its end. He funneled some of that wealth into generous benefactions to the impecunious local Baptist seminary, Richmond College. He was deemed the richest man in town by his death more than a decade later.

As repairs to wartime damage proceeded apace, the owners of the railroads that carried the city's iron, flour, and tobacco renewed their antebellum passion for expansion and consolidation of lines. General William Mahone had risen to the presidency of the Norfolk and Petersburg Railroad before secession. When war came, this diminutive man with a long beard and abundant energy served the Confederacy in uniform, most controversially as commander at the 1864 Battle of the Crater at Petersburg, where his men massacred surrendered soldiers of the United States Colored Troops. Mahone returned to railroading after Appomattox and became president of both the Norfolk and Southern and the Southside Railroads. His plans in 1866 for a merger with a third line ran up against the power brokers of Richmond and northern Virginia. Feuding would continue for years and pit Mahone against the traditional elite in politics as well. Despite his contentious wartime record, he would go on to champion a biracial coalition that briefly defeated the conservative establishment and pursued a progressive agenda. But that was far into the future. In the winter of 1866, he had just begun to joust with competing business leaders for mastery of the railroads.[13]

As commerce and industry rebounded, other hopeful signs followed in the city's cultural life. The evidence was there in growing churches, educational institutions, professional organizations, and entertainments.

The Medical College of Virginia (MCV) was fortunate that its Egyptian Revival–style building stood far removed from the Burnt District. In July 1865 the college's board met to fill vacant faculty vacancies. The chair of surgery went to Dr. Hunter McGuire of Winchester, who borrowed three hundred dollars to start his new career in the capital. He was renowned as a Confederate army doctor, though he was not able to save his wounded commander, Stonewall Jackson. With hope for the future, the college announced it would resume classes in November. For teaching purposes, its faculty controlled the large hospital for poor freedmen at Howard's Grove, the City Alms House Hospital, and the Richmond General Dispensary. By March 1866 MCV was able to hold its first postwar graduation ceremony at First Baptist Church. McGuire gave the main address. He praised chloroform as "God's boon to the suffering" and heaped even greater plaudits on the work of Confederate army surgeons.[14]

In recognition of their expanding presence and importance for the city, later that year Richmond's attorneys organized a bar association named for the great chief justice, John Marshall. It also testified to how tightly knit the leading elements of Richmond were. Meeting in the council chamber of city hall, the lawyers chose James Lyon as their president. He had enraged northern opinion the previous year at the mass meeting to proclaim Richmond's loyalty to the nation. The first vice president was William Macfarland, the banker who had taken Richmond's promise of loyalty to Washington in the fall. Second vice president was longtime city councilman and attorney Gustavus Myers, who had spoken to Lincoln the day after the fire. The corresponding secretary was James Dooley, whose father had rebuilt his burned hat factory. Except for Dooley, they all had taken a leading role in the city's economic life before the conflagration and continued to do so afterward.[15]

Ida Vernon, the darling of the Confederate stage, frequently returned to perform in Richmond after the war. (National Portrait Gallery)

The theaters reopened before the fires cooled in April and at first featured mostly blackface farce and vaudeville shows offering similar racist stereotypes. These continued but by fall were joined by selections from Shakespeare and Italian opera featuring actors like twenty-two-year-old Ida Vernon, who had been the darling of the Confederate stage. A famous beauty as a young woman, Vernon became even more striking in appearance as she aged, with a penetrating gaze and aristocratic bearing. She appeared with all the leading American players of the midcentury, including the towering thespian of the age, Edwin Booth, her sometime fiancé and brother of Lincoln's assassin.

During the war, Vernon had settled her large family in Richmond and supported them after her father lost his property. She founded a hospital for Confederate soldiers, helping treat them by day and acting at night. When her house burned to the ground on April 3, 1865, she joined the refugees huddling on the green of Capitol Square to escape the flames. She fled north but by October reappeared to accolades at the New Richmond Theatre. Though she spent most of her six-decade career in New York, she kept returning to the Virginia capital, where she had enjoyed her greatest acclaim.[16]

Recovery was hard for other cultural and literary figures. John Reuben Thompson, an ardent poet with a penchant for dapper clothes, had edited the *Southern Literary Messenger.* Tubercular and impoverished, he ran the blockade to England in 1864 to publish the *Index,* a Confederate propaganda sheet designed to sway British opinion. A few days after word of Richmond's fall reached London, where Thompson rubbed shoulders with Dickens and Tennyson, he learned from his sister that the family business had fallen victim to the evacuation fire. Worse, all of his books had perished.[17]

Thompson's friend and fellow secessionist George William Bagby had succeeded him as editor of the *Messenger.* He had had some success as a humorist before the war with stories that sentimentalized the dialect of backwoods characters. He fled Richmond on the same train as Jefferson Davis. Before he returned, his father, a pious shopkeeper, warned him that in the capital "ruins, broken hopes and sad memories meet you at every step." The son struggled to revive his literary career, but eye disease threatening complete blindness forced him to give up writing. "I had to lecture or starve," the acerbic essayist recalled. "Ah! How I hated and dreaded it." He achieved some success in 1866, but speaker's fees proved inadequate to support his young family.[18]

As wealthy and once-wealthy families strove to reassert their leadership in the economy and politics of the city, they invoked new social distinctions to signify their prominence. At the end of 1866, they founded the German, an exclusive dance club named for its Prussian dance figures. Their first event took place in the Linden Row townhouse of insurance broker John Montague. To gain admittance, it took more than white gloves, a Prince Albert frock coat, and five dollars for membership. Founding members included Tredegar's Joseph Reid Anderson and assorted Haxalls, Warwicks, and Cabells, all free of unionist taint. They allowed no mention of German attendees in the newspapers because it was unseemly for a lady's name to appear in print.

Much further down the social scale, the city's working people faced their own troubles trying to make a living. The racial divide in the skilled trades grew with economic revival. White carpenters and painters formed rudimentary unions and tried to freeze out Black artisans. In response, the latter began to organize their own unions. One of them predicted "an irrepressible conflict between the white and Black mechanics of the South." Tredegar proved to be an exception in part. Joseph Reid Anderson rehired many of his formerly enslaved workers and spurned northern laborers who were willing to come to Richmond but did not want to work alongside African Americans. Though Anderson held the same views about race as most white southerners, he claimed he paid his workers the same wages regardless of color. He may have considered his Black workers socially inferior, but he rewarded their skill.[19]

The chimera of imported white labor continued to beguile business leaders even after repeated attempts to bring Europeans to Virginia failed. The radical Baptist minister James Hunnicutt criticized the effort because it slighted African Americans. Why try to encourage a colony of immigrants from Europe, he argued, when there were so many capable Black people? "To ignore them, and drive them out from us, by refusing to give them adequate wages for their labor is cruel, heartless, diabolical," Hunnicutt wrote. Another source of labor closer to hand was convict leasing, which accentuated the racial divide. Starting under Governor Pierpont and continuing under his successors, the penitentiary on the west side of town began filling requests from companies for inmates to labor on railroads, turnpikes, and rock quarries. Here was another form of involuntary labor much like slavery in all but name.[20]

Almost before the ashes of the Burnt District had cooled, a drumbeat of exhortations from past, present, and would-be future leaders of Richmond pleaded with young people, in particular Confederate veterans, to go to work and rebuild their city and state. Caustic as ever, Henry Wise directed pointed admonitions to the sons of the gentry. At the reorganization of the Richmond Light Infantry Blues in February

1866, the former governor urged his audience not to think of emigrating. They should "go to work; not to be idle, not to loaf about the streets."[21]

Nearly a year after the fire, tourism still produced a stream of visitors and a minor source of income for locals mining the battlefields of central Virginia for the seemingly inexhaustible supply of relics. A northerner noted that as yet no publisher had produced a guidebook to the seat of war. He archly suggested that there should be two, one for each side "to suit the prejudices of the reader."[22]

Those prejudices were present at a reception Julia and Francis Pierpont held on February 27, 1866. On that Tuesday evening, the governor's mansion filled with members of the legislature and the US Army. Prominent among the former were Speaker of the House of Delegates John Brown Baldwin and gadfly Richmond state senator John Gilmer. Former mayor Joseph Mayo, planning his return to office later that spring, showed up as well. General Terry attended with officers of his headquarters staff. Unrepentant Confederates and representatives of northern victory alike, they had all accepted the Pierponts' invitation. It had been scarcely three weeks since Henry Rives Pollard provoked outrage over his snide report on the dance sponsored by army officers. It had been even less time since Baldwin and Terry had given stunningly antithetical testimony before the Joint Committee on Reconstruction. The tension between civil and military powers in Richmond was as acute as ever. What could the Speaker of the House Delegates and the commanding general have said to one another that evening under the glittering gaslit chandeliers of the governor's parlor? Whatever the subject and tone of their conversation—acrimonious, stilted, icily correct—none of them likely anticipated the next chapter in Richmond's postwar story. That would be fashioned by people who were not invited to the governor's reception but who were even then planning to make their opinions known, and in dramatic fashion.[23]

14

Observed and Remembered

March to April 1866

At fifty-two, James Hunnicutt looked remarkably like a younger John Brown before his rendezvous with destiny at Harpers Ferry—down to the same pinched, menacing scowl. Hunnicutt swept his generous shock of salt-and-pepper hair up in an alarming pompadour to give him the appearance of height. The stern, thin-lipped face he showed the photographer marked him as a man of scant humor and grim purpose. Like many southerners, the Fredericksburg minister had espoused a bewildering range of political opinions during the tumultuous 1860s. He earlier believed slavery was the best condition for Black people. Later, he denounced secessionists for unwittingly inflicting emancipation on the South. The Confederate majority in Fredericksburg drove him from town in fear of his life, and the experience thoroughly radicalized him.

In March, after testifying before Congress's Joint Committee on Reconstruction, he moved to Richmond and began publishing the *New Nation,* a radical journal fueled by his evangelical passion and newfound solicitude for freedmen. The paper ran on a shoestring, with the proprietor living in a garret and reduced to begging for contributions throughout its brief run. He employed sarcasm and outrage without a hint of subtlety to flay the Confederacy, former slaveholding aristocrats, and the postwar establishment. With a fondness for capital letters and a bottomless supply of exclamation points, his paper delighted in insulting Richmond's traditional leaders. He had been ostracized by Fredericksburg and openly courted the same reception

Baptist minister James Hunnicutt founded the *New Nation* newspaper, which advocated equal rights for all citizens. (Virginia Museum of History and Culture)

in the former Confederate capital when he arrived to advocate equal rights for all.[1]

To celebrate Washington's birthday, on February 22 General Turner and staff reviewed smartly turned-out detachments from two infantry regiments, while artillery fired a thunderous salute. After the review, they marched into town from the west behind flags waving and brass bands playing. At the end of the procession, the soldiers and their followers crowded around the Washington statue on Capitol Square.[2]

African Americans had watched similar displays for almost a year. At the end of the war, they saw seemingly endless ranks of blue-coated soldiers marching through town on the way to victory parades in Washington. In the summer they watched the local garrison, when it still numbered more than ten thousand men, perform resplendent reviews. They saw similar displays at the Fourth of July celebration. And now they watched the army, even with diminished numbers, commemorate the birth of the first president. In all of these events, they had been spectators. True, they were the principal actors in the jubilee celebrations of the previous April and at the anniversary of the Emancipation Proclamation. But those events had taken place inside their churches, not on public streets. Now, at the beginning of the new year, they began to anticipate an anniversary even more important to them than all that had come before and that they meant to celebrate publicly in full view of the white population.

Whether they took inspiration from General Turner's men on Washington's birthday or not, only days after that holiday, the city's Black leaders began their planning in earnest. What they envisioned was a grand parade from west of town along Broad Street and into Capitol Square, replicating the soldiers' line of march. It would put on display the many social organizations they had secretly fostered before 1865 and expanded after emancipation. They purchased a banner that cost one hundred dollars, a considerable expense for an impoverished community. They meant to celebrate the first anniversary of their manumission—not by a wartime proclamation having no practical effect within the Confederacy but by their actual liberation from servitude amid fire and smoke on the morning of April 3, 1865. By this demonstration, they meant to assert the blessings of freedom against the continuing threats to its realization.[3]

By the first week of March, the parade organizers formalized their plans and notified Mayor David Saunders of their intentions. They were aware that what they proposed would spark controversy, and they reassured him of their intention "to turn out in a Gentle manner with no Dezire of boasting." They promised to keep good order among their own people and asked him to ensure the city police would do the same for white citizens. Governor Pierpont approved and told the mayor to coordinate security with General Terry.[4]

At first the press lightheartedly mocked the planning. One account chided the organizers for not inviting Frederick Douglass to address them. Were Fields Cook and other local leaders afraid of being upstaged by the nation's leading Black orator? But by the middle of March, the white community was alive with sinister rumors about what the celebration would entail. "The whole thing," some people worried, "might wind up in a terrible tragedy of blood and death." They claimed intelligent African Americans considered such an event in bad taste. They professed to believe that the parade could not have been envisioned by local people. Only "maliciously and mischievously disposed persons" from outside Richmond could be behind it.[5]

Editors warned the planners they ran a grave risk of offending and alienating "those who are and have always been their friends, and without whose continued good will and patronage their lot will be miserable beyond expression." If, against all good judgment, the event took place, those who participated "will be observed and remembered." Henry Rives Pollard's revived *Examiner* said white Richmond would tolerate many changes because they had to, but they would not stand for insults from African Americans.[6]

A petition from white citizens convinced Governor Pierpont and General Terry to reassess their original approval. The petitioners cautioned that April 3 invoked painful memories not just of the immolation of their city but also of "the defeat of a cause they believed to be just." If General Grant had chosen not to march triumphantly through Richmond the previous April out of respect for the defeated, the petition argued, why should freed people not show the same sensitivity now?[7]

Given the heightened unease, Terry agreed that the parade was ill-advised and convinced the planners to back down. The press expressed pleasure and congratulated the organizers for their good judgment. Their relief did not last long. At a meeting on March 27, African Americans reversed their decision and restated their intention to go forward. Bessie Canedy, a sympathetic northern teacher, approved of the decision. She attributed it to younger men who insisted on celebrating despite the caution of grayer heads in the African American community. Those elders worried as much as their white counterparts about stirring up racial antagonism.[8]

Terry telegraphed Grant's headquarters in Washington that he had advised the leaders not to proceed because their plans were creating "great excitement among the whites." He expected serious unrest and asked for instructions. He closed with a personal request saying he was due a leave of absence and hoped to begin it on March 30. Grant replied the same day and told his subordinate that if the parade was likely to create disorder, he should stop it. He left it to Terry's discretion but pointedly told him not to leave town until after April 3.[9]

Tensions rose as rumors coursed through the city. For whatever reason, Terry decided not to ban the event, but he did close the bars and kept soldiers and police on heightened alert for signs of trouble. As the day approached, employers threatened to fire workers if they took time off to attend. This would become a standard tactic in the coming months to stifle Black political expression. The Rev. William Harris reported he had heard of businessmen saying they would "wade through blood before the niggers shall celebrate that day." Tobacco manufacturer John K. Childrey fired forty-three employees for leaving their posts to take part in the parade or just watch it. He did not stop there but sent their names to other business owners to prevent them from finding work quickly. A northern Black journal claimed that President Johnson himself had ordered the procession suppressed. There were wild rumors that the organizers planned to drag the Confederate flag in the dust and at the end of the parade route burn effigies of Robert E. Lee and Jefferson Davis.[10]

It was Holy Week, the most somber of the Christian calendar. On March 31, the night before Easter, Second African Baptist Church near Gamble's Hill burned to the ground until all that remained of it and two adjoining houses was "a heap of smoking ruins." The church played host to a large school but, more to the point, was known to be one of the venues where parade organizers met. At the same time, and knowing the strenuous objection of many white people, the organizers posted a handbill around town in an attempt to allay apprehension. "The coloured people of the city of Richmond," it read, "would most respectfully inform the public, that they do not intend to celebrate the failure of the Southern Confederacy, as it has been stated in the papers of this city, but simply as the day on which God was pleased to liberate their long-oppressed race."[11]

These two events—the church burning and the posting of handbills—evoked different interpretations from white and Black communities. The former dismissed the church fire as accidental. African

Americans saw it for what it was—a brazen attempt by arsonists to intimidate them. They were not convinced by the admonitions of the press. Nor, in turn, were whites convinced by the broadside's logic. There was no way to separate marking the downfall of the Confederacy from the date that emancipation came to Richmond.

The parade, long expected and much talked about, took place as originally planned. It had been the all-consuming topic of conversation for weeks. Richmond had burned a year before, one journalist wrote, and now it blazed again with banners, gaudy dresses, red ribbons, and a host of other colorful garments. The parade formed up at the fairgrounds west of town, progressed along Broad Street, and ended at Capitol Square. Ten thousand or more spectators had queued up from an early hour to watch. First in the line of march came a body of sixty mounted men in uniform, sabers drawn. A brass band followed them and took special delight in ending the spiritual "Kingdom Coming" with a long, drawn-out exclamation "Massa run, aha-a-a." Spectators on either side of the procession rushed around to get close to the musicians. Their surging mass threatened to disrupt the march, but horsemen with batons galloped up and down the route, shouting and huzzahing and preventing disorder.[12]

After the band came the marchers, maybe 1,500 in all. They represented the dozens of fraternal and charitable societies that African Americans had founded in secret before the war and expanded in the year since. They had added labor and political organizations since the past summer. One pennant, with a blue-and-white inscription, bore the legend "Peace, Friendship, and Liberty with all mankind." Another contingent carried a standard that read "Union Liberties Protective Society, organized February 4, 1866." These and other formerly secret societies were the motive force behind the parade. The marchers dressed largely in remnants of US Army uniforms and identified themselves with rosettes, badges, stars, and large letters on their breasts. There were the Young Sons of Zion, Teamsters Star of the East, Reform Sons of Love, Rising Christians, Union Sons of Liberty, and perhaps a dozen more, including the Humble Christian Benevolents from the Chesterfield coal pits. It was the first time white Richmond realized the extent of these organizations.[13]

After reaching Capitol Square, they passed by and saluted Governor Pierpont in his mansion and then gathered around Crawford's equestrian Washington to hear speeches. The crowd now swelled to as many as fifteen thousand. Waiting for them at the statue was the stern radical editor who had recently testified before the Joint Committee on Reconstruction. When an anonymous writer warned James Hunnicutt to leave town, saying the North would be "safer for your miserable carcass," he printed the letter. It was an example, he sneered, of what to expect from the city's not-so-genteel gentry. He gloried in the abuse and scoffed at threats to kill him. He promised to continue speaking out for "the equal rights of all loyal American citizens before the law without regard to race, caste or color." His *New Nation* was the only publication that forthrightly advocated for Black Virginians, and that was why a delegation of their leaders had invited him to give the main speech. Hunnicutt's curious postwar political odyssey would follow a crooked path forward, just as it had before the war, but for the present he had found his voice and intended to be heard.[14]

Writing in the first-person plural, Hunnicutt recalled that "never in all our life, had we addressed so many thousands of persons." The prospect energized him. He immediately began addressing his audience as his fellow citizens and repeated that salutation over and over during his speech. Even though he was not yet ready to champion votes for Black men, his remarks unnerved Confederate Richmonders. He urged his audience to work hard. In doing so they could command respect. Before last April, he said, it was dangerous to teach a Black man to read, "but now . . . with education you may become creditable doctors, lawyers, skilled mechanics, or clergymen." He appealed to their common southern identity. "My home is in the South. Your home, my 'fellow-citizens,' is in the South. In the South we have lived and in the South we must die."[15]

Even if Hunnicutt was not yet ready to advocate votes for his audience, he said he favored "freedom of the negro without compromising the freedom of the white." A year later, with the benefit of hindsight, he said that when he spoke to the crowd that day, he was confident they

Peter Randolph, minister of Ebenezer Baptist Church and leader of the effort of Black people to claim ownership of their churches. (Wikimedia Commons)

would become voters. But even at the time, his remarks dispelled for his audience any doubts they may have had whether there could be freedom and citizenship without the vote. His support of Richmond's freedmen would stand him in good stead the next year, when they did gain the franchise.[16]

It is unclear why the organizers chose a white man as the principal speaker. Perhaps it was simply because his paper was the only megaphone in town for broadcasting their point of view. Perhaps they thought it prudent to give a white man that role. But whatever the reason, they made sure other forceful leaders of their own race made remarks after Hunnicutt. One was the Rev. Peter Randolph, pastor of Ebenezer Baptist Church. Despite the pleasant appearance of his bland, round face, he was anything but a meek shepherd of his flock. He intended to achieve equality for his people despite the obstacles. A few white bystanders heckled him and asked him what his motto was. In answer, he smoothly replied, "peace and good will to all men." Other Black leaders followed and received an enthusiastic response. Reporters from the conservative press demeaned them by printing their words in exaggerated dialect. And yet the sense of their comments and the pride in their voices shone through. One speaker told the audience to "'hav themselves, and show dey war worthy with to be trusted of their freedom."[17]

All observers, those who approved the march and those who opposed it, agree that the day's events passed off without serious incident. There was only a single minor episode when a drunken opponent fired his pistol at one of the horsemen in the parade. He missed, and before he could shoot again, the police hustled him off to jail. The police chief received credit for the good order of the day because he had stationed his men at almost every street corner.

Ralza Manly, the education superintendent of the Freedmen's Bureau, commented optimistically that the marchers comported themselves with such dignity that they won praise from their enemies. But he admitted that if General Terry's infantrymen had not been present, the day would have been "a baptism of blood and fire" even before the procession entered the city. The presence of soldiers, the closure of the bars, and, indirectly, a newspaper compositors' strike all helped suppress the possibility of violence. In the last case, it meant that because no papers were printed in the first week of April, there was no chance for more inflammatory editorials to further stoke the fears of the white populace.[18]

When the newspapers resumed publication six days after the parade, they scoffed at the affair by ridiculing the dress and deportment of the marchers. They claimed most local Black people opposed the event, minimized the number of participants, and asserted that in any case most were outsiders imported for the day. The leading paper lampooned the effort of the parade marshals to form up individual units into proper order. It opined that when the parade reached the equestrian statue on Capitol Square, "Washington, in bronze, fairly trembled as he heard the shouting of the many-headed 'emancipated.'"[19]

According to the press, most Richmond Black people objected to the parade and did not leave their work to spectate. Those who did watch only jeered at the procession. They evinced "a great contempt for those of [their] own color who put on airs." The participants in the parade were common, or they were impressionable young hotheads who wanted to disport their sartorial finery, or they were mere hangers-on of the Freedmen's Bureau. The better sort, the so-called colored aristocracy, disdained the celebration. In the racist words of Henry Wise, "hardly a respectable darkey engaged in it." But such fanciful comments could not gainsay the massive display of enthusiasm for the parade.[20]

The lack of untoward incidents was attributed to the good behavior of the population and the police presence, but no credit was given to the army because it had allowed the parade. The striking pressmen, who had shut down the capital's newspapers, joined in the ridicule with a thinly distributed sheet of their own that mocked participants as "field hands in jeans walking in squads."[21]

Unsurprisingly, northern and Black commentators took a different view. A Boston journal said Black citizens deserved the right to commemorate "the downfall of treason." The African American clergyman William Harris called the parade respectable and orderly. He counted fifteen secret societies participating in the procession. "They took Richmond the second time," he wrote, inadvertently validating the claim that it was not just practical emancipation but also the fall of the Confederacy that was being celebrated.[22]

A week after the parade, parishioners of Second African Baptist held a fundraising fair to collect money for rebuilding their burned church. A reporter went to the Freedmen's Bureau building, where the fair took place. In condescending words, he described both the patrons of the fair and the cakes, dolls, and craft items they offered for sale. He said it was all harmless fun in a good cause, but his conclusion revealed his incomprehension of what life for African Americans was like before freedom came to the city. "Let them for a while forget all their troubles," he wrote, "and fancy themselves once more living in that time when they were happy, although not 'emancipated,' and when 'Old Virginia' was 'Old Virginia' still."[23]

A few weeks later, the white Second Baptist Church, which had exercised guardianship over the Black church in the past, permitted the use of its building for a vocal concert to help raise money for rebuilding the burned church. The press used the event to reiterate its frequent assertion of who had the freed people's best interest at heart.

It wanted readers to see that, while Black parishioners could not find another Black church to host the concert, the white church magnanimously offered its hall: "Thus it ever will be. The negroes of the south will always find the southern white man their truest friend." This was only a few weeks after two more African American churches burned on the same night in Petersburg, and attempts were made to set others alight. This time, no one tried to deny that it was arson.[24]

Two weeks after Black men and women paraded down Broad Street, a similar event took place in Norfolk. There they were celebrating passage of the Civil Rights Act over President Johnson's veto. Many men in the procession carried weapons. Shots were fired; four people died. Interracial disturbances, discrimination, and abuse had sporadically occurred in Richmond ever since the US Army arrived the previous spring. But this was possibly the first time in Virginia that anyone had died in racially tinged violence. It was a grim prelude to more deaths across the South that summer. Opponents of the march were quick to blame Norfolk's African Americans for taking their inspiration from the Richmond celebration on April 3. That parade, they asserted, "was the example which these Norfolk brutes imitated." The presence of armed Black militiamen terrified them. "Woe unto those who put the devil in the hearts of these once humble people," warned Henry Rives Pollard. Easily offended and quick to assign blame, he believed the teachings of northerners misguided gullible freedmen and invariably produced evil outcomes. It all resulted, he charged, in the degradation of southern white people.[25]

In the capital, the press claimed, the April 3 parade had been "concocted for our humiliation more than the good of the negro." Only smart preparation and swift execution by the city police, the papers alleged, had saved Richmond from bloodshed. The same account concluded darkly with admiration for the calmness of white residents but implied that they would not indefinitely forbear from taking action against public demonstrations by their Black neighbors. The parade, and the opposition to it, demonstrated how divided the city was over the meaning of emancipation a year later.[26]

Mischaracterizations of the Richmond march and blaming it for the Norfolk disturbance were not the only ways opponents displayed their disapproval of the April 3 parade. In less than a month, a greater expression of Confederate defiance announced to the world a powerful and contrary interpretation of the events that surrounded that day. And it would be the creation of the white women of Richmond.

15
The Heroic Dead Reigned Supreme

May 1866

In 1847 a few forward-looking citizens created a rural burying ground west of town on the high bluffs above the James River rapids. Hollywood Cemetery commanded a spectacular view downstream toward the prosperous city of mills and foundries, with Jefferson's neoclassical capitol dominating the skyline. But lot sales languished, to the disappointment of the cemetery's directors. A decade later, they hit upon a novel marketing scheme to boost sales. It required disinterring a famous Virginian buried elsewhere and, amid great pageantry, moving him to Hollywood. President James Monroe had lived in New York after his second term and was buried there. He now served his native state one last time.

With the family's permission, Monroe's remains were exhumed and placed in a new coffin. Ten thousand people, including elite militia companies, accompanied the hearse down to the Manhattan waterfront for the steamship journey to Richmond. There, on July 5, 1858, the New York Seventh Regiment was greeted by its Virginia counterparts. Together, they accompanied the coffin to Hollywood for an elaborate ceremony. At the reburial, Governor Henry Wise gave the principal eulogy.

The reburial of Monroe worked, and for a few years the sale of lots was brisk. But then the war came. Thousands of Confederate soldiers, and Union prisoners who had died in captivity, were buried there. Hollywood received scant compensation. In 1865 the evacuation fire consumed both the cemetery's records and its investment in Confederate bonds. A year later, out of their grief for the loss of their soldiers and their devotion to the southern cause, white women fashioned at Hollywood a powerful symbol not just of remembrance but of defiance in the face of defeat. The Confederate dead, or rather what the living made of them, would transform Hollywood and, by extension, Richmond. Both would come to embody what even then, in that first year after the war, was becoming known among white southerners as the Lost Cause.

To many city residents, the familiar springtime symbols of rebirth seemed a special reproach in 1866 because of the deplorable state of soldiers' graves and the lack of money to do anything about it. On the eastern side of town, thirteen thousand Confederate soldiers lay in shallow graves, now becoming overgrown, in Oakwood Cemetery. On the western side, Hollywood's soldier section contained the remains of eleven thousand more, under equally melancholy conditions, rude wooden headboards rotting in the heavy Virginia clay. In the city's impoverished condition, there was little money to commemorate the fallen. Still, the need was great and weighed on the minds of white Richmonders, especially the women who viewed remembrance of the dead as their special province. Two developments that spring both troubled and spurred them to act.

The first was the effort by the federal government to gather the Union dead and rebury them in newly created national cemeteries. Congress provided ample funding, and in February work crews in and around Richmond began to identify and reinter Union remains. Some farmers outside the city worried they would lose their Black laborers because the government was offering more money than they could afford to pay. It "would almost ruin me," one of them cried. Although white Virginians might not want their soldiers buried by the federal government, the pointed exclusion of Confederates' remains by the US Burial Corps caused great anguish. The corps not only left the southern fallen to decay in unmarked obscurity, but it also was rumored to have dug up Confederate corpses and sold them to be ground into fertilizer. If reburying the Union dead in carefully designed, well-financed national cemeteries sprinkled around Virginia was meant to honor them, then denying southern soldiers that same respect implied they were without honor. That inference appalled white opinion across the state and beyond.[1]

The second event was the parade on April 3, 1866. Black people had become increasingly visible in public activity since the fall of the city, but this mass event troubled white citizens like nothing before. They took it as a direct challenge to their claim to be the natural rulers of the city. The effort to develop an organized commemoration of the Confederate dead was gathering steam even before the federal reburial program or the Black procession. But it was no fluke that Confederate women chose to hold their first ceremonies of remembrance in the following weeks.[2]

They did it first not at Hollywood but at Oakwood Cemetery. On April 18 women from Church Hill and Union Hill, both in east Richmond, met at the Third Presbyterian Church to preserve and perpetuate the memory of Confederate soldiers. They represented eight religious denominations, and they called the outcome of their gathering the Ladies Memorial Association for Confederate Dead of Oakwood.[3]

The Oakwood association's first commemoration began with a service at St. John's Episcopal Church on Church Hill on May 10, the anniversary of the death of Stonewall Jackson. Afterward, the assembly, mostly women and children, filed out toward Oakwood Cemetery in a procession a mile long to place garlands and wreaths on the graves. To deflect criticism from northerners, supporters of the event were quick to point out that the ceremony was "under the management of the ladies." This would become their standard shield to avert charges of politicized commemoration.[4]

On the same day, the Richmond Light Infantry Blues celebrated their anniversary by placing flowers on the graves of members who had died in the war. They wore civilian dress to avoid provoking the army but put distinctive blue ribbons in their buttonholes. They formed up and marched behind a band playing appropriately somber music, first to Shockoe Cemetery, then the Hebrew Cemetery, and finally to Hollywood. After discharging their solemn duty, the veterans retired to the Exchange Hotel, where an ample supply of mint juleps enhanced the retelling of wartime memories. In his remarks, former governor Wise pointedly praised three African Americans: restauranteur Tom Griffin and two of the regiment's wartime bandsmen, Lomax Smith and Reuben West. They had refused to take part in the parade on April 3, he claimed, because they did not want to insult their white friends. As honorary members of the Blues, Smith and Lomax had walked to the cemetery with the regiment—but at the back of the procession.

The veterans imbibed a headier elixir than juleps when they offered after-dinner toasts that would have incensed General Turner and his officers, had they heard them. The toasts saluted the Blues, comrades who died in the war in a cause "that they believed to be just," "Virginia! Right or Wrong!," Robert E. Lee, and "the Lost Cause." With the toast to "Henry A. Wise—prisoner of war—unforgiven and unforgotten," the former governor rose to reply with remarks that elicited hearty applause. He roused the assembly with defiant words: "The cause must not be spoken of as lost, because he looked upon that cause as the cause of civil and constitutional liberty, which must, and will be victorious throughout the United States."[5]

If the women of Oakwood took precedence by organizing first, more important for the future was what followed at Hollywood Cemetery two weeks after the Oakwood association's founding. At St. Paul's Episcopal Church on May 3, two hundred women, using words identical to those of their Oakwood sisters, organized a society to memorialize the soldiers buried at Hollywood. The pain of loss and the ache to make sense of it spurred them to act in a collective effort. Dr. Charles Minnigerode, a devoted Confederate, called the meeting to order and explained its purpose. The church's longtime minister and his parishioners had come far since the fraught early postwar days. They all viewed the present moment with expectation. With brief preliminaries, the women formed an organization to beautify the cemetery to honor the fallen. They called it the Hollywood Memorial Association of the Ladies of Richmond, Virginia, usually abbreviated to Ladies Memorial Association or Hollywood Memorial Association. They then elected a president, a treasurer, six vice presidents to represent the major denominations, and a board of twenty members.[6]

The president of the association, Nancy Bierne Macfarland, was married to one of the most powerful men of Richmond. A crafty lawyer, president of three banks, and former Confederate congressman, William Macfarland figured prominently in efforts to revive his city. He had spoken at the mass meeting the previous August to pledge Richmond's loyalty to the nation and was one of the three delegates to make that argument in person to President Johnson. In April 1866, he had been elevated to president of the city council.

At forty, Nancy was twenty years William's junior, but she was not in his shadow. She had made her home a center of Confederate high society during the war, and she had been active in raising funds for the cause, principally as president of the Soldier's Aid Association of Virginia. Her contribution extended beyond the state as she helped build a network among volunteer organizations across the Confederacy. These wartime soldier's aid societies, private hospitals, and sewing circles bequeathed to MacFarland in peacetime a potent network of women eager to pour their Confederate devotion into memorial work. As president of the Hollywood Memorial Association, she now had a more important role in fashioning the way her city would be viewed after the war. Her efforts and those of hundreds of other white Richmond women helped create a new incarnation of their city as the seat of Lost Cause commemoration.

The exhilaration of these events energized the city's white population as nothing had done since the end of the war. After the Oakwood day of remembering, the Hollywood association announced plans to hold a much grander event on May 31. In preparation, they announced a citywide effort three days before to clean up the cemetery's walks, pull up weeds, replace defective headboards, spread gravel on the pathways, and plant grass seed on the grounds.

Fifteen organizations, most of them militia companies, supplied eight hundred men armed with axes, spades, and picks. Freight companies and the city council lent their wagons and teams of horses and mules. At a break for lunch, German-born shoemaker and saloonkeeper J. G. Lange sent three barrels of lager to supplement the men's picnic meals. At the end of the day, buoyed by their accomplishment and undeterred by cuts, bruises, and poison ivy, they marched back to town, shouting and singing. Only one untoward incident marred the day when a US Army colonel passing by claimed he overheard insulting language from Confederate veterans and briefly arrested them.[7]

Three days before the workday, the memorial association adopted an appeal "To the Women of the South." It proclaimed that the association's work to preserve and consecrate the Confederate graves at Hollywood was the cause of the whole South. It could make that claim because of the large number of soldiers buried there from states other than Virginia. Nancy Macfarland and her officers signed this public letter announcing their intent to rescue the Confederacy's dead from oblivion.[8]

The morning of May 31 dawned bright and cloudless. Nearly all stores remained closed, many displaying portraits of Confederate generals draped in black. Clusters of young men gathered on street corners in worn gray uniforms. The day before at Grace Episcopal Church, women of the Hollywood association had woven masses of flowers into garlands, crosses, and wreaths. Now they carried these toward the cemetery. Wagons lent by hotels and freight companies bore floral tributes too large for any single person to carry. "The very houses of Richmond seemed asleep," marveled an eyewitness. "For one day . . . the living were forgotten and the heroic dead reigned supreme."[9]

At 10:00 a.m. the Virginia Life Guards and other units marched from their separate marshaling points toward Hollywood behind a brass band. There were twenty-three companies, most from Richmond but units from Norfolk and Hampton as well. Following them, upward of twenty thousand people, the majority of white Richmond, streamed toward the cemetery in a seemingly endless procession. Many of the bereaved wore mourning dress and some sobbed as they walked. Wounded veterans hobbled along on prosthetic legs or balanced with walking sticks. At the soldier's section, a large cross bore an evergreen arrangement with the unapologetic inscription "Dead, but not Forgotten." No addresses or speeches were given. A brass band played a solemn dirge.

For the participants, the sight of this reverent mass of devoted Confederates slowly converging on the cemetery brought up all over again the anguish they had experienced over the past five years. The catharsis of that shared experience gave them hope for the future.

The owner of one business on Broad Street had refused to close his store for the Oakwood commemoration on May 10. He said "he had no respect for rebels, living or dead." He must have decided it would be imprudent to repeat that performance for the Hollywood remembrance and shut his business along with the others. Special attention was paid to the grave of J. E. B. Stuart, which was temporarily decorated with a bust by the sculptor Edward Virginius Valentine. It bore the words "Stuart. Dead, Yet Alive! Mortal, Yet Immortal." A photography shop took a picture of the bust and promised to give 250 copies to the memorial association to help it raise money. Varina and Jefferson Davis had lost a son during the war, and his grave received special treatment, smothered in floral tributes.[10]

The sight of Confederate units marching to Hollywood and the knowledge of widespread store closings in solidarity with the event troubled the local army commander. General Turner brought two companies of infantry down from Fredericksburg to bolster the garrison in case of trouble. Governor Pierpont thought the commemoration showed that treason still ruled in the city. William Harris, pastor of the Third Street African Methodist Episcopal Church, was alarmed. He told a friend he was skeptical when he heard a rumor that a Confederate flag had been raised, and he went to the cemetery to see for himself. When he got there, he found the rumor confirmed by more than just one flag. If the revival of this sentiment continued, he feared, it would only lead to "war, blood, and death." Northern observers criticized the Hollywood observance as overtly political and clearly meant to extol the Confederacy, not just to remember the fallen.[11]

The events at Oakwood and Hollywood gave a resounding rebuttal to the Black celebration on April 3. They rekindled Confederate feelings and gave white citizens a new way to deal with loss and defy their conquerors. Through the ladies' memorial associations, white Richmond learned that it could use a collective expression of grief to show that Confederate nationalism still lived in the former southern capital. White men might still run afoul of federal authorities if they made disloyal political remarks, but gender convention shielded white women from censure.

That first Confederate Memorial Day began the long romance of commemoration that annealed the dedication of white Richmond to the southern cause. It also let African Americans know how the dominant culture intended the war to be remembered. At all the events of this first, rolling commemoration, stretching across the month of May, the phrase "Lost Cause" came into full flower. It had first been used several months before in advertisements for Edward Pollard's forthcoming eponymous book, and now Henry Wise gave it eloquent articulation. The journalist had given it currency, and the former governor took up the cry and proclaimed it unashamedly.[12]

As yet, neither those who honored the fallen wearing Union blue nor those who mourned sons of the defeated South were ready to accept the equality of death. It was too soon. For some, the war could still be fought through commemoration. It was only years later that North and South embraced reconciliation through a united Memorial Day. For the present, and for a long time to come, the dead provided an ideological purpose for many in both North and South. For white Richmond, memory of the Confederate dead offered a talisman of totemic power.

Shortly after it occupied the city in April 1865, the US Army had banned Confederate insignia from the streets. Southern veterans who had no other clothes could wear their uniforms in public, but they had to cover CSA buttons with cloth and could not display any marks of rank. This prohibition rankled then and long after. And it had significance for the letter the president of the Hollywood Memorial Association wrote sometime after the May commemorative events. Nancy Macfarland sent it to Francis Dawson, an English immigrant and ambitious Confederate veteran of twenty-five who had survived eleven battles. He was the secretary of the organizational meeting in May that elected her president. Rakish, dashing, and stylishly dressed, Frank Dawson was one of the wild young journalists of the *Examiner*. After the Englishman left the city for better prospects in Charleston, Macfarland wrote to express her gratitude for his "untiring efforts in our behalf." She enclosed as a token of thanks a gift that Dawson treasured for the rest of his life. Her little memento was a set of gold sleeve buttons and studs, each bearing an enameled, defiant Confederate battle flag.[13]

16

The Fires of Malice

Summer to Fall 1866

The stone Customs House at the foot of Capitol Square, which had housed Confederate executive offices a year before, had been the only building between the square and the river to escape burning. On June 6, 1866, Judge John Underwood, the most hated figure in the demonology of white Richmond, presided over its court. Dark circles under his eyes, a scraggly, unkempt beard, and rumpled waistcoat reflected an inattention to personal appearance. In contrast, his courtroom had been remodeled and repainted, sneered the local press, "to remove from loyal nostrils" the stench of association with southern jurisprudence. Underwood convened this Richmond session of the US Circuit Court in pursuit of his charge of treason against Jefferson Davis, now entering his second year of confinement at Fort Monroe, eighty miles southeast at the mouth of the James River. At an earlier session in Norfolk, Underwood had asked grand jurors to indict the Confederate president, and they had obliged. The judge moved the next session of his court to Richmond, a week after the Hollywood Cemetery commemoration.[1]

Spectators for this latest scene of the drama filtered into the courtroom at a leisurely pace during the morning. The leaders of the Richmond bar had personal as well as professional reasons for observing the proceedings. James Lyons, Gustavus Myers, and William Macfarland—all prominent in the rebuilding of their city—had each received a writ of confiscation from Underwood the previous year. Those writs

Unionist Judge John Curtis Underwood enraged Confederate Richmonders by trying to confiscate their property. He championed equal rights for African Americans when few public figures did and presided over the constitutional convention that gave Black men the vote. (Library of Congress)

had failed, and now their relieved targets came to see the devil incarnate for themselves.

It was not until 1:00 p.m. that Underwood, looking fidgety and cadaverous, according to a hostile witness, took the bench. Before he made his charge to the jurors, his opening remarks must have startled them. He said he was happy to see them again "and to know that you are still living," an unsettling reference to the threats some of them had received. Rumor had it that Underwood had received them too. Some said he had spread them himself, and the press scoffed at his "morbid love of notoriety." He assured the jurors he had alerted the local military commanders to the threats and promised the army's protection.[2]

He told them they should not be surprised at the animus of the Richmond newspapers. He repeated his denunciations of the Virginia capital, whose press, politics, and pulpits, he claimed, had become infamous through the stain of slavery. Treating the audience to an overblown harangue of the sort that drove his critics to apoplexy and embarrassed his friends, he blamed newspapers for everything. They were responsible for all the Confederacy's "murders, duels, assassinations, violent and ungoverned passions, ending in self-conflagration and self-immolation unparalleled in any heathen country."[3]

Davis's attorney, William Reed of Philadelphia, wanted to know if his client would be tried for high treason, as the indictment alleged, or if the charges would be further delayed or even withdrawn. He asked for a speedy trial, as Davis wished and as the Constitution guaranteed. The prosecution could not say. The Johnson administration was still unsure what course to take with the former Confederate leader. And so the prisoner of Fort Monroe, still aloof even in confinement but now haggard, graying, plagued by blindness in one eye and wracking facial pain, remained incarcerated and in limbo. His plight mirrored that of Richmond, an anticlimactic metaphor of uncertainty that discouraged optimism for the future.

In time, Davis would give a revived Confederate nationalism a rallying cry. For the present, the summer of 1866 brought heightened racial tension in the city against a backdrop of physical rebuilding and explosive racial violence across the South. Antagonism between civil and military authority took on renewed intensity until a change of army command in August. That change heralded worse prospects for Black residents, who continued to fear a very real threat to the promise of emancipation. By the end of summer, the leading voices of the Lost Cause would give its devotees more cause for hope as President Johnson tried to rally his supporters against the proposed Fourteenth Amendment, then making its way through state legislatures toward ratification.

Shortly before Underwood came to town, the parishioners of Second African Baptist Church laid the cornerstone of a new brick building to replace the wooden one that had burned under suspicious circumstances on the eve of the April parade. Black masonic fraternities from as far away as Norfolk and Petersburg joined their Richmond brethren to celebrate. The Rev. Fields Cook, who had represented the African American community to President Johnson the previous year and looked to a day when Black and white children would grow up together in peace, gave the opening prayer. The event testified to the vibrancy of his community. In its reports to Washington, the Freedmen's Bureau agreed. It applauded the progress of the formerly enslaved people of Richmond and praised their industry and pride in self-reliance.[4]

It would take more than prayers, however, to usher in the New Jerusalem of racial harmony. In fact, the signs of the times pointed mostly in a contrary direction. The city had witnessed a gradual increase of unease in race relations that spring. The first anniversary of slavery's demise in April had heightened those tensions. The parade on April 3 and then the first Confederate Memorial Day at Oakwood and Hollywood cemeteries established the chief holy days for years to come on which the different communities commemorated their divergent interpretations of what the war had meant.

To the dismay of Black residents, the April city election returned Joseph Mayo to the mayor's office, with the explicit blessing of President Johnson. All fifteen of the councilmen elected were also members of the traditional elite. Mayo's friends might praise his old-fashioned social graces as he resumed office, but the sentences he meted out to African Americans in his Mayor's Court proceeded with undiminished severity. By summer Black men and women faced increasing hostility with waning support from the army and the Freedmen's Bureau. In spring, the Bureau closed its freedmen's camps. With restoration of civil courts, the Bureau had to close its own court, which had given some measure of redress. Congress extended the life of the Bureau and gave it an appropriation, but its scope narrowed as time passed.[5]

The day after the cornerstone ceremony at Second African Baptist Church, Black people met to thank the local agent of the Bureau, Halstead Merrell, on his retirement but also to express concern for the future. Doubtful of the course of President Johnson's policies, they lamented that it had become "useless for us to expect justice." The Bureau still helped with schools and relief for the poor, but its influence over how the city treated Black people on a day-to-day basis gradually declined. The Richmond press had always exaggerated the Bureau's power to demonize it, and now what little it possessed was shrinking. Former governor Henry Wise admitted that the Bureau had done some good. But, he added with sardonic understatement, "it has the semblance of a military power kept over us, and this you know can hardly be pleasant." The irony was lost on the city's traditional leaders that their anxiety increased even as their grip on power tightened. A surfeit of bad feeling pervaded on all sides as spring yielded to the enervating humidity of Virginia summer.[6]

In the late spring and summer of 1866, racially charged violence detonated across the South. These events, plus Andrew Johnson's repeated vetoes of congressional action, pushed the congressional Republican majority in a more radical direction. The first explosion occurred in early May, when forty-five people died in clashes between African American soldiers and white residents in Memphis, Tennessee. In the wake of this unrest and after Johnson's veto of the Civil Rights Act, Congress passed the Fourteenth Amendment and sent it to the states in June. The amendment became the centerpiece of congressional policy, and the ratification process agitated national politics for months to come. Congress concluded that Johnson and the state governments he created in the South could not be trusted to protect the rights of freedmen. The worst incident occurred later that summer when a white mob broke up a political convention in New Orleans, Louisiana, leaving dozens of African Americans dead. The Richmond press blamed it on seditious revolutionaries. But for many in the North, the massacre served as further evidence that the South remained unrepentant.[7]

For months white southerners had known the Fourteenth Amendment was being drafted, but its passage left them stunned. Black citizenship and suffrage were now likely to become enshrined in the US Constitution unless they could rally around the president and help him somehow to thwart the wishes of Congress. That was the great worry on the national stage, and it undergirded white concern locally as the tempo of Black political activity increased.

At 11:00 a.m. on July Fourth 1866, a battalion of blue-coated soldiers paraded down Franklin Street to Capitol Square accompanied by a band playing "Yankee Doodle" and "The Star-Spangled Banner." At noon they fired a 36-gun salute as General Terry and staff observed from horseback. Unlike the past year's celebration, no one took the place of Dr. Mary Walker to read the Declaration of Independence. American flags flew from a half dozen public buildings, but none from any private home.[8]

The most notable aspect of the day was not the military salute on Capitol Square but the participation of African Americans, who filled the streets from dawn to dusk. As many as four thousand made up the procession that wound its way through downtown. First came two hundred mounted men. The members of dozens of Black societies turned out in their colorful regalia, just as they had done on April 3. The parade promenaded through the city behind a drum and brass band, making stops to cheer at the homes of leading unionists.

At her mansion on Church Hill, former spy master Elizabeth Van Lew delighted at the public honor shown her. She said her secessionist neighbors closed their shutters on the unwelcome scene but nevertheless peeped through them to catch a furtive glimpse of the spectacle. Her brusque associate Burnham Wardwell provocatively told a gathering how much he valued the United States Colored Troops. The square-jawed native of Maine, boorish and unlettered, had lived in Richmond for decades and now delighted in antagonizing former rebels. Union general Benjamin Butler called him uncouth but self-sacrificing in the northern cause, "not always judicious in his methods as enthusiasts rarely are." For Wardwell's impertinence, Confederate veterans warned him that when the US Army left town, they would string him up within twenty-four hours.[9]

Another Union general wrote his wife how impressed he was at the large turnout of Black spectators on the Fourth—he estimated fifteen thousand—and the nearly complete absence of white people. The local press reported the commemoration with disdain as "a day long to be remembered by our citizens, who never wish to see its like again" because Black citizens had taken possession of the city and the holiday. "Ethiopia held high carnival and saturnalia on Capitol Square," the papers sneered, and freedmen crowded around the Washington statue "like maggots over a carcass." It would be hard to dispute James Hunnicutt's characterization of these remarks as motivated by anything but vindictive racial animus. Because of the press, he later wrote, "the fires of malice, deep rooted hate, and revenge are kept burning in the hearts of the people."[10]

Much had changed since the previous Fourth. In 1865 Confederates were still stunned by the enormity of their defeat. A year later, their defiance was more obvious. The army banned Confederate flags, but residents learned that they could make known their true sentiments in other ways. The coach of the Ballard House Hotel cleverly bore a portrait of Grant on one side and Lee on the other. More daring shopkeepers put portraits of Lee in their windows. Others displayed framed copies of his Appomattox farewell address. But they felt the city no longer belonged to them on the Fourth. Many had still not become accustomed to seeing large numbers of African Americans on the city streets. Some white residents left town for picnics or excursions on the river. They left, said an unrepentant Confederate, because they were "disgusted with the dust and heat of the city, and the blackened condition of the streets."[11]

It was no coincidence that the women's memorial associations published a request for volunteers to go out to the cemeteries for a day of work on the Fourth. Several units of Confederate veterans lent their hands, and the northern press took notice. It did not begrudge the desire to decorate graves but saw how these events had become overtly political. "This Southern spirit grows with wonderful rapidity," mused the *New York Times*' man in town, "and its most fruitful feeders are the Memorial Associations."[12]

The change in their city that most frightened white residents was the sight of armed Black men on the streets. Denied legal ownership of weapons in the past—though they often ignored that regulation—African Americans came to value guns as tools of self-defense and symbols of freedom that they could now proudly display in public. Since early in the year, there had been reports of Black men parading with weapons in militia units on Navy Hill and in the Chimborazo freedmen's camp. In the summer, accounts of nightly drilling disturbed the sleep of white Richmond. Some of the units in the April 3 parade openly carried firearms. Even more did so on the Fourth of July.[13]

For their part, Black people grew restive about unfair treatment at the hands of the city government. They held a mass meeting on Navy Hill to petition General Terry to intervene. They denounced Joseph Mayo as the "tyrant that now rules in the Mayor's Court." He, in turn, repudiated their charges as "false from foundation to apex stone." That summer the courts convicted a number of Black residents for petty larceny and sentenced them to be whipped and jailed. The African

American community was appalled, and Hunnicutt took up the cry to protest whipping as a barbarous practice.[14]

General Terry acknowledged the validity of their complaints when he passed along their petition to O. O. Howard at the Freedmen's Bureau in Washington. Caught between Black protests over ill treatment and white anger over Black militias, Terry issued an order on July 30 banning all militia units not specifically authorized by the governor.[15]

In the governor's mansion, Francis Pierpont soldiered on, despite being rejected by the small band of unionists who believed he had betrayed them and by the conservatives who dominated the state legislature and city council. He had hoped to bring together men like Speaker of the House of Delegates John Brown Baldwin and former congressman John Minor Botts. But Baldwin spurned his overtures and barred Union men from office. (Pierpont eventually called him the worst man in the state.) Botts was no radical, but he did try to get Congress to replace the Pierpont regime. Beyond those differences, the governor should have known that acute personal animosity between the two men precluded any cooperation. The governor's hopes for a middle way, never a likely outcome, withered and died.

For the city's white unionists, the past year had relentlessly confounded their expectations when they welcomed Godfrey Weitzel's army the previous April. Despite that brief moment of acclaim on the Fourth of July, Elizabeth Van Lew saw little reason for optimism. Her prewar wealth had gradually dissipated. Although her brother John, like others in her espionage network, found modest work as a detective for the army, he barely managed to keep the family hardware store afloat. It angered former Confederates when northern journals began extolling Van Lew for her wartime role ministering to Union prisoners. They would have been even more incensed if the articles had revealed her spying exploits. For the moment, though, that contribution to the Union war effort remained hidden.

Van Lew, now looking drawn and pensive, with deep-set eyes and dark hair in ringlets, toyed with the idea of writing a book. But she held back, knowing the harsh condemnation that would greet it. She received an undated note that could have been from wartime but more likely came from the period immediately after. "White Caps are around town," it threatened. "They are coming at night! Look out! Look out! Your house is going at last. FIRE." Van Lew's northern friends tried to secure public compensation for her as a reward for service. After whittling down the proposed amount, Congress finally approved five thousand dollars, though that was inadequate to support her family. She hoped for a teaching post with the Freedmen's Bureau but was disappointed when all it offered was a lowly clerk's position.[16]

After months of declining health, Van Lew's fellow unionist, the foreign shipping agent Charles Palmer, died on July 31. As a teenager, he had come to Richmond from his native Gloucester County east of the city and made his way in commerce. He suffered imprisonment for his unionist sentiments, welcomed Governor Pierpont to town, and worked unstintingly to rebuild his business and his city. Despite personal popularity, his minority political views meant he had no chance to win the state senate seat against conservative lawyer John Gilmer. Even so, at Palmer's death the Richmond Tobacco Trade organization met to express its affection for him. They may not have been so charitable if they had known the extent of Palmer's work in Van Lew's spy network against, to use his own words, "Treason & the infernal Rascals" of the Confederacy.[17]

Among those native white unionists who believed most Virginians still harbored Confederate loyalties was Charles Palmer's garrulous friend John Minor Botts. The former congressman had warned Governor Pierpont not to trust former rebels who sought to influence him. He felt vindicated, if saddened, when the General Assembly replaced Pierpont's appointees with others more to its liking. At the beginning of the war, Confederate authorities had believed Botts was writing a denunciation of the southern quest for independence. They ransacked his house but failed to find incriminating evidence. Botts had hidden his papers well, but they threw him into jail anyway. A year after Appomattox, Botts got his revenge when he finally published the book his persecutors feared, *The Great Rebellion: Its Secret History, Rise, Progress, and Disastrous Failure.*

It was, Botts said, an explication of how a handful of wicked and selfish men gradually seduced the people of the South until a majority succumbed to the effort to dissever the Union. The book ended with a burning condemnation in words of incandescent rage stoked by knowledge of the colossal loss of life and property caused by secession. In a final, fulminating sentence of more than two hundred words, he damned Confederates for the hatred they had engendered between North and South. With rolling cadences, he flung his final execration at secessionists, who, "as I firmly believe, have to answer hereafter, both in this world and in the world to come, for the most atrocious and stupendous crime that has been committed since the crucifixion of our Lord and Savior Jesus Christ."[18]

The rebuilding of Richmond became more apparent that summer. It did so as politicians of the old order jockeyed for control with proponents of a new vision that included freed people. Arguments over who would control the city and over the Fourteenth Amendment competed for attention with new fascinations. The craze for baseball, for example, already being heralded as the national sport, arrived that summer in force in Richmond. On the Fourth of July, the Enterprise Base Ball Club of Baltimore played an exhibition game to promote interest. By the middle of the month, numerous local clubs had been founded. So many Black and white youths took up the sport that they were warned against the hazards of playing in the streets.[19]

After years of disappointing setbacks, the Atlantic telegraphic cable was finally completed by the end of July. This dazzling technological feat, hailed as the wonder of the age, astounded Americans. Now international traders had a powerful new tool to gauge markets across the ocean. At lightning speed, the undersea cable could tell Europe about American wheat and cotton prices. But it could also report on the latest violence in the South.

A year of rebuilding produced notable accomplishments. In May 1866 ceremonies marked completion of the rebuilt Richmond and Petersburg railroad bridge across the James. Finally, the stigmata of blackened stone piers from the ruined bridge were superseded by a gleaming new structure. With connections now reestablished to Petersburg, Richmond was linked to commerce with the Carolinas and the wider South below. But rivalry among Virginia cities over railroads continued unabated. Richmond power brokers opposed General William Mahone's efforts to consolidate three lines across the southern part of the state for fear that the capital city would be left out. The summer of 1866 saw establishment of the Richmond Tobacco Exchange, as well as new iron-front buildings along Main Street that gave it a modern facade. Construction began on rebuilding the street railway, which the following spring would become a lightning rod for disputes over segregated seating.

Despite these advances, reconstruction in the city proceeded at a slower pace in the last half of 1866. The lack of outside capital continued to retard growth, and then an outbreak of cholera in the summer further derailed economic growth for months. Farmers and merchants were reluctant to come into town, and residents who had the means to do so left. Poor understanding of contagious diseases hampered efforts to contain the epidemic. The doctor in charge of the board of health claimed that improper consumption of vegetables was the cause. He urged his colleagues to report cases so the board could map the incidence of disease and target the disinfecting campaign. The preferred tactic—burning tar—was unlikely to succeed.[20]

With summer came a change in the local army command that had momentous consequences later. The son of a Baptist minister in upstate New York, John McAllister Schofield was one of the youngest major generals of the Civil War. He served ably in both the western and eastern theaters, though controversy dogged his path. His talent, drive, and connections enabled him eventually to cap his service as general in command of the entire US Army. That was for the future. In summer 1866, he was an ambitious, youthful-looking thirty-four, with a very long beard that contrasted with his premature baldness. He had just returned from Paris, where he helped negotiate removal of French forces from Mexico. He would need those diplomatic skills to deal with his next posting as successor to General Terry. Schofield had

John Schofield succeeded Alfred Terry as the general in command in Richmond and supervised the 1867 referendum on a constitutional convention. (Library of Congress)

crossed swords with radical Republicans in wartime Missouri, and their Richmond colleagues worried about his influence in the former Confederate capital. James Hunnicutt warily welcomed him. He publicly prayed, in vain as it turned out, "God grant that he may prove a second General Terry."[21]

Schofield thought it folly to expect former rebels to recant their beliefs quickly. Any such act on their part, he thought, would be hypocrisy. Because he opposed African American suffrage and the disfranchisement of whites, he received a hopeful welcome from former Confederates. Within days of his arrival, they were hailing him for establishing more agreeable relations between civilians and the army. Their demeanor toward the departing General Terry had been, in the blunt words of an observer, "one of cold respect—very cold." Black Richmonders, correspondingly, feared the worst from Schofield. William Harris, the Methodist pastor who was alarmed to see Confederate flags at Hollywood Cemetery, worried that the change of command heralded "a *very great calamity* on the Loyal whites and especially the colored people of Virginia."[22]

Schofield revealed his conservative opinions soon enough. But like Terry he would brook no disloyalty from former Confederates. If white Richmonders welcomed the new commander, they still pined for the day when his soldiers would leave town. Terry, for his part, welcomed the chance to be done with the city. He could now stamp the Richmond dust off his boots and head west to his next posting in the Dakota Territory, where he hoped to face more tractable problems.

Despite the focus on rebuilding and other purely parochial matters, Richmond could not ignore national events. When Congress submitted the Fourteenth Amendment to the states for ratification in June, former Confederates saw it as an assault on the supremacy of white men and on the authority of states to define their citizens' rights. The report of the Joint Committee on Reconstruction, filled with accounts of the violation of freedmen's rights, provided damning evidence to justify the amendment. When the president condemned it, white southerners clung to the hope that he would somehow derail it.

Johnson's supporters put out a call for a national Union convention in Philadelphia in August to marshal support against the amendment. Among the contingent from Virginia were the conservative Richmonders William Macfarland and John Gilmer. The timing was awkward for the organizers, coming only weeks after deadly racial violence in New Orleans further discredited Johnson's Reconstruction policy. By now few Republicans supported the president. The Philadelphia meeting appealed to a handful of the party's conservative members but mainly to the Democrats, North and South. The convention urged Americans to elect a Congress that supported Johnson. The white South gambled that he could thwart rising sentiment in the North to give full legal rights to African Americans. The fall congressional elections would, in effect, be a referendum on both the Fourteenth Amendment and the president. With no representation in Congress, Virginia could only watch and wait.

Philadelphia played host to another political gathering the following month. It was meant to be a convocation of Republican loyalists from all sections of the country. The Virginia delegation, sixty-some strong, was the largest from the South but was riven by faction. It pitted John Minor Botts, who led the delegation, against the radical editor James Hunnicutt. Botts did not believe giving uneducated Black men the vote was prudent. Like many white unionists, he thought African Americans would be too easily swayed by former owners to vote the way they wanted. (In that opinion he was greatly mistaken.) But Hunnicutt's resolution in favor of universal manhood suffrage without distinction of race carried the day and set a marker for the continuing clash between these two very different white Virginia Republicans.[23]

Edward Pollard had begun work on his long-awaited book, *The Lost Cause,* the previous summer, shortly after the Union army arrested him on the streets of Richmond. With his close-cropped hair, long red beard, furrowed brow, and high forehead, he presented a stern appearance that matched his adamant views. A rash of advertisements in early 1866, months before publication, indelibly linked Pollard's name with the book's title. Now, in August, *The Lost Cause* codified for all the world to see the attitudes that its title embraced: the righteousness of the Confederacy, the superiority of the South, the positive good of slavery, the perfidy of the North, the correctness of states' rights, and the necessity of white men to continue wielding power over four million people set free by the war. Here was a catechism of faith, a canonical creed that resonated with many white southerners and that they embraced with fervor.[24]

In a tome of more than seven hundred pages, the angry exegete of southern defiance narrated the rise and fall of the slave republic down to its fiery, Richmond-centric ending. There, he bristled, "all the hopes of the Southern Confederacy were to be consumed in one day, as a scroll in the fire!" He ended with the assertion that the southern cause of constitutional liberty was separate from secession and slavery and thus not lost. In that claim, Pollard conjured up the man he called "the orator of the South," former governor Henry Wise. Pollard did not think much of Wise's wartime record as a Confederate brigadier. But like Wise, he called for a war of ideas, which he believed the South would eventually win.[25]

Secessionist newspaper editor Edward A. Pollard, whose book *The Lost Cause* gave a name to the postwar Confederate creed. (Wikimedia Commons)

Pollard now had his revenge. *The Lost Cause* was said to have sold fifty thousand copies in its first month, an astounding figure, if it can be believed, considering the impoverished state of the South. He saw the Confederacy die and Richmond burn, but he now gave a name to the defiance he had first declared in April 1865 while he watched fires consume the business district.

The greatest exponent of that cause was Henry Wise. He would not be silent. He held no office. He never applied for a pardon. Even so, gauged by the number of times the Joint Committee on Reconstruction asked about him when it interviewed other Virginians in early 1866, the unrepentant Wise had thoroughly spooked the congressmen.

Wise's blunt pronouncements and his sheer theatricality kept him in the limelight. He apparently never turned down an invitation to speak. Whether it was a talk in aid of the Richmond Female Orphans Society, at a militia gathering, or for a church group, he always brought the subject around to defense of the South. His remarks at the dinner of the Richmond Light Infantry Blues after the first Confederate

Memorial Day fused his name as much as Henry Pollard's to the Lost Cause faith. Later that fall he went to Winchester to speak at the reburial of southern officers in a cemetery there. He repeated his claim from the Blues dinner that the cause was not lost. He left no doubt where he stood. Though his stories by now had acquired the patina of age through frequent retelling, he showed he still had that magical gift for the apt phrase. His exhortation reverberated throughout Virginia and beyond when he thundered, "I invoke, then, the mighty Confederate dead."[26]

17

Obliterate All Distinctions

Fall 1866 to Spring 1867

The northern congressional elections in autumn 1866 presaged doom for Andrew Johnson. The president's inept and, at times, incoherent efforts to campaign for his supporters in Congress led to disaster at the polls for them. The outcome magnified the existing Republican majority in the national legislature. The elections, effectively a referendum on the Fourteenth Amendment, were unambiguous. White southerners had bet on Johnson and his veto, and they had lost. Aghast, they resigned themselves to more years of what they denounced as a corrupt and unscrupulous congressional majority intent on inflicting a heartless system of penalties on the South.[1]

Congress, in turn, was increasingly frustrated by the intransigence of the white South. The case of Dr. James Watson illustrated that displeasure. In November 1866 Watson had shot and killed William Medley in Rockbridge County. The perpetrator was white, the victim Black. A local court quickly acquitted the doctor, but General Schofield voided the verdict. He ordered a military commission convened in Richmond to try Watson again. The doctor's supporters protested and got President Johnson to order his release. It was a pyrrhic victory, however, because it showed Congress the dubious prospects for justice for Black Virginians.[2]

Despite the clear outcome of the fall elections, and its likely consequences, white opinion in Richmond remained adamant in opposing the Fourteenth Amendment. When the General Assembly convened in December, Governor Pierpont urged it to ratify the amendment as the only way to restore Virginia's congressional representation and avoid more extreme measures from Congress. General Schofield thought the amendment flawed, but he echoed the governor's request.

Richmond power brokers, however, expected the General Assembly to reject the amendment as a point of honor. Radicals might well impose their will on the South, they argued, but it was their duty to resist humiliation. To do otherwise "would damn us to everlasting infamy." The city's most influential opinion-makers vowed continued resistance. Southern newspapers misled their readers by overestimating the strength of Johnson's allies and dismissing the power of his opponents. "Let us be patient—we have endured much—we can endure more," they bluffed. "Let's see what our rulers in Washington will do." On cue, the state senate rejected the amendment unanimously; it garnered a single vote in the House of Delegates.[3]

Despite the bravado of their defiance, however, the editors and the legislators allowed the initiative to pass to other, less well-known actors. The pace of political change in the city accelerated with dizzying speed. The signs were unmistakable in pointed speeches at the Emancipation Proclamation commemoration in January. In March, Congress imposed its long-awaited sweeping imprint on southern policy, galvanizing Black people and their white radical allies. The ascendancy of radicals in the Republican Party was manifest in the second April 3 parade, in the Black response to an appeal by conservatives, and in the state Republican convention. Politics spilled out into the streets that spring, with protests against segregation and sometimes violent clashes with police.

Richmond's Black citizens welcomed 1867 full of hope that, when it convened, the Republican Congress would strengthen their rights as citizens. They began the new year with another parade and mass gathering on Capitol Square to celebrate the Emancipation Proclamation. James Hunnicutt used the occasion to advance his vendetta against Governor Pierpont. He approvingly published an anonymous letter that called the governor "mentally weak and constitutionally vain." He and African American businessman Albert Brooks collected 2,400 signatures on a petition to have Pierpont replaced with a new provisional governor. Hunnicutt did not give the governor credit for urging the General Assembly to endorse the Fourteenth Amendment. Pierpont had not been able to satisfy the city's establishment leaders. He now found himself in the crosshairs of Hunnicutt's rising radicals.[4]

With the exception of Tennessee, all the former Confederate states made the same futile acts of defiance as the Virginia General Assembly. In the face of such resistance, as the governor correctly predicted, Congress acted decisively to void President Johnson's plan for Reconstruction and replace it with one of its own. On March 2 the first Reconstruction Act divided the former Confederates states into five military regions under the supervision of army generals. Virginia had the distinction of being one all by itself. It was now converted into Military District Number One. Under a supplemental law, the generals in charge of these districts were directed to register all males, Black and white. This expanded electorate would choose delegates to write new state constitutions. These must include the right to vote without regard to race, and they must endorse the Fourteenth Amendment, something the former Confederate states had so adamantly resisted. The amendment would not be ratified until 1869, but its effect on the South was immediate through the provisions of Congress's Reconstruction Acts. This stunning and revolutionary change was what the combination of white southern resistance and radical activism had wrought in a short span of time. As a result, in little more than two years, Virginia was on course to move from a society based on slavery to one experimenting with radical change, even interracial democracy.[5]

While Congress's action alarmed the Richmond establishment, it electrified African Americans and ushered in a season of intense political activity. It encouraged their erroneous belief that the federal government would distribute land to freedmen. It heightened their sense of destiny because they would soon have the right to vote. It revived that millennial sense they felt at the jubilee of deliverance in April 1865. Once more, it seemed to them that a new age was dawning.[6]

The new order decreed by Washington formed the backdrop to the second anniversary of the fall of Richmond. Like the previous year, African American social clubs and militias organized a large parade through the city, ending at the Washington statue on Capitol Square where a throng gathered to hear speeches. Once again, the keynote speaker was James Hunnicutt. Black militia units, though wearing elaborate uniforms, bore fewer arms than in the previous year because of federal strictures. That may have alleviated some concerns of conservative Richmonders; the speeches did not.

After excoriating Governor Pierpont for betraying unionists, Hunnicutt devoted his address to the new dispensation created by the Reconstruction Acts. He urged his listeners to register to vote and admonished them to resist the appeal of candidates who had supported the Confederacy. Any vote for them, he said, would be a vote to bring back the whipping post and the chain gang. "The Southern Confederacy is lost," he exhorted them, "don't you help to regain it." He reminded his audience that it was the former enslavers who were responsible for racial mixing, not Black men and women.[7]

Another speaker, Lewis Lindsay, a short man about thirty years old with wavy hair and a long, drooping mustache, represented a rising cohort of more militant African American leaders who had begun to eclipse men like Fields Cook and John Oliver. Born a slave in rural Caroline County, Lindsay went to Richmond as a child, played the bugle in a Confederate artillery battery during the war, and had his own brass band afterward. He married a woman once enslaved by Congressman John Minor Botts. African Americans, he told the gathering, should "vote for a good man without regard to color; but whatever you do don't cast your vote for a rebel." He urged his listeners to obey the law, respect magistrates, and deal fairly with white people. Such reasonable advice impressed the newspapers, but before long they regretted their praise and denounced him for his increasingly radical pronouncements in favor of social as well as political equality.[8]

Two weeks later, an extraordinary gathering at the New Richmond Theatre offered a different perspective. Thirteen Black men called the meeting to ask the city's white leaders to give African Americans their views about the future. The political agitation of the spring made the objectives of radical Republicans well known. These more cautious men wanted to hear what alternative vision the white establishment could offer their community.

Many white people refused to have anything to do with congressional Reconstruction. The more practical among them, like the speakers at the New Richmond Theatre, believed they could not afford to stand aside out of devotion to an Old South that was gone and boycott the process Congress had decreed. That meant accepting votes for African Americans and then appealing for their support. It did not mean, however, that they would bow to demands for social equality. And it did not mean they would relinquish their attempt to exert as much authority over Black people's lives as they could, only that they would need to find different means to that end.

The notice announcing the meeting suggested the conveners as well as the invited speakers had not shed outmoded attitudes. In deferential terms, it spoke of the "circumstances both novel and embarrassing" that African Americans found themselves in. And it hoped the event would give them the "salutary and impartial advice" they needed.[9]

Even so, it was an event that could not have been imagined before the war. Never before, gushed supporters in the press, had there been such a large gathering of both races under one roof. The white speakers did not accept their African American audience as equals, but the changed circumstances in their city compelled them to view them as fellow voters. The hall was filled to capacity. Solon Johnson, a respected barber, called the meeting to order and introduced the three scheduled speakers, all attorneys. Marmaduke Johnson had commanded Confederate artillery at Antietam and was a popular orator. The other two—Raleigh Daniel and William Macfarland—had spoken at the meeting on Capitol Square in August 1865 to proclaim their loyalty to the nation. Later in the program, Nathaniel Sturdivant, the Confederate officer who had been elected mayor the previous year but was barred from serving, was asked to add his comments. The speakers warned the audience against being taken in by strangers who would turn them against the native white people of the city. These, the speakers pleaded, had their best interests at heart. In a poorly veiled rebuke of Hunnicutt, they spoke of white demagogues who had "suddenly been seized with great love for the colored man, and told him he must hate his neighbor."[10]

From the heated questions asked from the floor of the theater, however, it was clear that few African Americans in the audience would be dissuaded from supporting the radical agenda of universal male suffrage. The speakers received some support with their pleas for unity and mutual respect, but they encountered objections when they questioned the intentions of Republicans. At one point Marmaduke Johnson posed a rhetorical question—what had Black people's new friends done for them? A shout from the audience gave a reply that could not be refuted: "Dey fed us all de winter." In an attempt to appeal to shared wartime privation, Sturdivant praised two Black men who had accompanied him in the Confederate army as servants. That evoked a dismissive voice from the floor: "They ought to be hung; they wanted to die slaves." Sturdivant seemed to enjoy parrying objections from the audience, but his attempt to sow doubts about Hunnicutt failed. The editor of the *New Nation* was an imperfect vessel for preaching the gospel of equal rights for Black people, but he was their standard-bearer for the moment. They tolerated his long speeches and contributed to support his newspaper. Despite his awkward, strident voice, the grim-faced former preacher with the alarming coiffure articulated their aspirations for fair treatment and equal rights.[11]

Afterward the men who called the meeting came in for sharp criticism. One of them, Wyatt Lewis, said he looked for the same results from the proposed constitution as most other African Americans. He hoped it would guarantee free public schools and would "level and obliterate all distinctions of color before the law." But he said they would be unworthy of their freedom if they gave up the right to hear both sides of an argument. He reminded his readers of an uncomfortable fact—Black men were in a minority among voters statewide. They could not count on tipping the balance in their favor without some support from white laborers and mechanics who had worn gray uniforms.[12]

The political winds, however, strongly favored the radicals, as the first Republican state convention demonstrated two days later. Two-thirds of the delegates were African American. Most of them supported

Hunnicutt as their leader because he now endorsed equal suffrage and civil rights. And his newspaper was the sole organ in the city promoting those views. He and his allies dominated the convention, which took place in part in the African Baptist Church and in part as an outdoor rally on Capitol Square. The firebrand editor now gloried in the sobriquet of "Friend and Hero." He pushed aside the minority of moderates, mainly white men who supported John Minor Botts and who questioned universal suffrage and opposed social equality. Hunnicutt said he now wanted to revolutionize Virginia and divide up the land belonging to what he called "negro-oligarchs." These opinions troubled moderate Republicans; they horrified the city's conservative leaders.[13]

Frequent meetings and mass rallies kept the political temperature high. Four days after the state Republican convention, the national Republican Party sent US Senator Henry Wilson of Massachusetts to heal the division between the radical Hunnicutt faction, mostly Black, and moderate Botts Republicans, mostly white. That fissure set the Old Dominion apart from other southern states and alarmed national leaders who feared they would lose control of Virginia. An early foe of slavery and its devotees, Wilson was a driver of congressional plans for Reconstruction. He spoke to an immense crowd from the steps of the capitol. Most of the six thousand or more were Black, but many legislators and other white citizens came to hear what the celebrated northern radical had to say. Wilson made the expected denunciation of Andrew Johnson and of "men who still had the virus of secession in their veins." He encouraged his Black listeners "whose hands had been weaponed with the ballot" but discouraged any talk of confiscating former Confederates' property.[14]

Richmond was a pedestrian city. The majority of its people could not afford the expense of keeping horses and so walked to work, school, and worship. Beginning in late 1866, a horse-drawn streetcar began operating on rails laid between Twenty-Eighth Street in the East End to Eighth Street just west of Capitol Square. Segregation of the races was the norm on the cars, as it was in hotels, bars, and other public spaces. Black men were permitted to stand on the outside platforms of the six streetcars but not to sit inside. In April three members of the Mounted Negro Guard, wearing their militia unit's badges and ribbons, contested this arrangement. When police arrested their leader, Christopher Jones, a crowd of several hundred surrounded the car and shouted, "Let's have our rights." A show of force by the police thwarted an attempt to rescue Jones, but the crowd continued to make threats to the streetcar as it continued on its route.[15]

When questioned by a magistrate, Jones and defense witnesses repeated their assertion that anyone paying the fare had the right to sit in the cars. Another attempt by a Black man to ride inside a streetcar a week later was thwarted. In the face of this turmoil, the directors of the Street Railway Company reached a compromise adjudicated by General Schofield. Four of the company's six cars would be open to both African Americans and whites, and two were reserved for the use of white women and children. These latter two would be distinguished by a white ball on top of the car. Over the course of the following spring and summer, Black people made other sporadic efforts to occupy segregated sections of streetcars, ferryboats, and railroad carriages.[16]

On a sunny May morning a large contingent of visiting firemen from Delaware paraded with the Richmond fire brigade through the city streets behind a brass band. It was a popular event that attracted thousands of onlookers. The audience swelled even larger in the afternoon to watch a demonstration of the pumping capacity of each city's fire engines. Toward the end of the contest, a shoving match between a Black spectator and a white fireman quickly escalated into violence. When police arrested the Black man, others tried to free him. The confrontation degenerated in a roiling melee of shouting and rock throwing. A crowd broke into the police station and freed the man under arrest. Police reinforcements failed to dispel it. Mayor Mayo arrived and commanded the crowd in the name of the commonwealth to disperse. It took the presence of Orlando Brown and General Schofield—or, more accurately, the soldiers they commanded—to force the demonstrators to disperse. Six additional infantry companies brought into town later that night drove the point home.[17]

The increase in Black people's political activity, and the certainty that the Reconstruction Acts would lead to more of the same, troubled white Richmond's sense of the proper balance of affairs. The massive display of disorder in the streets on the day of the firemen's demonstration was unnerving in a new and disturbing fashion. A greater shock came two days later when a northern speaker at one of the increasingly frequent political meetings at First African Baptist Church appeared to exhort his listeners to violence in the streets. In his speech, Jedekiah Hayward praised his audience for demanding equality. But then he alluded to the possibility they might take reckless action to achieve their goals. He said they would not want to embarrass Judge Underwood while he was holding court in town. But "as soon as he leaves you may have a high carnival for what you please." He went on to give oblique approval for whatever they did, saying to prolonged cheering, "It is useless for me to advise you as to what to do; for great masses generally do what they have a mind to."[18]

Whether Hayward had incited Black people to violence or merely encouraged them to assert their rights as citizens became a matter of dispute when the northerner appeared before a city magistrate. A hostile press certainly thought he was inciting a riot. General Schofield dismissed the unrest and called the troubles only a temporary excitement that he easily suppressed. But that was not true. Two days after Hayward's remarks, a minor incident showed how volatile the situation was and how easily violence could erupt. When police tried to arrest a drunk and disorderly Black man, his friends showered the officers with bricks. Shots were fired on both sides. A squad of infantrymen from Libby Prison came to the aid of the policemen, who arrested twenty participants in the disturbance. The frequency of disorder in the streets, even of riots, not just public political meetings, ratcheted up the sense of unease felt throughout the city.[19]

Into this volatile mix, a Confederate apparition, lurking in the wings for two years, descended unbidden on Richmond in the febrile spring of 1867. The whole nation, North and South, once again looked on the former rebel capital with the same intent fascination it had when fire consumed the shrunken remnant of the southern republic.

18

The Prisoner

May 1867

When Abraham Lincoln walked through smoldering ashes the day after the great fire, crowds of African Americans greeted him on his way up from the waterfront. As if by magic, word spread that the president had come. On the fringes of the swelling crowd, some thought that meant Jefferson Davis had returned. Shouts went up of "Hang him, hang him." That was not a surprising reaction from people who had been enslaved not forty-eight hours before, but many Confederates were hardly more charitable. The dour southern assistant secretary of war, John Archibald Campbell, who had remained in town and met with Lincoln, later called Davis unfit for leadership, "filled with petty scruples and doubts . . . an incubus and a mischief." Archsecessionist editor Edward Pollard, scribbling away a year later on his book to glorify the Confederacy, heaped the blame for defeat on Davis. He had frittered away great assets. These, in Pollard's caustic enumeration, included "a servile Congress, a Cabinet of dummies, and a people devoted to his person." By the end of the war, Davis's reputation among the Confederates of Richmond had sunk low.[1]

Now the passage of time transmuted Davis's image into something entirely different among those same people. Alone among leading rebels, he remained in prison two years after his ignominious flight from Richmond. His position had become much like what John Brown imagined for himself at Harpers Ferry. In defeat, Brown had said he could recover all his loss "by only hanging a few moments by the neck." Davis would not hang like Brown, but the threat of martyrdom had the same effect. By the time of the first Confederate Memorial Day at Hollywood Cemetery in May 1866, the transformation was complete. As much was clear in the floral tribute placed on his son's grave. It read "Joseph, son of our Beloved President, Jefferson Davis. Erected by the Little Boys and Girls of the Southern Capital." Those sentiments could not have been imagined by die-hard Confederates when they damned Davis in April 1865 for bringing ruin to their city. Now, two years later, he returned to his former capital, if not exactly in glory, then at least in vindication in their eyes. White Richmonders saw more hope for the future than at any time since the close of the war.[2]

The federal government charged Davis with treason soon after his capture. At first it seemed he might be brought to trial quickly. But there was no consensus within the government about how to handle a treason prosecution. The politically ambitious chief justice of the Supreme Court, Salmon Chase, was assigned to circuit duty for Virginia, but he invoked every reason he could think of to avoid going to Richmond to try the Davis case. It offended General Schofield to hear that Chase was concerned about his personal safety in the former Confederate capital. He assured the chief justice he would be "as free from molestation in this City as in Washington."[3]

For the time being, federal prosecutors thought it better to leave Davis in the hands of the army, beyond the reach of his attorneys' requests for bail. Davis could have asked for a pardon but refused. Like Henry Wise, he believed he had done nothing that demanded atonement. As the months passed, it became apparent that Washington did not know what to do with its distinguished prisoner. It might have been better for all concerned, as some wished at the time, including Lincoln, if he had made his escape abroad rather than be captured fleeing south. But there he was, the inconvenient loose end of Fort Monroe.

Davis's lead defense counsel was Charles O'Conor of New York. Although he refused to accept compensation, he did use funding for expenses from a variety of parties, including southerners who still controlled money from former Confederate sources. For two years, this stern, white-haired elder of the New York bar, a proud Irish immigrant and ardent Democrat, had played a long game, bluffing the government that he wanted a trial for Davis to justify secession. He knew federal prosecutors feared the result of such a contest even more than he did. O'Conor had no desire to contest the legality of secession even though his client initially did. Davis gradually gave up that hope and allowed O'Conor to maneuver behind the scenes with feints and misdirection to achieve his ultimate goal to have the charge dismissed.[4]

O'Conor's main worry focused on the federal judge whose court would hear Davis's case. John Underwood had sought indictment of leading Confederate military figures at the end of the war and, separately, the southern president. Underwood was becoming an embarrassment to Republicans, not so much because of his poor grasp of the law but because of his intemperate remarks and blatant contempt for judicial evenhandedness. When the Joint Committee on Reconstruction interviewed him the previous year, he told the congressmen he probably could not find a jury in Virginia to convict Davis. But that was a problem easily solved, he breezily assured them, by simply packing the jury. There was also his unsavory reputation for self-dealing in confiscated property. At the end of the war, he praised President Johnson for his declaration to punish rebels. Johnson soon disappointed the judge's desire for wholesale confiscation, but Underwood took advantage of at least one case that did go through. He had condemned and put up for sale the Richmond properties of a convicted rebel. Underwood and his wife then quietly bought them up at knock-down prices.[5]

With Underwood's volatile personality and open animus toward Confederates in mind, Davis's legal counsel needed to make sure the judge would not thwart them when they renewed their efforts. In their favor, they knew Davis's fragile health was creating sympathy for him. Because they knew the government was still not ready to go to trial, even after two years, they were able to make an agreement with the prosecution team. They arranged for prominent Republicans, notably Horace Greeley, celebrated editor of the *New-York Tribune,* to appear in Richmond as sureties for Davis's good behavior. That was clever window dressing. The most crucial bit of advance planning was to ensure that the administration would not object to the writ of habeas corpus or to bail. And in that effort, O'Conor succeeded.

These men were members of the unprecedented integrated jury pool for the abortive treason trial of Jefferson Davis. (The Valentine Museum)

All was in order on May 4, when O'Conor requested a writ requiring the army to release the prisoner into the custody of Virginia authorities. It was signed and countersigned in Richmond and taken to Fort Monroe, where the army gave assurances it would comply. Shortly after 3:00 p.m. two days later, Judge Underwood took his seat, and the marshal called the court to order. The clerk read the names of twenty-four prospective jurors, six of them African American. They included Lewis Lindsay, John Oliver, Fields Cook, and Albert Brooks, all leading members of the Black community in Richmond. It was little more than two years since slavery's demise, and now, incredibly, Black men were sitting in an integrated jury pool to hear the case against the former Confederate president. John Minor Botts, prominent wartime unionist and now the chief white moderate Republican of the state, served as foreman.

In his charge to the jurors, the judge treated his listeners to a colorful harangue on the Confederacy's perfidy. "In the very rooms we now occupy," he insisted, "dwelt the fiery soul of treason, rebellion, and civil war." With a flair for awkward metaphors, he poured special contempt on Richmond, "looking as comely and specious as a goodly apple on a gilded sepulchre, where bloody treason flourished its whips of scorpions." Underwood's opening tirade enraged local opinion, as he knew it would. Northern newspapers were no less appalled by "its foul-mouthed abuse of Richmond, with its spluttering poetic quotations . . . such a farrago of rant." Even the radical New York *Nation* said that the cause of justice would be better served if the judge stifled his rhetorical outbursts.[6]

It took five more days after Underwood convened his court, but on the morning of May 11, the elaborate performance that O'Conor had taken such pains to engineer began. It started when Davis embarked from Fort Monroe on a Richmond-Norfolk packet boat. The journey soon took on the aspect of a royal progress. People gathered at the packet's numerous stops along the James River. Crowds gathered to raise their hats in greeting and send flowers aboard. They showed him a reverence they had rarely displayed when he was in office. When they reached their destination, Varina Davis remembered her husband saying, "I feel like an unhappy ghost visiting this much beloved city."[7]

The army command sent a detachment from two infantry regiments down to Rocketts Landing to greet the boat. Davis disembarked wearing a plain black frock coat and large slouch hat. He walked slowly with the aid of a cane, and his sallow complexion and short, iron-gray beard bore witness to the toll the war and confinement had taken on his stooped figure. He had fled his capital before the evacuation fire began and had never seen firsthand the extent of destruction. Now as his carriage passed through the Burnt District, he could see how many blocks had been leveled. But he could also see many newer, taller buildings rising from the ruins. Despite the authorities' injunction not to gather, the excitement proved too much, and an immense crowd assembled along the streets to catch sight of him.

Davis was ensconced in the same suite of rooms at the Spotswood Hotel that he had occupied when he first arrived in Richmond in 1861. The excitement reached fever pitch on his day in court. Large crowds assembled at both the hotel and the Customs House three blocks away. An infantry guard flanked the entrances to both buildings to provide security, though the orderly demeanor of the spectators made their presence unnecessary. At the Customs House, Davis waited for an hour in the room that had been his office during the war. The courtroom filled beyond capacity with notables. Among these were Governor Pierpont; the commanding general of Military District Number One, John Schofield; the head of the Virginia Freedmen's Bureau, Orlando Brown; James Lyons; John Minor Botts; and Dr. Charles Minnigerode, rector of St. Paul's Episcopal Church and Davis's friend and pastor during the war.

Just before 11:00 a.m., Judge Underwood took his seat, but it took a half hour of preliminaries before Davis was escorted into the chamber. Most observers thought he looked frail. Despite it being warm inside the packed courtroom, he asked a soldier to close the window behind him. The tightly choreographed judicial minuet, planned so carefully and agreed upon in advance by the defense and prosecution teams, now began. The writ of habeas corpus was read, in which the president of the United States addressed those who had custody of the prisoner and said, "We command that you deliver the body of Jefferson Davis" to the circuit court for the District of Virginia. The writ had been witnessed in Washington by the chief justice of the US Supreme Court. Its date—May 8—let even the most clueless spectator know that this event had been orchestrated at the highest level days before.[8]

The deputy marshal then served the writ to Davis, who acknowledged it. The indictment on which the writ was based was then read. It had been hurriedly and faultily written in May 1866 at Underwood's insistence and was based on thin testimony by questionable witnesses. Even so, after listening to Underwood's diatribe against the "selfish and wicked aristocracy" of Virginia, the grand jury had responded to the judge's charge to it and had returned the indictment against Davis.[9]

O'Conor confirmed that defense attorneys had received a copy of the writ. William Evarts, a skilled litigator who served as President Johnson's counsel the following year during the impeachment trial, spoke for the prosecution. He accepted that Davis had now passed into civilian custody and admitted that the government did not intend to prosecute him during the current term of the court. In reply, O'Conor drew attention to the long duration of the defendant's imprisonment and the Constitution's guarantee of a speedy trial. He disingenuously stated that he was not there to question the government's failure to prosecute because he accepted that there might have been good reasons to delay. But he played upon the prisoner's poor health. He reminded the court that two years in judicial limbo had not been kind to Davis's weak constitution. He stated what everyone present knew, that the defense could furnish ample security to guarantee Davis's appearance when the government eventually was ready to go to trial. Because the defense could bring pledges from prominent men of every political stripe, he begged the court to grant bail. He perhaps went too far when he said those making that offer were willing to pledge their whole estates.

The court next asked Evarts for the prosecution's response. He said it was up to the judge whether to allow bail. If he did, the amount and terms of bail needed to be decided. Evarts and US Attorney Chandler proposed an amount of $100,000. Chandler said there were eighteen men present willing to offer surety of five thousand dollars each and two more who had yet to appear.

After making clear that he thought the need for further delay in prosecution was a decision of the government and not his court, Underwood announced that the amount of bail was agreeable to him. The judge asked those agreeing to offer sureties to make themselves known. O'Conor first invited Horace Greeley to step forward. One after another the eighteen were introduced to Davis and shook his hand. They included some of the most prominent white men of Richmond—William Macfarland, Gustavus Myers, James Lyons, Abraham Warwick, James Thomas Jr., and Isaac Davenport Jr. Even John Minor

Botts, whom Davis had imprisoned during the war and who served as foreman of the grand jury, offered surety for his old tormentor.

Courtroom decorum collapsed as the clerk called the names of the sureties, and they came forward to sign the bond. Greeley received the loudest approval from the audience. The presence of Botts among the guarantors surprised many. (He later denied that there was hissing when his name was called.) When Chandler said that enough had signed, the judge ordered the marshal to discharge the prisoner. The hall erupted in pandemonium. Escorted by his friends to the portico of the Customs House, Davis greeted the mass of well-wishers who cheered him noisily. The night after his release, a huge crowd of Black and white citizens filled the First African Baptist Church to hear Horace Greeley speak. His conciliatory remarks reinforced the good feeling of the Davis affair—the only sour note being the presence of Judge Underwood, who was loudly booed by white people and applauded by Black people.[10]

White Richmond had not known such joy since before the end of the war. Local leaders thought Davis's release on bail would do more to resolve the acrimony that still lingered between North and South than anything that had happened since Lee surrendered. Although Davis's case had just been postponed, few believed it would ever come to trial—and indeed it did not. (Before President Johnson eventually pardoned Davis, his attorneys had the ironic pleasure of arguing that the Fourteenth Amendment exempted him from future prosecution.)

To some residents, it seemed as though the outcome at the Customs House heralded a turning point and gave hope that optimism would return to stimulate enterprise in their city. That sunny view was only possible, however, if they overlooked the continuing unrest in the streets that did not stop, even for the Davis trial. Just two days before the court granted the former Confederate president bail, an African American newspaper reported that soldiers quelled a fracas that erupted when a crowd of Black men, using clubs, bricks, and pistols, tried to rescue one of their number from the police. Then, on the following day, Jedekiah Hayward made his incendiary speech that allegedly incited Black people to violence.[11]

Two weeks later, more of the sectional good feeling from the court proceedings dissipated in the face of greater restriction on public expression of Confederate sentiment. After the first Reconstruction Act turned the southern states into military districts in March, US Army officers limited processions and speeches they thought might encourage disloyalty. They did not ban memorial activities in cemeteries, but Confederates understood they needed to be more careful than they had been in the previous year to avoid provoking a crackdown. As a result, the second Confederate Memorial Day displayed a different tone than the first. Thousands still participated in decorating soldiers' graves at Hollywood Cemetery. The Ladies Memorial Association announced in advance, however, that there would be no parades or speeches. Unlike in the previous year, the commemoration featured no procession of men in Confederate uniform or bands playing solemn music. The participants understood why. One observer wrote approvingly that nothing could subdue the women's passion to remember the fallen, but "if the management had not been under the control of the Ladies, [a] thousand bayonets would have bristled to prevent the celebration."[12]

Unlike in 1866, the majority of participants were women and children. Comparatively few were men, none in organized military units. Out of respect, the larger stores in town closed, but the city was not as deserted as the past year. Although the established portions of Hollywood had densely wooded sections and elaborate tombs, the Confederate soldiers' section lacked trees. The tightly packed rows of graves with wooden headboards there formed a barren view that looked from a distance like a plowed field with long furrows. The mass of mourners decorated them with, it seemed, every flower growing in Richmond. On that day the soldiers' section became, in the words of a journalist, "one great republic of sorrow."[13]

That same month the Ladies Memorial Association resolved to erect a monument to commemorate the South's dead soldiers. At a charity bazaar they raised an astonishing eighteen thousand dollars to fund the project. Later that summer they chose a design submitted by engineer Charles Dimmock, who had put Crawford's bronze Washington on its plinth before the war. When completed, a stone pyramid of dry-stacked James River granite would tower ninety feet over the soldiers' section. It was meant to proclaim to the world the city's veneration of the Confederate dead, a sentiment no federal restriction could stifle. Their devotion to the southern cause and their sorrow over the loss of their fallen sons and fathers, heavy and inconsolable, underlay all their hopes for the postwar city. The tragedy was that the society they envisioned admitted scant room for the aspirations of Black Richmonders beyond the subservience of a subordinate class. That was a status those soon-to-be-enfranchised citizens refused to accept.

19

Fit Them for Citizenship

Spring to Fall 1867

In the two years since the war, Richmond's press had mentioned the Freedmen's Bureau mainly to disparage its work. But in May 1867 the city's widest-circulation newspaper appealed for teachers for the many African American schools outside the city that stood empty for want of instructors. The *Dispatch* approvingly cited those sent by northern charities and also southern white women who volunteered to help. To support these schools, the editors wrote with patronizing sympathy, was important because "to fit them for citizenship, the colored people need to be educated." Such a positive statement would never have been made before it finally became clear, even to die-hard Confederates, that Congress would settle for nothing less than giving votes to Black men. Even so, it was a statement for public consumption, not an indication of any change of heart. In private the more common reaction among former Confederates was still to condemn extension of the franchise, as one of them wrote, "a crowning outrage [that] must be avenged." This was the climate in which the unprecedented electoral campaign took place to fashion a new constitution for the state.[1]

Since coming to Virginia, General Schofield had been suspicious of extending the vote to Black men. He nevertheless had urged the state legislature to endorse the Fourteenth Amendment to avoid stronger measures. They did not heed him, and now, with the Reconstruction

Acts, those stronger measures were law. He dutifully set about enforcing them. The head of Military District Number One wielded supreme power in Virginia. He could appoint or remove any state official he wished, suspend any law, or impose any regulation. The most important task Congress set for him was to conduct the vote for the mandated constitutional convention.

The general began in April by setting up voter registration boards in each jurisdiction composed of citizens with unimpeachable unionist credentials. Like a good army bureaucrat, he specified the precise details of their tasks, down to stipulating the times when notices should be posted. He also decided, controversially, that Black and white voters should be listed in separate columns. Orlando Brown, now a brevet brigadier general, sent out orders to his Freedmen's Bureau officers. He directed them to counteract the influence of anyone trying to prevent freedmen from registering. More pointedly, he told his men he would consider them derelict in their duty if any Black man failed to register to vote out of ignorance of the process.[2]

Schofield announced that all male citizens at least twenty-one years of age and Virginia residents for at least a year were qualified to vote. The exceptions were those convicted of felony and, significantly, those who had previously taken the oath to uphold the US Constitution but later supported the Confederacy. That provision barred the wartime political class from participating but not the mass of ordinary Confederate veterans. The general worried that the unprecedented campaigning leading up to the election would cause civil unrest. To maintain order, he appointed army and Freedmen's Bureau officers as military commissioners in the seven subdistricts of the state. All civilian law enforcement officers were subject to the orders of these commissioners.[3]

Schofield's boards of registration finished their work by mid-September. By election day in October, they had enrolled 120,101 white and 105,832 Black electors. The process had gone smoothly. Few people complained of injustices, and the military commissioners did not have to try anyone for infractions. As a check on the accuracy of the registration, Schofield compared the electoral rolls with tax lists. This exercise revealed 17,649 more Black men registered to vote than were named on the tax lists. The general directed his officers to conduct a census in the Richmond ward that had the greatest disparity and found that the registration of voters was correct. It was the tax rolls that were in error. The closeness of the totals between Black and white voters statewide increased the already high level of tension that had prevailed since the first of the year.[4]

During the monthslong process of registration, the enthusiasm of Black men in Richmond for the opportunity to vote was apparent. The city's Monroe Ward caused special concern for white observers. There, they claimed, fraud had produced a much larger number of eligible Black men than expected, far in excess of the known population. Further, there was an improbable claim that white voters were underrepresented in the ward because of intimidation. The latter cause allegedly arose from the perjury prosecution of a Confederate veteran who had improperly taken the oath of allegiance. That case, the press claimed, "hangs like a scare-crow in the field to frighten away people [from] the registry." The real reason why fewer white men registered than expected had nothing to do with fraud or intimidation and everything to do with Confederate apathy. Just as with the fall 1865 elections, diehards wanted nothing to do with rules decreed by the radical Republican–dominated Congress, to the frustration of more pragmatic conservatives.[5]

From the beginning of the registration process, it was clear that white men could not compete with the energetic mobilization of newly enfranchised Black men for the radical Republican cause. If they hoped for better luck in rural areas, a meeting in Amelia County disabused them. There a group of self-styled conservative Black men copied the format from the April event at the New Richmond Theatre and invited local white leaders to speak to them. At the county courthouse about two hundred Black people, many of them women, gave a positive welcome to the invited speakers. They also heard from two African Americans from Richmond known for their moderate Republican opinions, John Oliver and Fields Cook.

Moderate he may have been, but Oliver frankly told his mostly Black audience their place was with the Republican Party. He distrusted men who had fought to the bitter end to preserve slavery. He criticized the people of Richmond—and General Schofield too—for not allowing equal access to the streetcars. And he pointedly said freed people "owned a large portion of the soil of Virginia that they had earned by the sweat of their brow and by the sale of their children." These remarks must have made the county gentry who shared the platform with him squirm with discomfort. They likely breathed easier when Oliver switched to thanking God for freedom and said he was willing to drop questions about land. He dismissed talk of a race war and schemes for confiscation. Instead, he urged his audience to focus on equal rights before the law.[6]

Most white Virginians eventually rejected the die-hard view and bowed to the new reality created by the Reconstruction Acts. They did not like it, but it was no longer possible to think, as they had for so long, that they could somehow avoid Congress's dictates. The sooner the work was done, they came to accept, the sooner Virginia could emerge from what they called the humiliation of being Military District Number One and be readmitted to Congress, giving them the best chance to regain their former ascendancy. They had to accept the right of Black men to vote and the need to appeal for their support at the polls, but they did not abandon their intent to control them.

There was as yet no formal conservative party or organization. White men divided between pragmatists who wanted to participate and reactionaries who opposed the election. But the Republicans, who did have a party, were divided as well. The split in their ranks on display at their April convention had widened since then. It pitted the dominant, mostly Black faction under Hunnicutt's leadership against the smaller, mostly white faction that looked to former Whig congressman John Minor Botts for guidance. Senator Henry Wilson came down from Massachusetts again in the summer to try and heal the rift. The two factions agreed to hold a second state convention in August, and it took place amid great excitement and turbulence in the capital city.

Two days before the convention, word circulated through the tobacco factories in the lower portion of the city that an impromptu outdoor mass meeting would be held in the evening at the corner of Main and Twenty-Fourth Streets. Hundreds of workers assembled there to hear radical speakers, principally John Given, a Black minister from Brooklyn, New York. He denounced conservatives and exhorted his audience to elect only radical delegates to the convention. He made a vigorous pitch for confiscation ("the rebels should be made to disgorge their ill-gotten gains") and denounced President Johnson. Given was interrupted when shouts of "Kill him! Kill him!" arose from the edge of the gathering, where a group of African Americans was beating a white man. With some difficulty, the police rescued him from the crowd. The following day the magistrate who heard the case determined that the man had been roaring drunk, had made threatening remarks, and had waved a pistol at the speaker before the crowd knocked him down and disarmed him.[7]

At the same time, a different radical meeting denounced John Oliver and Fields Cook for betraying Republican principles and consorting with former Confederates. Oliver rejected the charges as fabrications gotten up by "low white men" around James Morrissey, an Irish immigrant who, Oliver charged, was trying to buy African American votes "by bootlicking and 'rotgut' whisky."[8]

This was the setting in which three hundred Black and one hundred white delegates from across the state streamed into the city by canalboat, carriage, and rail to attend the Republican convention. Moderate whites allied with John Minor Botts and Governor Pierpont checked into the Exchange and Ballard House Hotels, white radicals chose the Spotswood, and African American delegates found accommodation at three Black hotels and the many Black boardinghouses. A nonstop series of mobile conversations to discuss the issues of the day swirled around each hostelry. It was supposed to be a united Republican Party, according to the compromise agreed to by the factions earlier. But the prospect for harmony faded when it became known that Hunnicutt had asked all his political supporters, not just official delegates, to come to the African Baptist Church on August 1.

Thousands answered his call and filled up the church on Broad Street. These included hundreds of workers from tobacco factories who told their bosses not to expect their labor that day. With complete dominance of the gathering, Hunnicutt denounced the moderates. Few if any delegates from the Botts faction or from anywhere outside the city were there to hear his taunts. Lewis Lindsay, ordinarily a firebrand radical, deplored the insult to delegates who had come at personal expense from distant counties, but his remarks were not well received. A few dissatisfied delegates gave up, abandoned the church to Hunnicutt's supporters, and went to the capitol, where they reassembled in the House of Delegates chamber. They appointed Fields Cook their chairman. He deplored the failure to harmonize the discordant factions and denounced the cult of leadership that surrounded Hunnicutt and had nearly destroyed the party. But his conciliatory stance was out of fashion.[9]

In the meantime, Hunnicutt directed the crowd inside the church to adjourn and re-form on Capitol Square, where they held an unruly mass meeting. In the words of a sorrowful white delegate, reporters for the establishment newspapers watched the proceedings from windows in the capitol, gloating over the disarray, which they hoped anticipated the dissolution of the Republican Party. In the proceedings that day and the next, Hunnicutt demonstrated his influence with the African Americans of Richmond and his mastery over his moderate opponents. Of the latter, he boasted, they could not see as far into the future as he could. When he was assured that the party would adopt his platform, he graciously encouraged Botts to speak.[10]

The former Whig congressman began with his familiar castigation of prewar Democrats for causing the war and bringing ruin to Virginia. Their embrace of secession had left the state in a parlous condition: "thousands of useful citizens killed or crippled on the battle-fields, fences and crops laid waste, dwellings destroyed, the whole country impoverished, and our hearthstones left desolate." Botts had his say, but the convention sealed the domination of the Hunnicutt faction over the party. With stubborn ways easily subject to caricature, Botts personified a backward-looking perspective. He only grudgingly came to accept unrestricted male suffrage. Even so, Hunnicutt's failure to make common cause with Botts's moderates would come back to haunt him. But at the zenith of his power, the *New Nation* editor had no equal for political influence in Richmond, or indeed in Virginia. The United States Ex-Officers, Soldiers, and Sailors Association met to denounce him for attempting to dominate the party. The city's white power brokers could only marvel at his sway and grind their teeth at what they denounced as his "egotism, profanity and low scurrility."[11]

While the political metronome ticked off the days toward the fall referendum, the city's physical reconstruction continued. Because they must submit to a process decreed by Congress that was distasteful to them, business leaders focused on economic recovery rather than politics. "It will be a delightful diversion from events of the day," promised the *Dispatch*. Because rebuilding of the Burnt District was steadily moving ahead by mid-1867, some commentators predicted unlimited growth and prosperity for the future. Others demurred, citing a continuing lack of capital and Richmond's failure to keep up with competing southern cities. Still others out in the surrounding countryside, like George Fitzhugh, the judge of the Freedmen's Court who doubted the capacity of Black people, believed landowners were still living in uncertainty about the tenure of their property and arrangements for adequate labor. All was indecision and chaos, he exaggerated. In town, optimists pointed to creation of the Corn and Flour Exchange that summer and of a chamber of commerce in the fall. General Mahone finally secured legislative approval for his scheme to consolidate railroad lines across southern Virginia, though powerful interests in Richmond still opposed him. The Gallego and Haxall Mills increased production over the past year, though they would never reach their antebellum levels because of increasing competition from Baltimore and midwestern mills.[12]

No bank had survived the evacuation fire two years before. Two of the earliest created afterward, the National Exchange Bank and the First National Bank, received their charters even as thin coils of smoke still rose from the Burnt District. They planned to merge by the end of 1867, the better to meet competition from newer financial institutions. The National Exchange Bank could trace its roots to the prewar Exchange Bank and chose to consolidate operations in a new building erected on the site of the bank's original 1841 building. Unlike other casualties of the fire that left only forlorn iron safes surrounded by rubble, the old Exchange facade survived, preserving two tall, classical granite columns and the pediment they supported. Featured prominently in photographs of the destruction, these dramatic sentinels seemed to outsiders to epitomize Confederate failure. But to white Richmonders, they represented not failure but the presence of the revered past in a new enterprise that looked toward the future.

If life went on beyond electioneering for ordinary Richmonders, hard-pressed in hard times to scratch out an adequate living, the divisions that politics inflamed were never far away. In a sign of the times, Frances Harper gave a public address that August, three days after the Republican convention ratified Hunnicutt's ascendancy. Residents were unaccustomed to women speaking in public, but Harper did, and in the House of Delegates no less.[13]

Harper was a celebrated speaker for abolition and women's suffrage. Born of free African American parents in Baltimore, she published poems in abolition papers and lectured across the North before the war. She gave a fiery speech at the National Women's Rights Convention in May 1866 that denounced Andrew Johnson as "the incarnation of meanness." She declared that the great social upheaval America had just experienced would not be complete until the nation became truly color-blind. By 1867, when she toured the South, she had become well known as a charismatic speaker with a poet's gift for metaphor and irony. She acknowledged the painful memory of injustice that lingered for those who had formerly been enslaved. But she offered her presence in the Virginia capitol as evidence of a brighter future ahead. The journalist who reported on her address gave Harper credit for her genteel appearance and articulate delivery to the audience of about a hundred, mostly African Americans. But he dismissed it all as abolitionist

Poet Frances Ellen Watkins Harper typified the changing times when she spoke in the Virginia capitol in 1867 on equal rights for all. (Library of Congress)

"cant and fanatical claptrap, plausibly arranged and dressed up." Even so, he could not deny the revolution in social and racial relations that she represented as well as preached.[14]

Another meeting a week later proved more disturbing to the sensibilities of white residents. The Rev. Peter Randolph, born enslaved in Virginia, had returned to the state after the war and became minister of Richmond's Ebenezer Baptist Church. He had been instrumental in the effort of the city's Black people to wrest power over their churches from white trustees. He was the founding president of the Shiloh Association of Black Baptist churches. Delegates from the members of the association gathered in August for their annual meeting in Manchester, the suburb directly south across the river from the capital. A journalist reporting on this otherwise anodyne event expressed horror when the meeting gave special recognition to delegates from Southampton County. There, the association proclaimed, "Nat. Turner struck the first blow for freedom." It appalled the writer that men of the cloth would validate this "most barbarous and brutal of all the human butcheries of this century." He was referring to the fifty-five white people killed in Turner's 1831 insurrection, but not to the similar number of African Americans who died in the paroxysm of revenge that put down the revolt. It was a stark reminder to him that Black men and women viewed the unsettling events of the past—and of the present—in radically different ways from him. And it hinted at great changes in the offing.[15]

20

The Disgrace Is Inflicted

October 1867

As the supreme authority in Military District Number One, General Schofield announced on September 12 that the referendum on the constitutional convention would take place six weeks later. He determined that there should be 105 delegates and divided the state into districts as equitably as he thought possible. There was some complaint about the shape of the districts, but Schofield's plan of apportionment seemed fair enough. At the close of voter registration, white men held a statewide majority over Black electors of almost fifteen thousand. But the distribution of the population concentrated the Black vote so that it held the advantage in fifty-nine districts that would elect delegates, to only forty-six with white majorities. The huge disparity in energy between the races was even more pronounced.[1]

It was a curiosity of the process that the men selected to run as convention delegates were not chosen until after the electioneering was nearly over. Even so, the summer of 1867 was filled with articles and speeches to acquaint anyone paying attention with the issues at hand. Then, barely a week before the election, candidates were selected. By then it was assumed on all sides that voters would approve the convention. Even the conservative press agreed. It warned that those who hoped they could somehow avoid having to produce a new constitution were delusional.[2]

With complete control over Republicans in the state capital, Hunnicutt directed how candidates for each of Richmond's five seats in the convention would be chosen. Each of the five wards in the city selected its nominees and presented them to a citywide Republican meeting on Capitol Square, where the five delegates would be chosen. The militants had the wind at their backs. When the moderate African American minister Fields Cook tried to propose an alternative to the radical slate, angry opponents shouted him down.

Albert Brooks, one of the most successful African American businessmen in the city, also illustrated the eclipse of moderate Black opinion. He had given a deposition in 1865 to protest the discriminatory pass system. He had gone to Washington to petition Republican congressmen for the vote in January 1867. He had been a delegate to the April state Republican convention. And in June he was a potential juror for Judge Underwood's stillborn trial of Jefferson Davis. But in October, when he was nominated to be a delegate to the convention, more radical men superseded him. After the vote, he regretted the puny white turnout for Republicans and appealed for moderate and radical white Republicans to overcome their differences. They ignored him.[3]

As widely expected, the five successful candidates selected to stand for election as delegates were all radical Republicans: James Hunnicutt, John Underwood, Lewis Lindsay, Joseph Cox, and James Morrissey. These five were, in the mocking words of the *New York Times*, the men "who will most surely represent the haughty and aristocratic people of the proud City of Richmond."[4]

The great majority of white Richmonders warmly detested the two best-known of the five—Hunnicutt and Underwood. In style and substance, the fiery Hunnicutt was utterly unlike the cool, well-mannered gentry who assumed a natural right to rule the city. He was a "half-phrenzied and erratic character," according to a northern opponent, and he earned his notoriety honestly. His writing in the *New Nation* and, even more, the influence he seemed to exert over the city's Black citizens were enough to make him despised by both the traditional elites and by the white moderates in his own party. General Schofield's confidential assessment of him was succinct: "Has some ability—a great deal of energy, and unbounded influence over the negroes."[5]

Underwood earned equal scorn in the same quarters. Confederates loathed him for indicting their leaders and attempting to confiscate their land. They reviled him even more for the insulting way he disparaged Richmond as beautiful but corrupt. Though he had lately tempered his denunciations of Confederates, they had not forgiven him. As an enemy wryly noted, "People rarely pardon insults offered to their wives and daughters and mothers and sweethearts."[6]

Lewis Lindsay first came to public attention when he spoke at the April 3, 1867, celebration and then served as a delegate to the Republican state convention. The white press began to take notice of, and feared, his powerful oratory as he campaigned in the capital and in outlying counties. He couched his demand for equality in blunt, provocative terms. "My friends," he allegedly said, "vote for the man who will bring you into his parlor, who will eat dinner with you, and who, if you want her, will let you marry his daughter." Given that these charged words appeared in the conservative press, they were likely fabrications to frighten white readers. But what was not in question was Lindsay's fervent desire for social as well as political equality, a prospect that underlay all white fears.[7]

Joseph Cox had been a free resident of Powhatan County before the war and had worked at Tredegar as a blacksmith. A tall, thin, affable, but serious man, afterward he became president of the Lincoln Union Aid Society, one of the largest Black organizations in town. He emerged as a leader of the radical faction and served as a delegate to the Republican convention and on the federal jury to hear Jefferson Davis's treason case. From that point on, he helped push aside moderate leaders like Fields Cook and John Oliver. General Schofield privately called Cox "A better man than Lindsay, but fully as ignorant."[8]

Little is known about the fifth radical delegate, James Morrissey, an Irish veteran of the British army who came to Richmond in 1866. A friend of Hunnicutt, he went into the saloon business and was disliked by the moderate Black leader John Oliver, who called him one of the "low white men" attempting to buy African American votes with bad whiskey. Embarrassingly for Governor Pierpont, Morrissey defeated the governor's attempt to be one of the five Richmond delegates for the convention.[9]

If the Republicans were tardy in choosing their candidates for the convention, conservative white men were even more disorganized.

They waited until barely a week before the election to select candidates. The five conservatives on the slate were all well-known: Marmaduke Johnson, William Taylor, Nathaniel Sturdivant, Thomas Evans, and Alexander Sands. Their supporters admitted they were late in organizing and feebly confessed that the ticket was the best they could do. They said it was the only choice for those opposed to the Hunnicutt forces, "the pandoras box of evil passions and proscriptions."[10]

The traditional leaders of Richmond denounced Hunnicutt as a traitor to his race, a lickspittle acolyte of northern radicals like Thaddeus Stephens, and a turncoat who incited violence between Black and white. In the last fevered weeks of campaigning, they veered between threats and supplications. They warned African Americans that if they elected the radical ticket to represent the city, they should not expect continued employment by white-owned businesses. If they persisted in supporting Hunnicutt's faction, "they should not eat our bread and drink our blood." But the same leaders also argued that the prosperity of Richmond was in everyone's interest. "Break your fetters, honest blacks," they pleaded with unintended irony in word choice, "and take your side with the conservatism, prosperity, and peace of the community." They sensed that the advantage in energy and enthusiasm lay with the radicals. They deplored the lassitude of white voters, even as they urged them to thwart their opponents.[11]

Unorganized moderate Republicans made one final, futile effort to wrest power from Hunnicutt. Four days before the polls opened, a notice circulated inviting disgruntled Republicans to gather at city hall and nominate an alternative slate to the radicals already selected. Many of these moderates were former Union soldiers who had settled in Richmond. At a mass meeting on Capitol Square the same day, Hunnicutt urged his supporters to disrupt the gathering at city hall. Amid the confusion, a former US Army major stepped up to the podium and bravely, if foolishly, denounced Hunnicutt as a traitor, demagogue, and archvillain. Black radicals, now a majority in the hall, hooted him down and forced him to withdraw.[12]

On the eve of the election, James Lyons wrote President Johnson an importunate, almost hysterical letter. Lyons was a prosperous attorney, veteran of the legislature, and a die-hard Confederate. He had been indicted for treason and pardoned by the president. At the meeting on Capitol Square two years before to proclaim the city's loyalty to the Union, Lyons had sarcastically wished Virginia rid of its African Americans. Nothing that had happened since then had convinced him to change his mind. The letter begged Johnson to thwart the looming threat of Black hegemony that Lyons feared and praised the president's "fearless and patriotic defence of the white men."[13]

The night before Lyons wrote the president, his former brother-in-law, Henry Wise, gave a two-hour address about the coming vote. It took place before a prominent audience at a horticultural exhibition, where he began with his familiar exhortations on the state's agricultural and manufacturing potential. The plantation system was irretrievably broken, he said, and he was glad of it. But now a new threat yawned before them in only a week's time—Black domination to be secured through the constitutional convention. The formerly enslaved people were deluded and misled by demagogues, he said. And now, he improbably argued, they were about to be set up as masters over white Virginians.

He then reverted to a favorite theme. The war, he said, could only be regarded as a message from God, for it was the instrument that finally removed the evils of slavery. From that conclusion, which must have been uncomfortable to his audience, he repeated his unlikely panacea of imported white labor. He bluntly told his listeners that the death of their Old South was both irrevocable and a good thing. And he urged the breakup of large estates, just as the New York colonel, William Kreutzer, did two years before to an equally dubious audience. But Wise could not take the next step of accepting a postemancipation world where African Americans were equal citizens. Instead, he could only conjure up a Hobbesian dystopia where "the leopard of hate and enmity" would be loosed among Black and white Virginians.[14]

Because this would be the first statewide election to use the ballot, no longer voting viva voce, General Schofield left nothing to chance. He directed the police to suppress disorderly conduct on polling day. He specified separate voting places for Black and white voters in jurisdictions of more than five hundred voters. Each precinct had to provide

In October 1867, Virginia voters approved a referendum to call a constitutional convention. Black men cast votes for the first time in the election. The document the subsequent convention drafted affirmed their right to vote. This engraving from the cover of the November 16, 1867, *Harper's Weekly* illustrates the historic referendum vote. (Library of Congress)

separate ballot boxes for white and Black voters. This generated controversy because it accentuated racial and class distinctions. Each man was to present himself to the polling officer, who had to be satisfied that the voter belonged to that precinct. The voter received a ticket to vote for or against the constitutional convention and one listing the names of the delegates he endorsed. Electors who chose to oppose the convention could cover their bets by voting for delegates to it if it passed.[15]

The polls were open between 7:00 a.m. and sunset on October 22. Richmond was an exception. Because of its large population, there were to be two days of voting. The police chief, John Poe, assigned four men to each polling place except city hall, where six would be stationed, ready to ring the alarm bell to call out more officers if a major disturbance broke out. General Robert Granger, the career officer who succeeded General Turner as Richmond army commander under General Schofield, prudently ordered all bars closed on voting day. He posted 1,500 troops on Capitol Square and other places. They formed a rapid reaction force to quell any disturbances. A mounted guard patrolled the city day and night.

On election day voters thronged the polls as soon as they opened. Hunnicutt's detractors warned against violence by his "noisy and turbulent bullies." In Jefferson Ward a rumor spread that a Black man named David intended to vote the conservative ticket. He ran away but was caught by an angry crowd. The police tried to rescue him, but it took cavalrymen and a squad of infantry with fixed bayonets to clear the streets. At another precinct, a Black man named Edward Kennedy admitted that he had voted for Franklin Stearns, the moderate white Republican candidate in neighboring Henrico County. The police arrested a man who threatened Kennedy, but a crowd of men and women menaced the officers, who had to be rescued by a detachment of cavalrymen. Stearns lost to a radical whose victory was assured, the press claimed, by intolerant African Americans, secret societies, and agitators from other states. James Hunnicutt's son was arrested for tearing up tickets for the conservative slate. The bars may have been closed, but a good many noisy drunks still marred the voting, and it took Schofield's soldiers to preserve order.[16]

At the end of each day, election commissioners took the ballot boxes to the Mayor's Court, where a company of soldiers guarded them. After the second day, General Schofield decided it was necessary to keep the polls open for a third day. In all, 10,063 votes were cast in Richmond, and in the end, more African Americans voted than whites. The racial disparity in turnout reflected the difference in enthusiasm statewide as well as in the capital city. Only 63 percent of eligible white men in Virginia voted, compared with 88 percent of African Americans. The establishment press attributed the low turnout to white indifference to Congress's desire to humiliate them. Northern observers thought the losers had only themselves to blame. The *Dispatch* agreed: "The work is done," it fumed, "the disgrace is inflicted." Of 105 delegates, the resounding majority were Republicans, including twenty-four African Americans. The five-man Richmond delegation, radicals all, would exert an outsized impact on the convention because they represented the capital and because of the influence of Hunnicutt and Underwood.[17]

John Gilmer, who had defeated Charles Palmer for the Richmond senate seat in 1865, immediately began a public feud with Schofield. The general's conduct of the election infuriated him. White votes had been slightly ahead on each of the two days set aside by Schofield's previously announced guidelines. But when the general added a third day, the total of Black votes edged ahead. Gilmer also accused Colonel Thomas Rose, the superintendent of elections, of gross misconduct, intimidation of voters, and incitement of Black men to commit violence. If Rose took off his uniform, Gilmer promised, he would thrash him in a fair fight. He claimed further, without evidence, that Orlando Brown had directed the Freedmen's Bureau to import Black men from surrounding rural counties to swell the vote in the city. The senator also complained to President Johnson about Brown's involvement in the election. When shown Gilmer's letter, Schofield dismissed it and its author as beneath contempt.[18]

The radicals won because of the disparity in energy between the two camps. They had the organization to bring out the African American vote. More importantly, Black Richmonders were highly motivated at their first opportunity at the ballot box. They had been agitating for the franchise almost from the moment freedom came and did not need Hunnicutt or other white radicals to remind them what they had achieved. In addition, the apathy of many whites and the intentional boycotting of the election by others led to a lower percentage who registered and a markedly lower percentage who turned out to vote.

Given the tenor of the campaign, few observers on either side were surprised at the Richmond outcome. General Schofield's provision for separate ballot boxes by race gave a quick, public way of assessing the result. Out of the more than ten thousand ballots recorded in the city, only twenty-two Black men voted for conservative candidates. The white vote offered a mirror image: a scant thirty-four whites endorsed the radical Republican ticket. In May 1865, when Governor Pierpont first came to town, he received a list of supposedly reliable unionists in Richmond. It contained only 132 names. Two and a half years later, Republican candidates for the convention could muster barely a fourth of that meager number from white voters.

Among the Virginians horrified by the outcome, few were more outraged than the two loudest proponents of the Lost Cause—Henry

Wise, with his impassioned speeches, and Edward Pollard, with his eponymous book. They agreed on little more. Pollard's publisher sent Wise a review copy of his newest book in the hope of receiving an endorsement from the former governor and Confederate general. Instead, Wise denounced Pollard's appraisal of his military career as a travesty and called the historian an insolent parasite. Pollard replied in kind that Wise's bilious critique was filled with "deceased rhetorical tumors, which have made the ex Gov. a literary stink and nuisance in the nostrils of decent men." The governor's son, John Wise, took offense and tracked Pollard down in Baltimore. Later he said he intended only to chastise the author. But words were not enough when he accosted Pollard. Both parties drew revolvers and fired. Pollard was the only one hit, with a bullet to his right elbow.[19]

While they feuded, men they loathed threatened to take power in Virginia. Reactionaries had only themselves to blame. Whether through apathy or active boycott, many of them did not register or did not vote. They thus forfeited a chance to control the convention. Black people had displayed growing political awareness almost before the ashes of April 1865 had cooled, but their votes were not counted until October 1867. With that election, a core of white radicals and their numerous African American allies took over the assembly that Congress required to write a new fundamental law for the state. While this momentous change unfolded, it was unclear which faction would triumph—the traditional power brokers who had been back in firm control of the city of Richmond and the state legislature for nearly two years or the new men who would dominate the convention. The same question unanswered in April 1865 still pertained: who would rule Virginia and its capital city? A revivified conservative movement, jolted into action by the election and unbending in opposition to equal rights or a colorblind constitution, was about to form. But it would run up against Richmond's African Americans and the expansive document they and their white radical allies meant to write.

21

Deus ex Machina

Fall 1867 to Spring 1868

Five days after the election, African Americans gathered at the capitol to hear James Hunnicutt congratulate them on the radical victory. He asked rhetorically why he had not been killed after receiving so many death threats. The answer, he said, was that the instant he died, many more white men would be killed, and he implied that would happen at the hands of his audience. He denied that he was in favor of a race war but cautioned employers who had fired their workers because of the vote. He threatened to record the bosses' names and send them to Congress. They should take their workers back; otherwise, he said, "If the whites go on as they have been doing, I don't say what will come, but I do say that something worse than has ever yet been will come." He concluded with a further threat that could not have been plainer: "There must be an entire revolution in this city."[1]

Lewis Lindsay, now delegate-elect to the convention, made similar provocative remarks at another meeting a few days later. Like Hunnicutt, he was incensed by stories of employers firing Black workers for voting the Republican ticket. He allegedly threatened that before his children would lack food, "the streets of Richmond should run knee-deep in blood." If that was not incendiary enough, he also thanked God that Black people "had learned to use guns, pistols and ram rods." The city's traditional leaders accused him of inciting insurrection. He disavowed making any such threat with an unconvincing response: "No, I did not intend to encourage any acts of violence," he replied. "I said that if the whites wanted a war of races, they could have it."[2]

Hunnicutt, who had implied the same outcome, came to Lindsay's defense but recognized that his colleague had chosen his words poorly. The more temperate African American leader John Oliver said in Lindsay's behalf that he knew how badly the newspapers perverted everything Black people said, but he hoped Lindsay would moderate his words in the future. The damage was done, however, and the police temporarily detained Lindsay for using language calculated to incite racial enmity.[3]

Two weeks later officials in Charles City County to the southeast of the city issued a warrant to arrest Hunnicutt for committing the same offense during the run-up to the election. In a speech before a mixed audience, he had allegedly encouraged Black people to burn their white neighbors' houses. He said some of them were too old and feeble to carry muskets but not too weak to start a fire. Though General Schofield disliked interfering in civil matters and despised Hunnicutt personally, he allowed him to be released from jail on bond so he could participate in the convention. These incidents involving Hunnicutt and Lindsay illustrated the volatile political climate in the city and on the eve of the convention and foretold more rancor to come.[4]

The convention first met on the morning of December 3 in the chamber of the House of Delegates. In preparation, the state redecorated the room. The floors were cleaned and rematted. Each desk received a new lock and key. Spittoons awaited being fouled by tobacco juice. Black delegates chose seats close to the speaker's chair; the minority of conservative white men claimed desks to the right of the speaker. "The line of division," an observer noticed, "was therefore distinctly drawn at the outset." African Americans crowded the galleries, so much so that the creaking of the floorboards panicked spectators below. This was a signal day for Black Virginians, and they would often return to watch the day-to-day proceedings. On days when important issued were debated, absenteeism at tobacco factories shot up. It was said that in large households employing servants, families had "to cook their own dinners, or content themselves with a cold lunch."[5]

The Virginia constitutional convention convened in December 1867 in the state capitol. Over the course of five months, the radical Republican majority crafted a revolutionary new foundational document for the state. It established equal rights for all citizens, universal manhood suffrage irrespective of race, increased power for the governor, and a system of free public schools. (*Frank Leslie's Illustrated Newspaper*)

At 10:00 a.m. the temporary chairman, James Platt, a former Union army officer who had settled in Virginia after the war, rapped the speaker's desk with his cane. He asked all who were not delegates to leave the floor so that the convention could select its officers. Among them were the lesser posts of doorkeeper and assistant. These went to William Davis and Edmund Johnson, two African Americans. These appointments were "the bone thrown to the negroes," in the dismissive words of a northerner. The most important post, that of president, went to Judge Underwood. That choice was no surprise, but it gave his enemies occasion to experience again the bile they had tasted when he came to Richmond two and a half years earlier in his attempt to confiscate their property. They had renewed their loathing for him the previous June at the Davis hearing. Now they denounced him as "a fit head-piece to a body whose controlling majority is notoriously incompetent, and as notoriously deficient in moral character."[6] The assembly and the constitution it produced would bear Underwood's name, though that designation overstated his role. That suited conservatives, who reviled equally the document and the man.

Traditional leaders of the state should have anticipated the extent of the radical victory. But they did not and fairly sleepwalked through the fall campaign for the convention. The result first stunned and then galvanized them into action. Richmond's white establishment conceded that Hunnicutt's forces had been better prepared. They warned that the next contest would be equally disastrous for them unless they organized too. By common consent, they said, it devolved on Richmond to rouse the people against the danger that menaced them. That meant, they baldly proclaimed, they must do whatever it took to perpetuate the rule of white men. To that end, barely two weeks after the October vote, a call went out from Henry Ellyson, Baptist lay leader, co-owner of the influential *Dispatch,* and now chairman of a group calling itself the executive committee of the Conservative Party in Richmond. It invited each city and county to send delegates to caucus in the capital on December 11. The goal was to organize a statewide Conservative Party to oppose the radical Republicans, who horrified them. They pledged merciless opposition: "We unfurl the standard of resistance to the wretched creatures who are soon to meet to complete the work of Africanizing Virginia."[7]

The gathering chose Thomas Randolph as its temporary chairman. To thunderous applause, this grandson of Thomas Jefferson denounced the convention of Black men and "a few renegades, [who] had ranged themselves against the white people of the State." Conservatives had no need to worry about adverse publicity: for its secretaries, it picked the editors of the leading Richmond newspapers, the *Whig, Enquirer,* and *Dispatch.*

Moses Drury Hoge, the chaplain to the Confederate Congress who had fled town on the Davis presidential train and returned a month later utterly cast down by defeat, gave the invocation. The meeting elected as its president Alexander H. H. Stuart of Staunton, brother-in-law of

John Brown Baldwin, the Speaker of the House of Delegates and uncrowned king of the General Assembly. In his remarks, Stuart echoed Randolph. The official convention, he said, subverted the natural order of things and brought "the land of Washington, Henry, Jefferson, Madison and Marshall, under the dominion of an alien and inferior race." He announced the purpose of the Conservative Party to save Virginia from disgrace.[8]

Conservatives could do nothing to prevent the convention from meeting or from producing a new foundational document for the Old Dominion. But they did hope to dilute its effect or possibly even thwart its ratification. To that end, they created a Central Committee to guide their strategy. The composition of that body showed the power of the capital city. It consisted of three consulting members from each congressional district but nine Richmonders in addition.[9]

After the convention adjourned its formal session, the delegates clamored for R. M. T. Hunter to address them. The corpulent former US senator and Confederate cabinet officer obliged. Much had changed for Hunter since summer of 1865. Then he was the jailed former Confederate secretary of state anxiously orchestrating a letter-writing campaign for pardon. He professed great affection for his Black neighbors but denounced the work of the official convention to enfranchise them. That would give African Americans control of Virginia "where the whites are superior in number, wealth, and intelligence." Rather than that, he said to great applause, he would rather continue to submit to military government.[10]

A week later, newspaper editors from across the state gathered at the Ballard House Hotel and founded the Associated Press of Virginia. Nearly every paper in the state was represented. The organization's purpose, in the words of a supporter, was "to stay the fanatical folly which would place the Old Dominion under the control of the ignorant and the vicious." It is unlikely James Hunnicutt received an invitation for the *New Nation*.[11]

From the day it convened, the official convention received abundant abuse from the Richmond papers. They warned readers not to be surprised by anything it might produce under the aegis of Underwood, who brooded over its proceedings like "a great sallow toad." The assembly's often-boisterous debates gave ample fodder for the press's taunts.[12]

The newspapers focused their animus on Black delegates, even though most radical men in the convention were white. Those they dismissed as carpetbaggers, who, they claimed, had come south after the war to despoil Virginia, and scalawags, natives of the state who supposedly did the same. The twenty-four Black delegates came from across the commonwealth, mainly from eastern and southern Virginia. Most, not surprisingly, had been free before 1865, as was the first cohort of postemancipation African American leaders in general. They developed close ties to the local Black community during their stay in the capital city. They attended Black churches and stayed in Black hotels and boardinghouses. They took part in mass political meetings. They influenced and were in turn influenced by the fervent opinions expressed by the city's outspoken radical Republicans.

Richmond's Lewis Lindsay became a favorite target for racist abuse in the press, in the North as well as the South. He had a strong voice and spoke at length, causing the *New York Times* reporter, as biased as any southern journalist, to sneer at his accent as "choicest Congo Billingsgate." General Schofield privately called Lindsay "an ignorant illiterate man, who makes fiery speeches to his class." Black delegates demanded respectful treatment but did not receive it. It outraged them to see how the press rendered their speeches in exaggerated, demeaning dialect. It was true that a few of them were illiterate, but far fewer than their enemies alleged. In response, they said it was the owners of the newspapers ridiculing them for poor grammar who were to blame. They were the ones who had robbed African Americans of a chance for education.[13]

Two incidents early in the convention's deliberations illustrated the hostility of white Richmond toward the radicals. The first concerned Jean-Antoine Houdon's white marble statue of George Washington in the capitol, where the delegates debated. Thomas Crawford's giant equestrian statue outside had been the focus of public gatherings for a decade, but Houdon's smaller, life-size likeness had stood inside the capitol even longer, ever since Washington's second term. A rumor circulated that the Houdon figure offended some of the delegates, who planned to introduce a motion to have it painted black. That, at least, was what the press claimed. It was likely just an attempt to malign African American delegates, and it showed how their opponents belittled the Black men earnestly engaged in writing equal rights into the fabric of Virginia's laws.[14]

The second incident arose from a visit to Richmond by one of the Confederacy's chief bêtes noires. No Union general raised hackles more than Benjamin Butler of Massachusetts, called "Beast" for his purported mistreatment of white southern women and "Spoons" for theft of their silverware. No man looked more villainous. With heavy jowls, drooping eyes, and censorious frown, Butler physically personified the corrupt, inept political general that he in fact was. But he also fiercely championed equal rights for African Americans, and the Black soldiers who served under him adored their commander.

His visit in January was sure to spark controversy. It appalled whites, but it gave Black people a chance to show their gratitude. At the First African Baptist Church, a rapturous crowd welcomed him, and prolonged applause greeted his vow that no one could take away their right to vote. A proposal for him to speak at the convention the following day almost disrupted it. Conservatives countered, without success, that they should be able to invite the former governor, Henry Wise, as a counterpoint. After the uproar abated and Butler arrived, his remarks turned out to be anticlimactic. But the minority of conservative delegates did not hear them because they all left the hall in protest. No incident showed them more clearly how completely their world had been turned upside down.

As the convention proceeded, fissures between Black and white radicals emerged. Led by Richmond's Lewis Lindsay, Norfolk's Thomas Bayne, and Princess Anne County's Willis Hodges, among others, militant Black delegates became increasingly independent of white radicals. They had already begun to chafe at the fact that the Republicans gave all leadership posts to white delegates. Black delegates vociferously advocated for integration in the new public schools that the convention's majority supported, but that was further than white radicals wanted to go. Outside the hall African Americans distanced themselves from their white allies at the parade marking the third anniversary of the fire and emancipation. The parade route that year went from the city across the rebuilt Mayo Bridge to Manchester. The new bridge became a flash point because it reinstated tolls, discouraging ties between the Black communities on opposite sides of the James River. Under the command of Ben Scott, colonel of the Lincoln Union Mounted Rangers, the African American marchers refused to pay the toll and, brandishing their swords, swept past the toll taker.[15]

While the convention debated, General Schofield faced the issue of how to fill city and state offices in light of the disfranchisement clause of the impending Fourteenth Amendment, which seemed headed for ratification. He suspended all elections for such posts and began to appoint men he believed were loyal to the national government. By late spring he had made five hundred appointments across the state, including Richmond city councilors, and would make more if he could find suitable candidates. Among those he had to replace was Joseph Mayo. As a very conservative Republican, the general had had little quarrel with the mayor's administration. As much was apparent from the kind personal note he sent Mayo in advance of the formal notification of dismissal.[16]

Schofield's most consequential decision came when he removed Governor Pierpont. The governor's term had ended in January 1868. The old constitution prohibited governors from succeeding themselves but implied they could continue in place until their successors were chosen. At first Schofield went along with letting Pierpont remain, a pitiful figurehead without support or respect. By April, however, Schofield believed the governor was maneuvering to get reelected, despite the constitutional ban. In his place, Schofield appointed a former Union general, Henry Wells, who had played a role in interrogating suspects in the Lincoln assassination conspiracy.

There was nothing the incensed Pierpont could do. Radical Republicans had long since lost faith in him. Hunnicutt personally reviled him. The white establishment neither accepted him nor forgave him for separating the western third of the state from Virginia during the war. He appealed in vain to Grant, accusing Schofield of acting in bad faith. The Richmond press delighted in paraphrasing the gospel of Matthew: "Thus has perished by the sword the official whom the sword inaugurated." Pierpont, normally unruffled but now boiling with rage, denounced opponents right and left, including Judge Underwood, the Freedmen's Bureau's Orlando Brown, and Richmond's white leaders, especially General Schofield. That Pierpont still maintained a house in Fairmont, West Virginia, was added proof to ungrateful eastern Virginians, if they needed any. To them, he was not a true native son, merely an ineffectual carpetbagger beneath their contempt and deserving of oblivion. He could do nothing but return to Fairmont, scorned on all sides and unthanked for his considerable role in reviving a devastated city and state after four years of internecine warfare.[17]

The draft constitution that emerged from the convention in April 1868 formally ratified the outcome of the war and altered Virginia government top to bottom. Few people were surprised at its main features, but together they demonstrated how utterly the landscape had changed. In addition to repudiating secession and its fruits, it accepted the supremacy of the US Constitution and the laws of Congress. It established equal rights under the law for all citizens, instituted universal manhood suffrage, increased the power of the governor, created a more democratic form for local government, decreed a system of free public schools, and outlawed discrimination in jury selection.[18]

Not all of the progressive ideas proposed made it into the final draft. African American delegates wanted the new schools to be integrated. They argued for it forcefully but failed to convince their white radical allies. Judge Underwood showed he was ahead of his time when he spoke out for votes for women on the floor of the convention. Though advocates for women's rights had been making their case since before the war, they had made little headway in Virginia. Two years before, John Brown Baldwin, the powerful Speaker of the House of Delegates, had reacted with horror when asked by the joint congressional committee about enfranchising Black men. Doing so, he said, would lead to an even worse innovation in the form of votes for women. Conservatives who shared Baldwin's views were a distinct minority in the convention, but most white radical delegates were no more in favor of votes for women than Baldwin. Nor were Black delegates.[19]

Some white Virginians later quietly admitted that some of the changes included in the draft constitution were positive. But they stridently denounced the clauses that, in their eyes, negated whatever good came from the rest of the document. Because it included an ironclad oath that excluded any man who had supported secession or the Confederacy, the constitution would disfranchise most white males. The Republicans feared they could never control the state without these provisions because Virginia was majority white. That majority knew disfranchisement would bar its return to power. It denounced the "negro and scallawag farce of a convention" that produced the document and vowed that it only made more certain the coming vindication of white rule.[20]

On April 17, 1868, three years after the funeral pyre of Confederate Richmond, General Schofield left his headquarters at Tenth and Marshall Streets and walked to the House of Delegates to speak to the convention. He wore a civilian suit, but his commanding presence and the three colonels from his staff who accompanied him let the delegates know he was the ultimate authority in the city and the state, whether he wore epaulettes or not. The convention had just concluded its work and adopted the constitution it had been crafting over the past five months. He considered parts of the draft objectionable and had said as much to delegates who had earlier informally queried him. But this was the first and only time he felt the need to express himself in person to the whole assembly.[21]

The disfranchisement clauses going beyond what Congress required were what most troubled him. He believed these provisions resulted from the same pernicious attitude that had elected "a majority of ignorant Blacks and equally ignorant or unprincipled whites to the convention." Those were the words he used in a private report to General Grant, but of course he did not put it to the assembly quite that way. In diplomatic but firm language, he urged the convention to remove the most obnoxious clause, the one requiring officeholders to take an ironclad oath that they had never supported the Confederacy. He told delegates that test would make it hard to fill the many posts of local government. There simply would not be enough qualified candidates for magistrate, sheriff, constable, and many other civil offices. Privately, he said the radicals in the convention could not hope to gain office except by disqualifying competent candidates.[22]

The delegates heard Schofield out in polite, stony silence (he called it "cold respect") and then ignored his advice. They refused to eliminate the provisions in the constitution that offended him. Not to be denied, the general asserted his authority as ruler of Military District Number One and refused to schedule a ratifying election. If they would not do his bidding, he would invoke the deux ex machina that was his to command and arbitrarily thwart their objective. As a rationale, he cited the state's lack of money and the failure of Congress to appropriate any. That was true enough as far as it went. Congress could have resolved the impasse by appropriating funds, but it had its own problems as the impeachment of President Johnson overshadowed all other concerns that spring. Schofield had no intention of letting the constitution go to a vote. He thought, incongruously, that it would result in a state government dominated by "worthless radicals, white and black" and by reactionary white opponents of congressional Reconstruction. Better, then, to let the draft molder on the shelf. His action, as nothing had done more forcefully before, showed the pronounced divide between military and civilian authority in postwar Richmond.[23]

Without the ratification referendum, the Republican and Conservative Parties had to shelve plans for electing a new governor and General Assembly that summer. And that meant the state could not proceed with the steps Congress demanded. With no new constitution, Virginia could not elect state or local officials. It could not call a new legislature to approve the Fourteenth and Fifteenth Amendments. It could not participate in voting in the 1868 presidential election. Virginians watched as other former Confederate states ratified new constitutions and once again sent congressmen and senators to Washington. The Old Dominion's status remained in agonizing uncertainty, where it had languished for the past three years.[24]

22

Left Undone

Summer 1868 to Summer 1869

The cityscape had slowly changed in the three years since Peter Michie and his surveyors began to limn their ambitious map amid the smoking rubble. The tall, thin spires of churches in the city center that survived the fire still punctuated the skyline. Thomas Crawford's bronze Washington still towered over Capitol Square. But newer and taller buildings had begun to fill the empty blocks below it. If the physical and commercial appearance of the city had changed, even more so had its social fabric. The statue had become the focus of civic events ever since its completion just before the war. Since then, it witnessed tumultuous gatherings by citizens who had previously been excluded. From Lincoln's impromptu speech to them the day after the fire, to the anniversary celebration a year later, to the mass rallies that followed, the statue became the epicenter of political and social upheaval in Virginia's capital city.

While politicians puzzled over how to move forward from the stalled vote on the constitution, everyday life in the city continued in its mundane course. After more than a year of increasingly rancorous political activity, public demonstrations, and even civic unrest, the summer of 1868 passed in comparative quiet. Joseph Mayo unsuccessfully lobbied President Johnson to reinstate him as mayor. Mayo's successor, George Chahoon, a twenty-eight-year-old Republican appointed by General Schofield, raised hackles by replacing Confederate veterans on the police force and in city government. The unfortunates who appeared before his Mayor's Court may have had less to fear from

Within three years, Black and white Richmonders had largely rebuilt the Burnt District. In this photograph from the 1870s, Thomas Jefferson's neoclassical state capitol still looms over the new business district that arose between it and the river below. (Wikimedia Commons)

him than from Mayo, but Chahoon, like his predecessor, regularly sentenced Black men to weeks on the chain gang for petty theft. The city council continued to wrangle over how little money to devote to poor relief. The press continued to shun the Fourth of July as a celebration fit only for the US Army and Black people. The rhythms of city life continued much as before. African American men employed their singsong chants to dispel the tedium of stemming and pressing tobacco in rebuilt factories along the river. The clangor and smoke rising from the Tredegar Iron Works testified to the city's restored heavy industry. Black and white Richmonders went to work, school, and church much as before, raising their families and vying for work in the gradually expanding city.[1]

Anyone looking down from Capitol Square could see the Burnt District being progressively erased. Rebuilding, however, did not follow a straight line. The United Presbyterian Church had been the only house of worship to succumb to fire in 1865. Three years later the congregation was still trying to raise money to pay for its unfinished new building. Economic recovery did not mean prosperity was evenly distributed. Railroads quickly rebuilt their war-ravaged lines, and Richmond soon boasted more freight tonnage than many northern cities. But waterborne traffic could not claim a similar resurgence, as coastal ports gradually outstripped fall-line cities like Richmond. The three biggest industries—iron, flour, and tobacco—remained along the river after they rebuilt from the fire. Of these, only the iron industry exceeded its prewar level, a sign that the Virginia capital was beginning to fall behind other southern cities. Even so, as the decade ended, optimism for the city's prosperity was on the rise. The expanse of new buildings in the heart of Richmond was a source of immense pride for its residents.[2]

Thanks to the influx of mainly Black rural Virginians, the population grew after the war, even allowing for the doubling of the city's area by annexation at the time of the constitutional convention. The horse-drawn streetcar system expanded to reach the western suburbs in 1869. It remained too expensive for the mass of laborers, who continued to live close to their work in the lower parts of the city near the canal and river. Within the expanded city limits, newer residential districts along Franklin and Grace Streets began to attract wealthier Richmonders, who gradually receded westward from their earlier concentration north of Capitol Square. The distribution of the races changed too. Before the war, they resided close to one another throughout the city. Afterward, segregated private housing increasingly followed the separation of Black and white people in public spaces.[3]

General Schofield's action to thwart a vote on the constitution frustrated the wishes of the radical majority in the convention. It halted Virginia's movement toward resuming a normal relationship within the Union. It meant no election of local and state government officials, no new General Assembly to elect judges or to revise laws. Thoughtful observers knew this stasis could not last. It only postponed resolution of the uncertainty that hung over politics. It denied African Americans their promised rights. It was bad for business.[4]

In December, Alexander H. H. Stuart, father of the Conservative Party, sought to break the logjam. He proposed a compromise based on a simple formula: universal suffrage and universal amnesty. It called for detaching the disfranchisement clauses from the draft constitution.

That would give the electorate the chance to vote the charter up or down and then separately decide whether former Confederates could vote or hold office. If, as most people expected, the constitution passed but the disfranchisement clauses failed, each side would gain half a loaf. African Americans would receive their most heartfelt desire of equal participation in the state's political life—but at the cost of restoring political rights to former Confederates. They, in turn, would regain the right to vote and stand for office—but at the cost of granting Black suffrage, the one thing traditionalists had sworn to prevent.

Reactionaries objected to this bargain. (Henry Wise said Virginians should "take death rather than dishonor.") Their boycott of the referendum in 1867 had allowed their opponents to dominate the constitutional convention. Now their opposition to the compromise offered the same do-nothing strategy and no solution to the impasse. More pragmatic conservatives recognized they had to come to terms with the dominant Republicans in Congress. These allies of Stuart came together with moderate, mostly white, Republicans led by Richmond distiller Franklin Stearns to move the state beyond the roadblock thrown up by General Schofield. A committee led by Stuart lobbied Andrew Johnson—impeached but not convicted and now the lamest of ducks—and President-elect Grant for their endorsements. The moderate Stearns group may have been even more persuasive in Washington than Stuart's committee. But together they were heard. Johnson, Grant, and congressional leaders all accepted the compromise formula. Once installed in the White House in March 1869, Grant announced that the vote on the Virginia constitution would go forward that summer, with a separate ballot on the disfranchisement clauses. On the same day, Virginians would elect a new General Assembly and governor.[5]

A kaleidoscope of personalities watched as their city rose from the ashes. Their collective hopes and disappointments, fears and achievements underlay the physical rebuilding. The burden of defeat and the promise of freedom gave definition to the lives of Richmond's people in the first years after the war.

Fields Cook witnessed those pivotal events as he worked to build the postwar African American community. He had moved to Richmond before the war, bought his freedom, and fashioned a leading role as both minister and political leader. Barely two months after emancipation, he stood before President Johnson in the White House to protest mistreatment of Black men and women. He prayed for a time when Black and white children would grow up together in harmony. Tireless, energetic, and hopeful, for five years Cook seemed to be everywhere making speeches for equal rights, for the Republican Party, for his Baptist faith. Though not formally educated, he later sat on the board of managers of the National Theological Institute and University in Washington, DC. For a time he served as cashier of the Freedmen's Bank and ran unsuccessfully as an independent candidate for Congress.

Cook urged Black people to work with moderate white Republicans, but the radical faction rejected him. After the 1867 referendum, he condemned the radical delegate Lewis Lindsay for provocative remarks that stoked racial animosity. After the convention drafted the new constitution, he continued to argue against confiscation of Confederates' property. He knew that because African Americans were in a minority in the state, they would need some white support to reach a majority. He sensed that the attempt to achieve it artificially by proscribing all Confederates or seizing their property would backfire. But Cook's moderate approach to politics, like that of other more cautious Black ministers, was in eclipse. For unknown reasons, after making his home in Richmond for more than two decades, Cook left town for a pastorate in northern Virginia.

Cook's sometime antagonist Lewis Lindsay was also born enslaved in rural Virginia and moved to Richmond early in life. Similarities between the two men ended there. Lindsay did not share Cook's upbeat attitude or his emollient personality or interest in compromise. On the contrary, he favored an unflinchingly combative style. His "knee-deep in blood" speech after being elected to the constitutional convention cemented his radical reputation. The white press, always eager to exploit divisions in the Black community, approvingly quoted another African American who called Lindsay ignorant and not at all representative of respectable Black Richmonders. Such talk did not faze Lindsay, nor did the newspapers' habit of presenting his remarks in exaggerated dialect to demean him. With a voice like a trumpet, he consistently argued during the convention debates, and after, for expropriating Confederates' land and denying them the vote. Unlike Cook, he remained in Richmond the rest of his life, continuing to participate in Republican politics for decades after the convention.

A man without a country, Commander Matthew Fontaine Maury abandoned his hapless Mexican project and forsook it for England in 1866. It had disheartened him when nearly all of his large family rejected his dream of starting over in a new land, bringing to it the economic system that underpinned the Old South. Few other Confederates answered his call, and he reciprocated their rejection, calling them "humble pie-eaters." At the beginning of the war, he was clean-shaven with rapidly thinning hair; after Mexico he was nearly bald, with a snow-white beard. When he arrived in London, bowed down by disillusionment and failure, his youngest children did not recognize him. He returned to Richmond in 1868 after the general amnesty but did not remain long. A spark of the old questing scientific spirit revived for him after he accepted the chair of meteorology at the Virginia Military Institute in Lexington. It was a modest niche for the internationally acclaimed oceanographer, but it gave him renewed purpose in his declining years, albeit in a narrower scope than his expansive, improbable dream of New Virginia below the Rio Grande.[6]

Governor Francis Pierpont's removal by General Schofield in April 1868 presaged the waning influence of his old antagonist, James Hunnicutt. The preacher-editor's actions during the secession crisis came back to haunt him during the constitutional convention's debates. A decline in support from African Americans outside his loyal base in the capital and his failed attempt to become Pierpont's successor signaled his eclipse. For two years he had blazed an incendiary arc across Richmond, energizing African Americans and horrifying the white establishment. Now, just as swiftly, came his demise. He managed to annoy nearly everyone. Snubbed by his former radical allies, the firebrand chameleon changed his colors yet again. He joined the Republican Party's moderate wing and ran for Congress, but all he accomplished was to garner the ironic endorsement of former enemies in the Richmond press and defeat at the polls.

William Harris, pastor of the Third Street African Methodist Episcopal Church, had arrived from Cleveland, Ohio, in the autumn of 1865. He took an immediate interest in expanding the church's role in educating freedmen, including establishing a night school for adults. He lent his talents to Black political organization and worried about white opposition to the 1866 anniversary parade and about secessionist resurgence after the first Confederate Memorial Day.

Later that year, political differences embroiled him in a personal dispute with Lomax Smith, one of the few but vocal conservative Black men of Richmond. Smith had Harris brought up before the Mayor's Court for the attempted abduction of his daughter, Eliza. Because of Harris's prominence in educating African Americans and even more because of his political work, the press found the sensational aspect of the case a useful tool to discredit him. The controversy blew over quickly, however. It turned out to be a contretemps generated by misinterpretation and mistaken identity started when Eliza imprudently became engaged to two young men at the same time. Once the facts were known, Lomax Smith printed a profuse and complete apology to the clergyman for maligning his good name, and Harris returned to educating and preaching.

In the following spring the Virginia conference of the African Methodist Episcopal Church held its annual meeting. Harris gave an upbeat report as presiding elder of the Richmond district, and the white press reported on the meeting in positive terms. But it could not resist telling its readers approvingly that, contra the nexus of church, schooling, and politics that Harris championed, the visiting bishop's sermon hewed strictly to religion. Harris left Richmond in 1867. But after years of often trying labor, he never lost his sense of exhilaration over teaching the newly emancipated.[7]

After the war Susan Hoge resumed her role of minister's wife. A diminutive figure, she brought energy and common sense to her partnership with Moses Drury Hoge. Together they had built Second Presbyterian into one of the largest congregations of the prewar city and one of the most devoted to the southern cause. No doubt theirs was one of the churches on Judge Underwood's mind when he denounced Richmond's fashionable pulpits as corrupt and prostituted. When Moses fled the city with Jefferson Davis, Susan saved their rambling parsonage at Fifth and Main Streets from burning. Like many Confederates, she bought into the myth of the disappearing freedmen. She thought African Americans were dying by the hundreds all over the South and concluded with a hard heart that it was a mystery of Providence.

Her stolid personality and head for business kept their household afloat, even though the church could pay Moses only a quarter of his prewar salary. She had little money and was grateful for gifts from friends in Baltimore and New York. While her disconsolate husband mourned the South's defeat, they both grieved over the death of another child just weeks after Appomattox. Trying to comfort a friend with a similar loss, she said she now had four children "laid side by side" at Hollywood Cemetery. Moses's eventual recovery was due in no small part to her support, but that did not last long. She died three years later, only forty-eight, after months of prostration and agony. Moses continued in his long pastorate at Second Presbyterian, but time dragged slowly for him. He confessed that in his loneliness he no longer felt alive after Susan died.[8]

In the dispiriting times that overtook the first hopeful days after the fire, Elizabeth Van Lew unburdened herself in long, importunate letters to northern friends. With great slashing pen strokes, she wrote about money troubles, about slights from neighbors, about the seeming abandonment of the now brokenhearted unionists. In partial compensation, she knew she had earned the affection of African Americans because of her support for their rights. As much was apparent in October 1867, on the day before voting began for the constitutional convention, when members of a Black militia unit assembled in front of her house. They had come to receive the loan of a special flag the Union army had given her. They thanked her and called her the Goddess of Liberty.

Two years later, her most powerful friend appointed her postmaster. It was one of Grant's first acts when he became president, and it outraged the city's traditional power brokers. The appointment, with its ample salary and wide patronage network, temporarily allayed her financial woes. Following the announcement, however, details of her wartime spying surfaced, increasing the scorn of former Confederates. To most of them, Van Lew remained the city's chief pariah, a lonely woman beneath their contempt, brooding in her Church Hill mansion that looked down on the city from the east.

Her neighbors would not forget or forgive her contribution to southern defeat, no matter how much they might credit her efficient running of the post office. When her mother died, she claimed she did not have enough white friends to serve as pallbearers. A Church Hill neighbor, the celebrated novelist Ellen Glasgow, recalled years later how as a child she caught a glimpse of this frail, white-haired old woman so thoroughly demonized. Glasgow wondered how such a wizened figure could have perpetrated the horrors attributed to her by Confederates. Van Lew never published her book.[9]

Joseph Reid Anderson fairly danced through the aftermath of war. He had met Lincoln on his visit to the city and laid claim to a leading role in rebuilding it. On all sides, people supported his quest for a pardon. Even some African Americans endorsed his effort. The drive and energy that suffused his prewar career continued undiminished afterward. Back in command of his company, he met the challenge of anemic funding by dissolving the Tredegar partnership and forming a joint stock company in 1867. With that more modern business model, he attracted enough capital to expand from northern businessmen, conservative

Republicans who, like him, gave strong support to Andrew Johnson. In his later years, Anderson looked the part he had created for himself, a supremely confident, silver-haired captain of industry. His reincarnated Tredegar Company enjoyed a long stretch of growth and profitability. Its chief entrepreneur continued to be the most notable Richmond business leader, a founding member of the exclusive Richmond German, vestryman at St. Paul's Episcopal Church, member of the House of Delegates, and president of the Chamber of Commerce. Important as these signifiers were in attesting to his prominence, nothing could increase his esteem more in the eyes of white Richmonders than his achievements as cannon maker for the Confederacy.

Mary Lumpkin returned to Richmond in April 1865. Since before the war, she had lived in the North with her children by the notorious slave trader Robert Lumpkin. He had enslaved her decades before and kept her in his slave pen, a two-story brick building with surrounding compound, in the Shockoe Bottom district where she worked for him and bore his children. Theirs had been a fraught relationship, carried out in the unequal tension between enslaver and enslaved, accentuated by the fact that she was twenty-seven years his junior. He bought her a house in Philadelphia and paid for their children's education with the proceeds from his repugnant profession. For whatever reason—she left no record—she returned to him after the war. She likely resumed keeping house for Robert and helped him run the hotel business that he hoped would replace the income lost from the death of the slave trade. When he died, he left everything in his diminished estate to Mary, though he never called her wife. In an ironic coda to her story, in 1867 she rented out the former Lumpkin slave jail to the Richmond Theological School for Freedmen.[10]

After his feuds with fellow journalists and the contretemps over insults to local army commanders, Henry Rives Pollard spiraled ever-further out of control. With a long, flowing beard and piratical squint, he grew more truculent as time went by. Morbidly sensitive to slights and increasingly eager to escalate verbal spats into violence, he alienated even staunch Confederates. In summer 1867, he brawled with his brother's in-laws over a perceived slight that ended up airing his sordid private affairs in print. Later he got into a scrap with a woman at a house the press smugly labeled "notoriously public." A month later, in a second dispute over the same woman, he shot and wounded another man. At the end of the year, he founded a new weekly and pledged that its columns would be entirely Confederate in outlook. *Southern Opinion* retailed thinly veiled personal attacks and staggeringly hateful racial taunts mixed with Old South romanticism. In November 1868, Pollard's penchant for insult and mayhem finally caught up with him in the shape of James Grant, the hot-tempered scion of a rich tobacco manufacturer. Grant believed Pollard had impugned his sister's honor, but no duel ensued. Perhaps he did not think Pollard was a gentleman worthy of an affair of honor. Instead, in cold blood he shot dead the angry exponent of Confederate virtue in front of his scandal sheet's office at the corner of Fourteenth and Main Streets. Pollard was thirty-five.[11]

Of all the outliers in Civil War–era Richmond, none was odder than Henry Alexander Wise. A bundle of contradictions, he alternately perplexed, offended, and charmed his contemporaries. The charismatic revolutionary who lit the bonfire of 1861 and rejoiced in the death of slavery could not abide giving votes to freedmen. Enfranchising the formerly enslaved, he said, would dishonor the memory of the glorious Confederate dead. The war had cost him his favorite son, his estate, and his fortune. He called Jefferson Davis a weak bigot. His restless fidelity to his standards, even at great personal cost, won him postwar admiration from such unlikely figures as Judge Underwood and James Hunnicutt.

Wise unsurprisingly denounced the grand compromise to bring Virginia back into alignment with the Union. He despised the new Conservatives who created it, just as he scorned the old gentry, who could no longer afford indolence. "No more lazy morning hours!" He scolded them, "No more cigars and juleps! No more card parties and club idleness!" When he pushed the 1861 convention to secede, observers said his wild hair looked like it was charged with electricity and his face shone like bronze. Now age and war had hardened that predatory appearance. Sickness had bleached his pale skin and etched his face with deep lines. Eccentric to the point of caricature, he spoke often of the Lost Cause, his lodestar. Above all, he obsessed about John Brown and told anyone who would listen how noble the abolitionist hero had been to reject clemency and die for the cause he championed. Like Brown, he would choose death over disgrace. He never did seek a pardon. Later he even improbably sided with the hated Republicans in a dispute over the Richmond mayoralty. It was said that when he died eleven years after Appomattox, no death save Lee's elicited a greater outpouring of respect and even love in the capital city.[12]

As much as any resident, Gustavus Myers endured the turbulent 1860s with equanimity. He had helped build the leading city of the antebellum Upper South as an enterprising lawyer, company director, and proponent of cultural enrichment. One of Richmond's pioneering Jewish leaders, he sat on the city council for more than three decades, twelve years as president. After secession, he supported Confederate Richmond at war. He met Lincoln on the president's surprise visit and argued for lenient treatment of his city.

It was in his person, however, more than in any civic attainment, that Myers most intimately embodied the complex legacy bequeathed by the peculiar institution. That was so for a poignant reason: that biracial youth who raised the first American flag over the state capitol as the fires burned their hottest on the morning of April 3, 1865, was his grandson.

Myers, like slave traders Bacon Tait and Robert Lumpkin and like so many white men in the antebellum South, had formed a relationship with a free woman of color, in his case with Nelly Forrester. That union produced a son, and they named him Richard Gustavus Forrester. He was openly recognized by the family and raised by Myers's two unmarried great-aunts, who left Richard a generous bequest. His father sent him to Canada for schooling, where he married Narcissa Wilson, also the child of Black and white parents. The couple returned to Richmond and had a son they named Richard Gill Forrester. At thirteen, young Richard became a messenger with the Virginia legislature, likely through the efforts of his grandfather, who then sat in the House of Delegates. Richard's duties included raising and lowering the Virginia and American flags over the capitol. When secessionists discarded the Stars and Stripes in 1861, he hid the flag under his bed. Four years later, he retrieved it and raised it once again over the state capitol while the business district burned below.

Three decades before the war, Myers had married Ann Augusta Conway, a widow and the daughter of Governor William Branch Giles. After a long illness, she died in 1867; Gustavus followed two years later. William Barksdale Myers, his son by Ann Augusta, followed his father into the law, served in the Confederate army, became a portrait painter, and designed the iron fence surrounding the section for Confederate soldiers buried in Richmond's Hebrew Cemetery. Richard Gustavus Forrester, Myers's first son by Nelly Forrester, also followed in his father's footsteps. In May 1865 he was a founding officer of the Colored Men's Equal Rights League of Richmond. He was the first man of color elected to the city council and served on the school board. He was a marshal for the 1870 parade celebrating ratification of the Fifteenth Amendment giving men the vote irrespective of race. That was in the hopeful time when African Americans voted, a time before the shadows lengthened as practice and then law relentlessly fixed segregation and caste on the South.[13]

These two half brothers, born sixteen years apart, were the joint heirs of the Richmond that arose from the death of slavery and the ashes of war. They were both legatees of the unequal society that followed and was in turn bequeathed to succeeding generations one day to overcome.

John Oliver came to the city from Boston two months after the fire to see how his fellow African Americans were building a new life after slavery. Soon after he arrived, he suffered verbal abuse at the hands of Mayor Joseph Mayo's city police and US soldiers. He was active in the effort to take Black grievances all the way to the White House. At the

1866 anniversary celebration of the Emancipation Proclamation, he pleaded, "We want justice, and to be protected by the same laws that govern the white man." For twenty months he advocated for African Americans in the Freedmen's Bureau court. He sat in the jury pool for the Jefferson Davis trial that never happened. He was a delegate to the Republican state convention. Radicals accused him of disloyalty for supporting the moderate Botts wing of the party. He escorted Ben Butler to the podium when that Union general, more loathed by white Richmond than any other, spoke at First African Baptist Church. With Peter Randolph, Oliver founded an African American Masonic lodge. He was the only Black man to receive a post with the city during Reconstruction, and that was the lowly position of messenger to the city council in 1868. He won election to the city's common council four years later and established the Moore Street Industrial Institution to teach Black children vocational skills.[14]

After two years in Richmond, Oliver wrote a public reflection on what had happened during the first season of freedom. It was tinged with sadness over missed opportunities, over real lost causes. "I wish I could not see a disposition in the white people of Virginia," he wrote in a moving lament, "which makes them appear as though they had nothing but hate and wrath for those who were once their slaves." Still, despite that regretful assessment and all the evidence that underpinned it, he hoped there might yet be a chance that one day his white neighbors in the former Confederate capital would come to treat African Americans with "kindness and not abuse."[15]

Epilogue

On Memorial Day 1869 businesses once again suspended operation. Thousands of white Richmonders converged on the city's premier Confederate necropolis. During the previous week organizers at Hollywood Cemetery asked everyone who lived within a hundred miles to send floral tributes in advance. Railroads, canal packet boats, and the Southern Express Company stood ready to transport them free of charge. Over the past few years, the loving attention of the memorial association had gradually replaced the forlorn wartime aspect of the soldiers' section with orderly rows of stone. Granite markers now identified each sector, and a cedar stake topped by a tinned-copper number plate graced every grave. Ornamental trees and shrubs had begun to fill the barren earth of earlier years. The stretches of bare hillside that remained drew special attention from the mourners on this day. Before it ended, they had decorated all of the soldiers' graves with flowers and greenery.

Rising above mourners and graves, the uncompleted granite pyramid bore the inscription "To the Confederate Dead." When finished, it towered ninety feet over the cemetery. In the words of its builders, it would teach unborn generations about "the heroic deeds of those who died in the Confederate war for independence." The white women of Richmond took it as their sacred duty to remember those who defended that cause. The sorrow the bereaved felt was palpable and deep. By stressing only the courage and sacrifice of their soldiers, however, they elided the issue that had caused the war. Their remembrance of the conflict and its meaning ignored the emancipationist perspective of Black Richmond. That outlook, held just as deeply, had developed in parallel to white commemoration and in distinction from it.[1]

As in previous years, the press covered Memorial Day with words of reverence. The *Dispatch* printed a large conjectural engraving of the finished pyramid and juxtaposed next to it another article reminding readers of their other duty, the one to the living. It listed the categories of citizens who were disqualified from voting in the election scheduled to take place in a month's time. More to the point, the article spelled out who was entitled to vote. The message was clear: all white men who could vote owed it to their community to do so.

At that election on July 6, 1869, by a large margin voters approved the new constitution written by Hunnicutt's and Underwood's Black and white radical Republicans. The state's basic law now guaranteed universal male suffrage, the goal that African Americans had longed for and struggled to achieve since the first uncertain days of freedom. At the same time, voters rejected disfranchising men who had served the Confederacy. Here was the half loaf for each side that the grand bargain promised. But there was no balance in the outcome. When the votes were counted, conservatives controlled power at all levels—the state legislature, the governor's mansion, and the delegation that Virginia once again sent to Congress.

The Old Dominion was the last Confederate state to send representatives to Congress after the war. But it was the only one to emerge from postwar limbo never having been ruled by radical Republicans. Those radicals did dominate the political scene in Richmond in 1867–68, thanks to James Hunnicutt's outspoken leadership and even more to the energized Black electorate. And they did craft a forward-looking constitution for the state. But very few Black or white radicals ever served on the city council, either during that fevered time or later.

Four years had passed since the great fire engulfed Richmond's commercial center. On that day, burning bridges collapsed into the James River with great hissing splashes, and flames raced up to lick at the green of Capitol Square in an incendiary finale to the failed attempt to secede from the Union. In the first months that followed, white residents lived in fear of expropriation, imprisonment, or worse. Black residents lived in doubt that emancipation could endure and feared that it might even lead to a bleak fate more akin to slavery than freedom.

In those four years Richmond changed beyond all recognition, and not merely or mainly in its physical aspect. By their actions, secessionists had wrought what they most feared—defeat, emancipation, the total upending of the traditional social order. At last, in 1869, the expanded electorate approved a new foundational document to guide the state forward, but the demons unleased by racial animosity boded ill for that future. An uneven, seesaw chronology ensued in which white politicians alternately appealed to and intimidated African American voters. For the rest of the century, Virginia's story was one of dueling visions of the future, between the cramped ideal of white domination and the hope of genuine equality for all Virginians. Richmond was the cockpit of that struggle, a contest that produced a progressively more segregated society as the years passed.

The road to that future, however, followed an uncertain path. In 1869 the route it would take was not yet determined. It was still possible to imagine a more expansive future. Indeed, a decade later, railroad magnate and former Confederate general William Mahone, whose men had butchered Black soldiers at the Battle of the Crater, briefly led an insurgent force of African American and white voters. It temporarily wrested political power in the state from the conservative establishment. That came later. Already in the first few years after the war missed opportunities abounded. In 1867 James Hunnicutt rejected the chance to work with moderate white Republicans in the run-up to the constitutional referendum. He chose instead to stress ideological purity, by mobilizing the Black electorate and preventing former Confederates from voting. That strategy worked temporarily for Richmond. But even in their stronghold in the capital, radicals never captured city hall. They failed to make common cause with moderate Republicans again in 1869. This time failure had greater consequences. Those moderates instead joined with pragmatic conservatives to defeat the radicals up and down the ballot.

The conservative victory in 1869 restored the traditional establishment in the city and the state, but it did not undo the enormous strides

African Americans had made over their past circumstances. They no longer needed to fear the auction block. They built a thriving parallel community of churches, schools, and social organizations. Above all, they controlled their own lives, no longer subject to the whims of enslavers. And now they had the vote and the right to run for office. Though a minority, twenty-nine African Americans served in the new General Assembly.[2]

Ten months after the Confederacy's defeat, a slender ribbon of smoke suddenly rose from the piles of blackened bricks where the *Richmond Dispatch*'s former building stood. It likely came from a buried coal bin that had been slowly smoldering until air somehow reached it and allowed the flame to blaze anew. The editors warned northern papers not to take this as a sign of "the Fires of Secession Still Burning." Rather, they said, it signified the revival of the *Dispatch,* the recuperative power of Virginia, and the indestructability of the press. But were they really concerned that outside observers might choose to ascribe that more sinister symbolism to the incident? The failing of Richmond's former Confederates was that their idealized self-image, as southerners and as Americans, was too constricted to imagine their neighbors of African descent as equals. The fires of racial discord, if not of Richmond's business district, still burned.[3]

ACKNOWLEDGMENTS

When I finished *Richmond Burning* more than two decades ago, I knew there were loose ends the book did not address because its tight time frame extended only a few days beyond the great fire. What was the state of affairs after the city center burned, slavery ended, and Abraham Lincoln walked through the smoking ruins? How did residents begin to put their lives back together? What kind of government followed Confederate defeat? How would emancipation and citizenship be defined? *After the Fire* attempts to answer those and other questions.

To begin to do so required examination of many collections of unpublished papers and many books and articles written by firsthand witnesses and later by those who have studied the Civil War and its aftermath. The range of sources, both primary and secondary, is daunting. Since *Richmond Burning,* many more have been digitized and are available online, some even in searchable form. But the unpublished sources that still need to be consulted in the flesh remain in the majority. My debt to the custodians of those sources, the librarians and archivists who collect and preserve the evidence of our individual and collective past, is accordingly immense.

Among the most important the repositories I relied on were the Library of Virginia, the Valentine Museum, the National Archives and Records Administration, and the Library of Congress. I want to express my gratitude to their staffs for thoughtful, professional, and courteous help. The most important archival source was the Virginia Museum of History and Culture (VMHC), formerly the Virginia Historical Society, where I worked for thirty years. I am so grateful to the VMHC's wonderful professionals, some of whom were colleagues from my time there and some who joined the staff more recently. I salute them all. They have been invariably helpful, kind, and professional, especially Cathy Boe, Jamie Bosket, James Brooks, Graham T. Dozier, Andrew Foster, Matthew E. Guillen, John McClure, L. Paige Newman, Eileen Parrish, Laura Stoner, Andrew Talkov, Chris Van Tassell, and Kate Weis.

Many other colleagues have assisted my research in a variety of ways, including Stephen V. Ash, Gussie Bannard, Cliff Dickinson, Stephen Engle, Mike Gorman, Michael Hoberman, Caroline Janney, Michelle Krowl, Jack McElroy, Keith Stokes, Sandra Treadway, Liz Varon, Minor Weisiger, Carol Wittig.

My special thanks go to those who took valuable time from their own busy lives to read earlier versions of the manuscript, in whole or in part. I am proud to call them friends and to name them here: Terry Alford, Ed Ayers, Mike Chesson, Brad Davenport, Harvey Lankford, Randall Miller, Jeff Schapiro, Dale Sorenson, and Brent Tarter. The final product is vastly improved because of their advice. I hope they agree. Any errors that remain—things done and left undone—are my own.

At the University of Virginia Press, my editors Nadine Zimmerli, Andy Edwards, and Clayton Butler expertly shepherded the book through the production process, and I thank them for their talent, advice, perseverance, and good humor. The Press's outside readers made numerous suggestions for improvement. Even when I did not agree, their comments enabled me to sharpen my argument, for which I am also grateful. I thank Susan Murray very much for giving the manuscript her expert copyeditor's treatment, leaving it much improved. And I thank David Robertson for an index that gives readers access to the myriad topics and individuals who populate these pages.

The initial—and ongoing—inspiration for this book came from my partner in life's journey, Betsy Stevenson. She suggested the kernel of the idea behind *After the Fire.* It would not exist without her, and I dedicate the book to her.

NOTES

ABBREVIATIONS

CR	*Christian Recorder,* Philadelphia
DU	Rare Book, Manuscript & Special Collections Library, Duke University, Durham, North Carolina
DVB	*Dictionary of Virginia Biography*
EV	Encyclopedia Virginia, Virginia Humanities
IHOR	In Her Own Right project, A Century of Women's Activism, 1820–1920, Philadelphia Area Consortium of Special Collections Libraries (PACSCL)
JAH	*Journal of American History*
JSH	*Journal of Southern History*
Jt. Comm.	*Report of the Joint Committee on Reconstruction at the First Session Thirty-Ninth Congress*
LC	Library of Congress, Washington, DC
LVA	Library of Virginia, Richmond
NA	National Archives, Washington, DC
NMAAHC	National Museum of African American History and Culture, Washington, DC
NYT	*New York Times*
OR	US War Department, *The War of the Rebellion: A Compilation of the Official Records of the Union and Confederate Armies*
RCB	*Richmond Commercial Bulletin*

RD	*Richmond Dispatch*
RE	*Richmond Examiner*
REnq	*Richmond Enquirer*
RNBP	Richmond National Battlefield Park
RNN	*Richmond New Nation*
RR	*Richmond Republic*
RSO	*Richmond Southern Opinion*
RT	*Richmond Times*
RW	*Richmond Whig*
UVA	Alderman Library, University of Virginia, Charlottesville
VC	*Virginia Cavalcade*
VMHB	*Virginia Magazine of History and Biography*
VMHC	Virginia Museum of History and Culture (formerly Virginia Historical Society), Richmond

PROLOGUE

1. *The Tempest,* act 1, scene 2 (first quotation); Perry, *A Bohemian Brigade,* 185–87, 210–12; "The City," *RW,* 22 April 1865 (second quotation).
2. Pollard, *Lost Cause,* 697 (first quotation); George A. Bruce, *The Capture and Occupation of Richmond* (n.p., 1918?), 18, VMHC (second quotation).
3. Varon, *Southern Lady, Yankee Spy,* 194.
4. Dispatch of 6 April 1865, in Blackett, *Chester,* 296 (first quotation); Linus Sherman to Alva Sherman, 4 April 1865, photocopy typescript, vol. 90, RNBP (second quotation).
5. Edward H. Ripley, "The Burning of Richmond, April 3, 1865," *Southern Historical Society Papers* 32 (1904): 73.
6. "Your loving daughter" to Ann Hull Herndon Maury, 24 April 1865, Maury Papers, LC.
7. Alexander, *Fighting for the Confederacy,* 519 (first quotation); Mary Burrows Fontaine to Marie Burrows Sayre, 30 April 1865, typescript, VMHC (second quotation); Susan Hoge to Moses D. Hoge, 4 April 1865, Hoge Family Papers, VMHC (third quotation); Pollard, *Lost Cause,* 698 (fourth quotation).

1. LAST DITCH OF THE REBELLION

1. Emma Mordecai to Edward Cohen, 4 April 1865, photocopy typescript of Emma Mordecai Diary, VMHC.
2. E. H. Ripley, *Capture and Occupation of Richmond,* 19.
3. Michie Report, 12 May 1865, in *OR,* ser. 1, vol. 46, pt. 1, pp. 1165–67; "Communication with Manchester," *RT,* 25 April 1865.
4. Badeau to Lt. Col. Edward W. Smith, 21 April 1865, in *OR,* ser. 1, vol. 46, pt. 3, p. 883.
5. Kreutzer, *Notes and Observations,* 323; George Bagby to George William Bagby, 24 May 1865, Bagby Family Papers, VMHC (quotation).
6. Janney, *Ends of War,* 109–10, 231; "General Orders No. 70, 10 June 1865," *RW,* 13 June 1865; Broomall, *Private Confederacies,* 87.
7. Sternhell, *Routes of War,* 165, 178; entries for 6, 12, and 14 April 1865, John Coles Rutherfoord Diary, Rutherfoord Papers, VMHC (quotation).
8. Grant to Weitzel, 4 April 1865, in Grant, *Papers of Ulysses S. Grant,* 14:345.
9. "Affairs in Richmond," *Daily National Intelligencer,* 11 April 1865; "From City Point," *NYT,* 9 April 1865 (quotation).
10. "The Pursuit of Lee," *New York World,* 7 April 1865.
11. Whitelaw Reid's dispatch of 4 April 1865, in Reid, *A Radical View,* 2:195.
12. Stevens, *A Trip to Richmond,* 8; dispatch of 9 May 1865, in Blackett, *Chester,* 339 (quotation).
13. Kreutzer, *Notes and Observations,* 350 (quotation); Marjorie Crandall, comp., *Confederate Imprints: A Check List Based Principally on the Collection of the Boston Athenaeum* (Boston: Boston Athenaeum, 1955), 1:xii–xiv.
14. Entries for 16 April 1865 (second quotation) and 19 April 1865 (first quotation), photocopy typescript diary, Daniel T. Nelson Papers, VMHC.
15. Daniel T. Nelson to Sarah H. Nelson, 28 April 1865 (quotation) and 4 May 1865 (photocopy typescript), Daniel T. Nelson Papers, VMHC.
16. Entries for 18 May 1865 (quotation) and 19 May 1865, Julia Wilbur Diary, IHOR; K. Green, *Devil's Half Acre,* 2–3, 35–36.
17. Weitzel to Butler, 26 April 1865, in Butler, *Private and Official Correspondence,* 5:585–86 (first quotation); entry for early April 1865, Sabbath Book, Lucy Muse Walton Fletcher Papers, DU (second quotation).
18. Marszalek, *Commander,* 228; Patrick to Dana, 19 April 1865, in *OR,* ser. 1, vol. 46, pt. 3, pp. 836–37 (first quotation); entry for 16 April 1865, Marsena Patrick Diary, LC (second and third quotations).

19. Marszalek, *Commander,* 221–34, 251–53.
20. Elizabeth Munford to George W. Munford, 2 May 1865, cited in Janney, *Ends of War,* 192.
21. George Alfred Townsend's dispatch of 9 April 1865, in *New York World,* 12 April 1865 (quotation); Stevens, *A Trip to Richmond,* 10.

2. NO LONGER WAY DOWN IN EGYPT'S LAND

1. Garland White to editor, 12 April and 22 April 1865, *CR.*
2. Ibid.
3. Irons, "And All These Things," 26–35; Ryland, "Reminiscences," 264, cited in O'Brien, *From Bondage to Citizenship,* 72; Rachleff, *Black Labor,* 23–24.
4. Dispatch of 6 April 1865, in Blackett, *Chester,* 297.
5. Dispatch of 9 April 1865, in ibid., 299.
6. "From Richmond," *NYT,* 11 April 1865. About 5,700 men enlisted in USCT regiments in Virginia during the war (Deal, Julienne, and Tarter, *Justice for Ourselves,* 48).
7. Dispatch of 30 April 1865, in Blackett, *Chester,* 328; Shaffer, *After the Glory,* 11–12.
8. "Richmond," *New York Herald,* 13 April 1865.
9. "Our Special Richmond Correspondence," *Philadelphia Inquirer,* 11 April 1865 (quotation); C. T. Chase to Rev. Dr. Joseph Thompson, *NYT,* 23 May 1865.
10. O'Brien, "Albert R. Brooks (c. 1817–1881)," EV; "Statement of Albert Brooks, June 10, 1865," Records Relating to Murders and Outrages, NMAAHC.
11. O'Brien, *From Bondage to Citizenship,* 28–33; Rachleff, *Black Labor,* 32.
12. "An Interesting Item," *CR,* 24 June 1865.
13. *New York Tribune,* 17 June 1865, cited in Rachleff, *Black Labor,* 14.
14. O'Brien, *From Bondage to Citizenship,* 328–33; Rachleff, *Black Labor,* 13–33; Taylor, *Negro in Reconstruction,* 64–65.
15. "Establishment of Schools for Colored Children," *RW,* 19 April 1865; letter from Lucy Chase, 18 April 1865, *Freedmen's Record,* 1 June 1865.
16. Garland White to editor, 12 April and 22 April 1865, *CR.*
17. *New York Tribune,* 17 June 1865, in Rachleff, *Black Labor,* 15.
18. Stephen Flemming to Francis Pierpont, 21 May 1865, box 1, folder 1, Pierpont Executive Papers, LVA (quotation). At the time, the governor

spelled his name "Peirpoint" but later changed it to "Pierpont," a spelling that historians have used ever since.

19. *RW,* 7 June 1865 (first quotation); *RW,* 9 June 1865 (second quotation); *RD,* 17 February 1866 (third quotation).
20. Rachleff, *Black Labor,* 15; C. A. Jones, *Intimate Reconstructions,* 62.
21. Letter from Sarah E. Chase, 5 May 1865, *Freedmen's Record,* 1 June 1865.
22. Gen. Orders No. 8, 27 May 1865, in *OR,* ser. 1, vol. 46, pt. 3, p. 1221; Halleck to Stanton, 26 June 1865, in *OR,* ser. 1, vol. 46, pt. 3, pp. 1295–97; Rachleff, *Black Labor,* 15.
23. Farmer-Kaiser, *Freedwomen and the Freedmen's Bureau,* 149; O'Brien, *From Bondage to Citizenship,* 52, 75; Foner, *Reconstruction,* 198.
24. Chesson, "John Oliver (d. 1899)"; John Oliver to editor, *RE,* 21 May 1867, reprinted in *New Orleans Tribune,* 8 June 1867 (quotations).

3. YOU CANNOT SUBJUGATE US

1. "From Petersburg," *NYT,* 30 April 1865.
2. Dispatch of 6 April 1865, in Blackett, *Chester,* 296 (first quotation); Harrison, *Recollections Grave and Gay,* 215 (second quotation); "R" to "My dearest Mother," 25 April 1865, Maury Papers, LC.
3. Entry for 12 April 1865, Margaret Brown Wight Diary, Wight Family Papers, VMHC (first quotation); Fanny Churchill Braxton Young to "dearest Mother & sisters," 11 April 1865, Young Family Papers, VMHC (second quotation).
4. Dispatch of 10 April 1865, *Philadelphia Inquirer,* 12 April 1865 (first quotation); Diana Fontaine (Maury) Corbin to "My dear Cousin," 7 May 1865, Confederate Memorial Literary Society, VMHC (second quotation).
5. Heinemann, *Old Dominion,* 241.
6. Dispatch of 16 April 1865, in Blackett, *Chester,* 308–9; Edward Crapsey's dispatch of 15 April 1865, *Philadelphia Inquirer,* 18 April 1865 (quotation).
7. "The News in Richmond," *New York World,* 18 April 1865; undated entry between 10 and 22 April 1865, Alice Fitzhugh Dixon Payne Diary, VMHC (first quotation); entry in diary book beginning 27 April 1865, Lucy Muse Walton Fletcher Papers, DU (second quotation); entry for 16 April 1865, in McGuire, *Diary of a Southern Refugee,* 356.
8. Entry for 23 April 1865, Diary, Henry S. Spaulding Papers, UVA (first quotation); James Hane to father and mother, 20 April 1865, vol. 80, photocopy typescript, RNBP (second quotation).

9. "The Secesh," *Philadelphia Inquirer,* 18 April 1865 (first quotation); Lankford, *Richmond Burning,* 148 (second quotation); dispatch of 15 May 1865, in Blackett, *Chester,* 347; Downs, *After Appomattox,* 64.
10. Marchant, "Maury's New Virginia, 1865–67," 370–76; William A. Maury to "Dear Cousin," 19 May 1865 (first quotation); "R" to "My Dear Cousin," 21 May 1865 (second quotation), Maury Papers, LC.
11. Susan Hoge to Moses Drury Hoge, 24 April 1865, Hoge Family Papers, VMHC (first and second quotations); Susan Hoge to Elizabeth H. Howard, 28 October 1865, Hoge Family Papers, VMHC (third quotation); Moses Drury Hoge to sister, 15 May 1865, in Hoge, *Moses Drury Hoge,* 235 (fourth quotation).
12. Hanna, "The Role of Matthew Fontaine Maury," 105–25.
13. Entry for 17 April 1865, Marsena Patrick Diary, LC.
14. "Richmond," *New York World,* 18 April 1865.
15. Entry for 21 April 1865, Marsena Patrick Diary, LC (quotation); Janney, *Ends of War,* 109–21.
16. Entries for 9, 11, 19, 27 April, 6 May, and 16 June 1865, Garidel Diary (quotation in 19 April), in Garidel, *Exile in Richmond,* 376–99.
17. Entries for 8 April (first quotation) and 17 April (second quotation) 1865, Fannie E. Taylor Dickinson Diary, VMHC.
18. Lankford, *Richmond Burning,* 123 (first quotation); entry dated 25 April 1865 (second quotation), "Little Red Book," Lucy Muse Walton Fletcher Papers, DU, cited in Barber, "Sisters of the Capital," 236, 436–39 (quotation on 236); entry for 16 April 1865, Margaret Brown Wight Diary, Wight Family Papers, VMHC.
19. Downs, *After Appomattox,* 33; "R" to "Dear Cousin," 18 June 1865, Maury Papers, LC (quotation).
20. Entry for 25 April 1865, in Strong, *Strong Diary,* 3:593.
21. "The Homeward March of the Army of the Potomac," *RW,* 8 May 1865; Garidel Diary, entry for 6 May 1865, in Garidel, *Exile in Richmond,* 393 (quotation).
22. Dispatches of 4 and 24 April 1865, in Blackett, *Chester,* 289, 320 (first quotation on 4 April); entry for 8 May 1865, Marsena Patrick Diary, LC; William Weston Patton, "Scenes in and around Richmond, Va.," 13, sermon delivered at First Congregational Church, Chicago, 23 April 1865, William Weston Patton Papers, Chicago Historical Society (second quotation); W. D. Jones, "British Report," 349 (third quotation).
23. "Special Correspondence," *Cincinnati Gazette,* 17 June 1865.

24. Entry for 9 April 1865, Anne Jennings Wise Hobson Diary, VMHC.
25. "Some of Our Contemporaries," *RD,* 1 April 1865 (first quotation); "R" to Matthew Fontaine Maury, 18 May 1865, Maury Papers, LC (second quotation).

4. CHARRED RUINS

1. Entry for 5 April 1865, in J. B. Jones, *Rebel War Clerk's Diary,* 2:471.
2. Michie to J. G. Barnard, 10 May 1865, in *OR,* ser. 1, vol. 46, pt. 3, pp. 1142–44; Ord to Grant, 19 May 1865, in *OR,* ser. 1, vol. 46, pt. 3, p. 1179; Ord to Grant, 6 March 1865, in Grant, *Papers of Ulysses S. Grant,* 14:110 (quotation).
3. Gustavus Myers to Conway Robinson, 2 July 1865, Myers Family Papers, VMHC; Gaines, *Biographical Register,* s.v. "William Hamilton Macfarland," 53–54 (quotation); entry for 9 June 1865, Julia Wilbur Diary, IHOR.
4. Chesson, *Richmond after the War,* 61–64; *RW,* 22 June 1865; *RCB,* 22 June 1865.
5. *New York Tribune,* 29 April 1865, reprinted in *Daily Evening Bulletin,* 3 June 1865.
6. "The Railroads," *RW,* 11 May 1865; Chesson, *Richmond after the War,* 68–71, 141.
7. Chesson, *Richmond after the War,* 68–70; "The Railroads," *RR,* 11 May 1865.
8. Chesson, *Richmond after the War,* 68, 76–77.
9. "The Signs of the Times," *RCB,* 4 August 1865.
10. Alford, *Fortune's Fool,* 64; "From Richmond," *NYT,* 14 April 1865; Lankford, *Richmond Burning,* 167, 177.
11. Norton Folsom to William A. Conover, 6 April 1865, RG 393, pt. 1, entry 5063, NA; *RW,* 18 April 1865; Margaret Wolfe, paper given at Southern Historical Association, November 1998, cited in Wyatt-Brown, *Shaping of Southern Culture,* 249.
12. Chesson, *Richmond after the War,* 81; "Vaccination for Small Pox," *RW,* 10 May 1865.
13. "Thieves, in Swarms," *RW,* 23 June 1865 (first quotation); entry for 20 May 1865, Julia Wilbur Diary, IHOR (second quotation).
14. Dispatch of 24 April 1865, in Blackett, *Chester,* 321–22 (quotation); Garland White, letter to editor, 20 April 1865, *CR,* 6 May 1865.
15. Bayliss, *Dooleys of Richmond,* 77–80; Carmichael, *Last Generation,* 216–17.

16. Robert Warren Powers, typescript memoir, 1905, VMHC.
17. Blackford, *Mine Eyes Have Seen the Glory,* 240–42.
18. Trent, *The Secret Life of Bacon Tait,* 1–5, 146, 161–64.
19. Entries for 30 May, 9 and 10 June 1865, Julia Wilbur Diary, IHOR.
20. D. W. Flagler to A. B. Dyer, 28 April 1865, in *OR,* ser. 1, vol. 46, pt. 3, pp. 1007–10; C. A. Dana to Halleck, 14 June 1865, in *OR,* ser. 1, vol. 46, pt. 3, p. 1266.
21. "Destructive Storm in Richmond," *Cincinnati Gazette,* 30 May 1865; "The Freshet on Sunday Night," *RW,* 23 May 1865; entry for 22 May 1865, Julia Wilbur Diary, IHOR.

5. ANGRY PASSIONS HUSHED

1. Lincoln to Pierpont, 10 April 1865, in *OR,* ser. 1, vol. 46, pt. 3, p. 703; Lankford, *Richmond Burning,* 47–48, 214–15; "R" to "My Dear Cousin," 18 May 1865, Maury Papers, LC (quotation); Escott, *Lincoln's Dilemma,* 21.
2. Lowe, "Pierpont," 34–37; Siviter, *Recollections,* 156 (quotation).
3. Levine, *Failed Promise,* 11; Foner, *Reconstruction,* 43 (first quotation); Carter, *When the War Was Over,* 24 (second quotation).
4. "Order Restoring Virginia," 9 May 1865, in Johnson, *Papers,* 8:53.
5. "Arrival of Gov. Peirpoint," *RR,* 27 May 1865.
6. Ibid.
7. "Letter from Richmond, Va.," *Cincinnati Gazette,* 2 June 1865; Siviter, *Recollections,* 165; entry for 26 May 1865, Julia Wilbur Diary, IHOR.
8. "Arrival of Gov. Peirpoint," *RR,* 27 May 1865.
9. Ibid.
10. Charles Palmer to George Moore, 6 July 1865, Palmer Papers, VMHC.
11. Stuart, "Colonel Ulric Dahlgren," 187–90; "New Concern," *RW,* 17 April 1865; "First National Bank," *RW,* 8 May 1865; "Official," *RW,* 13 June 1865.
12. "Mr. Botts," *RD,* 26 February 1866 (first quotation); Botts to Palmer, 27 April (second quotation) and 21 May 1865, Palmer Papers, VMHC.
13. Varon, *Southern Lady, Yankee Spy,* 195; Leveen, "Mary Richards Bowser," EV.
14. Entry for 31 May 1865, Marsena Patrick Diary, LC; Varon, *Southern Lady, Yankee Spy,* 195–96, 199 (quotation).
15. "The Flag of Our Union," *RW,* 10 April 1865 (first quotation); "Communicated," *RW,* 4 April 1865 (second quotation).
16. Mary Andrews West to Clara, 12 April 1865, VMHC.

17. Entry for 3 April 1865, in McGuire, *Diary of a Southern Refugee,* 345 (quotation); Wardwell to B. F. Butler, 19 April 1865, in Butler, *Private and Official Correspondence,* 5:598.
18. "A Monument," *RW,* 8 April 1865 (quotation); "From Richmond," *NYT,* 11 May 1865.
19. Entry for 9 June 1865, Julia Wilbur Diary, IHOR.
20. "List of the Prominent Union Men of Richmond and Its Vicinity," box 1, folder 2, Pierpont Executive Papers, LVA.
21. J. Woodward to Pierpont, 25 May 1865 (first quotation), box 1, folder 1, and C. Carazo to Pierpont, 28 June 1865 (second quotation), box 1, folder 5, Pierpont Executive Papers, LVA.
22. Foner, *Reconstruction,* 182–83; entry for 31 May 1865, Marsena Patrick Diary, LC (quotation).
23. Tarter and *DVB,* "John C. Underwood (1809–1873)," EV. Underwood's middle name is often incorrectly rendered "Curtiss."
24. "United States District Court at Norfolk," *RW,* 5 June 1865 (first and second quotations); Janney, *Ends of War,* 218–19.
25. Byrd Warwick Davenport Jr., "The Warwick Family: Richmonders in the Civil War: Gaines's Mill and Beyond: The Story of Bradfute and Barksdale," privately printed, courtesy of Bradfute Warwick Davenport, Jr. (first quotation); "Henry A Wise," *Norfolk Post,* 8 September 1865 (second quotation).
26. *Petersburg News,* 10 June 1865, reprinted in *Norfolk Post,* 22 June 1865 (first and second quotations).

6. OUR QUIVERING FLESH

1. Bratton, "Fields's Observations," 78; O'Brien, "Fields Cook," EV; "The Ballard House Bar and Restaurant," *RW,* May 5, 1865.
2. McFeely, *Yankee Stepfather,* 33, 40, 65.
3. O'Brien, *From Bondage to Citizenship,* 161–62, 212 (first quotation), 238 (second quotation).
4. Sternhell, *Routes of War,* 178–89; Carter, *When the War Was Over,* 159.
5. Halleck to Stanton, 11 May 1865, in *OR,* ser. 1, vol. 46, pt. 3, pp. 1131–32.
6. "The Holiday Season Past," *RW,* 19 May 1865 (first quotation); entry for 7 June 1865, Julia Wilbur Diary, IHOR (second quotation).
7. Randolph, *From Slave Cabin to the Pulpit,* 81 (first quotation); dispatch of 12 June 1865, in Blackett, *Chester,* 365; Rachleff, *Black Labor,* 35 (second quotation); "Jefferson Davis' Coachman on Reconstruction," *New*

Orleans Tribune, 5 August 1865; O'Brien, "Reconstruction in Richmond," 275 (third quotation).

8. O'Brien, "Reconstruction in Richmond," 272 (first quotation); *RCB,* 8 June 1865; *RW,* 19 May 1865; entry for 19 May 1865, Julia Wilbur Diary, IHOR (second quotation).
9. *New York Tribune,* 12 June 1865, cited in O'Brien, "Reconstruction in Richmond," 274.
10. "Statement of Albert Brooks," 10 June 1865 (quotation), and "Statement of Wm Ferguson," undated, June 1865, Records Relating to Murders and Outrages, NMAAHC.
11. "Statement of John Oliver of Mass.," undated, June 1865, NMAAHC.
12. "Statement of Thomas J. Hayer (concerning Thomas Chester)," after 8 June 1865 (quotation), NMAAHC.
13. "Statement of Jinny Scott wife of E. L. Scott, col'd," June 8, 1865 (first and second quotations) and "Statement of Richard Adams, col'd," June 8, 1865, NMAAHC.
14. Alex M. Davis to Col. O. Brown, 9 June 1865 (first quotation), NMAAHC; Brown to Howard, 9 June 1865, O'Brien, "Reconstruction in Richmond," 275 (second quotation).
15. O'Brien, "Reconstruction in Richmond," 275–76.
16. "The Richmond Negro Delegation in Washington," *RR,* 19 June 1865 (first quotation); *New York Tribune,* 12 June 1865, cited in O'Brien, "Reconstruction in Richmond," 274 (second quotation).
17. "Richmond Negroes at the White House" (reprinted from *New York Tribune*), *RW,* 19 June 1865.
18. "Reception of the Richmond Colored Delegation by the President," *Norfolk Post,* 22 June 1865.
19. Levine, *Failed Promise,* 21 (quotation), 42, 220; Foner, *Reconstruction,* 183.
20. Terry to Stanton, 16 June 1865, and Stanton to Terry, 17 June 1865, in *OR,* ser. 1, vol. 46, pt. 3, p. 1282 (quotation).
21. John W. Turner testimony, 23 January 1866, *Jt. Comm.,* 2:1–4; Turner to B. F. Butler, 7 May 1865, in Butler, *Private and Official Correspondence,* 5:616–17; O'Brien, "Reconstruction in Richmond," 280.
22. Halleck to Stanton, 26 June 1865, in *OR,* ser. 1, vol. 46, pt. 3, pp. 1295–97.
23. O'Brien, "Reconstruction in Richmond," 278.
24. "Treatment of the Freedmen in Richmond," *RW,* 17 June 1865; "The Richmond Negro Delegation in Washington," *RR,* 19 June 1865.

25. Orlando Brown, 16 February 1866, *Jt. Comm,* 2:123–28.
26. Entry for 5 June 1865, in Ruffin, *Diary of Edmund Ruffin,* 3:915–16.
27. Entry for 16 June 1865, in Ruffin, *Diary of Edmund Ruffin,* 3:946.

7. CORRECTION OF EVERY EVIL

1. George Bagby to George William Bagby, 3 July 1865, Bagby Family Papers, VMHC.
2. "Apprehended Negro Insurrection in Richmond," *New York Herald,* 6 July 1865.
3. "The Fourth at the Capitol," *RCB,* 6 July 1865 (first quotation); *Richmond Times-Dispatch,* 26 August 2023 (second quotation); Mary E. Thropp to "My Dear Father," 12 July 1865, *Washington Daily National Republican,* 19 July 1865, cited in https://civilwarrichmond.com.
4. "The Fourth at the Capitol," *RCB,* 6 July 1865.
5. "Virginia," *NYT,* 4 June 1865.
6. "Important Interview," *RR,* 31 May 1865.
7. Lowe, *Republicans and Reconstruction,* 37 (first quotation), 36 (second quotation).
8. "Organization of Cities," *RW,* 24 June 1865.
9. "Apprehended Negro Insurrection in Richmond," *New York Herald,* 6 July 1865.
10. *RR,* 24 July 1865; compare this perspective to that in "The Charter Elections," *RCB,* 27 July 1865.
11. "The Mayoralty," *RW,* 25 July 1865.
12. "The Municipal Elections," *RW,* 27 July 1865; "Richmond Election," *RR,* 26 July 1865; George Bagby to George William Bagby, 26 July 1865, Bagby Family Papers, VMHC (quotation); *Cincinnati Gazette,* 4 August 1865, cited in *New Orleans Tribune,* 24 August 1865.
13. Terry to Underwood, [July?] 1865, Underwood Papers, LC (quotation); "What the South Intends," *National Anti-Slavery Standard,* 5 August 1865.
14. *RCB,* 26 July 1865 (first quotation); "The Progress of Reconstruction," *CR,* 12 August 1865 (second quotation); "Vipers All," *RR,* 28 July 1865 (third quotation).

8. STERN EXACTIONS

1. "An Important Meeting," *RW,* 23 June 1865.

2. Entry for 9 June 1865, in Ruffin, *Diary of Edmund Ruffin,* 3:919; Myers to Conway Robinson, 23 September 1865, Myers Family Papers, VMHC; Richard Barton Haxall to "My dear Sir," 29 September 1865, VMHC; "Vast Accumulation of Pardon Petitions," *NYT,* 29 September 1865.
3. "Citizens Meeting at the City Hall," *RCB,* 29 June 1865 (quotation).
4. "A Petition from Richmond," *NYT,* 2 July 1865 (first quotation); "Adjourned Public Meeting at the City Hall," *RW,* 29 June 1865 (second quotation); "Mr Johnson, and the Amnesty Proclamation," *RCB,* 7 July 1865.
5. Interview with Richmond merchants, 8 July 1865, in Johnson, *Papers of Andrew Johnson,* 8:371–72; "$20,000 Exception—Mr. Johnson's Best Opportunity," *RCB,* 12 July 1865 (quotation); "Important Interview—The Richmond Delegation and the President," *RR,* 10 July 1865.
6. McFeely, *Yankee Stepfather,* 100.
7. Rives to Johnson, 12 July 1865, in Johnson, *Papers of Andrew Johnson,* 8:391–92 (quotation); Neumann, "Long Tried Patriotism"; "Meeting of Colored Men in Richmond," *NYT,* 3 October 1867.
8. "Salutatory," *RW,* 11 July 1865 (quotation) and 24 July 1865; "The Richmond Whig Suspended," *NYT,* 13 July 1865.
9. "From Richmond," *NYT,* 16 July 1865.
10. *RR,* 24 August 1865.
11. "The Jackson Statue," *RCB,* 29 August 1865.
12. Entries for 12 May and 22 August 1865, for "H. Exall," R. G. Dun & Co., VA 43, 291, Baker Library, Harvard Business School.
13. "Meeting of the Citizens of Richmond on the Capitol Square," *RR,* 30 August 1865.
14. Ibid. (first quotation); "Local Intelligence," *RCB,* 30 August 1865 (second quotation).
15. "A Mass Meeting in Richmond," *Staunton Spectator,* 5 September 1865 (quotation); *New York Herald,* 1, 2, 5 September 1865.
16. "Meeting of the Citizens of Richmond on the Capitol Square," *RR,* 30 August 1865 (quotation); "Local Intelligence," *RCB,* 30 August 1865.
17. Myers to Robinson, 17 August 1865, Myers Family Papers, VMHC.
18. "Meeting of the Citizens of Richmond on the Capitol Square," *RR,* 30 August 1865; *New York Herald,* 2 September 1865 (quotation).
19. "Property Libelled for Confiscation," *RR,* supplement to 7 September 1865 (quotation).

9. PHOENIX ARISING

1. Watterson to Johnson, 7 June 1865, in Johnson, *Papers of Andrew Johnson,* 8:198–99 (quotation); Foner, *Reconstruction,* 189–90.
2. Foner, *Reconstruction,* 188–91.
3. "Invitation from the People of Richmond," *RR,* 11 September 1865; "Judge Underwood—Federal Courts in Virginia," *RR,* 25 September 1865; "Pardons," *RR,* 9 October 1865.
4. Myers to Robinson, 9 and 23 September 1865, Myers Family Papers, VMHC.
5. Bromberg, "Joseph R. Anderson," EV; Pierpont to Johnson, 16 September 1865 (quotation), in Johnson, *Papers of Andrew Johnson,* 9:87; Dew, *Ironmaker,* 291–300.
6. Bayliss, *Dooleys of Richmond,* 84–87.
7. Ould to Brig. Gen. Winder, 17 March 1863, quoted in "The Trial of Capt. Wirz," *NYT,* 21 October 1865.
8. Rood, "Bogs of Death," 19–43.
9. Robert, *Story of Tobacco,* 103.
10. T. C. Williams to Thomas, 2 May 1865, quoted in D. T. Smith, "Tobacco and Its Role," 90.
11. Robert, *The Story of Tobacco,* 82, 130; Broadus, "Memorial," 47–51; D. T. Smith, "Tobacco and Its Role," 48–50.
12. "Richmond, Fredericksburg and Potomac Railroad," *RR,* 4 September 1865.
13. "There Was a Meeting of the Stockholders," *Alexandria Gazette,* 14 September 1865; "Election of President of Richmond & Danville R. R.," *Alexandria Gazette,* 15 September 1865; Maddex, *Virginia Conservatives,* 37.
14. "Trade between Richmond and Baltimore," *RR,* 1 September 1865; "A Bark Damaged by a Torpedo in the James," *RR,* 7 September 1865; "Shipping, Etc.," *RR,* 2 November 1865.
15. Myers to Conway Robinson, 23 September 1865, Myers Family Papers, VMHC; "Lot in the Burnt District for Sale," *RR,* 6 September 1865 (quotation).
16. "Removing the Dead," *RR,* 24 October 1865.
17. William A. Maury to Rutson Maury, 1 September 1865, Maury Papers, LC (first quotation); "The Negroes in Virginia," quoted from *RW* in *NYT,* 22 August 1865 (second quotation); "The Problem of Southern Labor," *RCB,* 29 July 1865 (third quotation).

18. "The Temper of Virginia," *NYT,* 6 August 1865.
19. Conversation on about 16 September 1865, in Trowbridge, *The South,* quoted in Rachleff, *Black Labor,* 23 (first quotation); "Tobacco Factory Mechanicks of Richmond and Manchester," 18 September 1865, in Trowbridge, *The South,* 210 (second quotation).
20. "The Labor System," *RW,* 17 October 1865 (quotation); "Virginia," *NYT,* 11 June 1865; "Virginia Central Immigration Society," *RW,* 6 December 1865.
21. Entry for 8 April 1865, Tompkins Diary, in Rachal, "Occupation of Richmond," 194 (first quotation); Susan Hoge to Elizabeth H. Howard, 28 October 1865, Hoge Family Papers, VMHC (second quotation); Francis Warrington Dawson to father, 4 October 1865, in Carter, *When the War Was Over,* 167 (third quotation).
22. "A Washington Despatch [. . .]," *Alexandria Gazette,* 2 September 1865; R. S. Davis, "Georgia Odyssey," 569–86; "The Gold Captured by Sherman," *REnq,* 25 April 1866.
23. Terry to Underwood, 30 September 1865, Underwood Papers, LC.
24. Downs, *After Appomattox,* 89–90, 100.
25. Entry for 7 June 1865, Julia Wilbur Diary, IHOR; "Virginia News," *Alexandria Gazette,* 16 July 1865.
26. Kreutzer, *Notes and Observations,* 358.
27. Ibid., 359; "City Intelligence," *RR,* 1 September 1865.

10. AN EQUAL CHANCE

1. "From Richmond," *New York Tribune,* 4 August 1865, quoted in *Boston Daily Advertiser,* 9 August 1865 (first quotation); "Jeff. Davis's Family in Albany," *Liberator,* 25 August 1865; *NYT,* 29 December 1878 (second quotation); "Overlooked No More: Edmonia Lewis, Sculptor of Worldwide Acclaim," *NYT,* 25 July 2018.
2. Foner, *Reconstruction,* 117.
3. Randolph, *From Slave Cabin to the Pulpit,* 77.
4. Lowe, "Local Black Leaders," 194, 201; O'Brien, *From Bondage to Citizenship,* 274–75 (quotation on 274).
5. "From the North," *New Orleans Tribune,* 10 August 1865.
6. Foner and Walker, *Proceedings of the Black State Conventions,* 2:267.
7. Ibid., 2:262 (first quotation), 2:272 (second and third quotations); "The Late Convention of Colored Men," *NYT,* 13 August 1865.

8. Foner, *Reconstruction,* 117.
9. C. P. Ripley et al., *Black Abolitionist Papers,* 5:346.
10. O'Brien, *From Bondage to Citizenship,* 240–41.
11. Ibid., 214–15, 218.
12. H. Green, "Ralza M. Manly (1822–1897)," EV; Alderson, "Freedmen's Bureau and Negro Education in Virginia," 64–90; H. Green, "Educational Reconstruction," 22–28; O'Brien, "From Bondage to Citizenship," 383–87, 396–407.
13. H. Green, "Educational Reconstruction," 46.
14. "Discourse by Rev. Dr. Bacon," *New-Haven Palladium,* 6 November 1865, quoted in "Virginia," *NYT,* 12 November 1865.
15. O'Brien, *From Bondage to Citizenship,* 230–35.
16. Fitzhugh, "Camp Lee and the Freedmen's Bureau," 349; Emberton, *Beyond Redemption,* 64–66; Schermerhorn, "George Fitzhugh (1806–1881)," EV.
17. "The Operation of the Freedmen's Bureau in Virginia," *RD,* 30 December 1865 (first quotation); "The Freedmen's Bureau of Virginia," *RD,* 30 December 1865 (second quotation).
18. "Letters from Richmond," 21 November 1865, *CR,* 2 December 1865.
19. "Off for Liberia," excerpted from *Lynchburg Virginian,* in *RCB,* 3 November 1865; "Expedition to Africa," *Washington, DC, Evening Star,* 3 November 1865.

11. EXTRICATE US FROM ALL OUR TROUBLES

1. Lankford, *Cry Havoc!,* 53, 122.
2. "Great Anxiety about the Oath of Loyalty—Impossibility of Understanding It," *NYT,* 6 October 1865; *Charlottesville Tri-Weekly Chronicle,* 14 September 1865 (first quotation), in Bromberg, "Virginia Congressional Elections," 83; editor of *RT,* cited in *RR,* 24 August 1865 (second quotation).
3. *Washington Daily National Republican,* 14 October 1865, in Bromberg, "Virginia Congressional Elections," 92; Foner, *Reconstruction,* 197.
4. "Candidates for Office," *RW,* 7 October 1865.
5. "To the Voters of Richmond," *RW,* 11 October 1865.
6. "The City Senator," *RW,* 14 October 1865 (quotation); Gilmer to Johnson, 16 October 1865, in Johnson, *Papers of Andrew Johnson,* 9:249–50.

7. Hildebrand, *Baldwin,* 190–92; Ayers, *Thin Light of Freedom,* 363 (quotation).
8. "City Intelligence," *RR,* 29 August 1865; "City Intelligence," *RR,* 23 October 1865; Chesson, *Richmond after the War,* 92–94; Turner to B. F. Butler, 16 October 1866, in Butler, *Private and Official Correspondence,* 5:672 (quotation).
9. W. A. Maury to William Hastinck, 20 November 1865, in Maury Papers, LC.
10. Chesson, *Richmond after the War,* 65–66; "The Burnt District," *RD,* 9 December 1865.
11. "The Past and the Present," *RD,* December 1865.
12. James Wesley Lewellen to John Packer, 5 April 1865, Lewellen Family Papers, VMHC (first quotation); Terry to Underwood, [July?] 1865, Underwood Papers, LC (second quotation).
13. Terry to Underwood, 7 October 1865, Underwood Papers, LC.
14. Maddex, "Pollard's *The Lost Cause Regained,*" 596, 598 (quotation); Hamm, *Murder, Honor, and Law,* 23.
15. Henry A. Pollard, 26 October 1865, letter printed in *Wheeling Daily Intelligencer,* 1 November 1865.
16. Blair, *Cities of the Dead,* 15–16; S.M.O, "A Letter from Richmond, Va.," *CR,* 20 January 1866 (quotation).
17. O'Brien, *From Bondage to Citizenship,* 467n223.
18. Ibid., 280–82.
19. "Christmas and Christmas Presents," *RD,* 22 December 1865; "The Great Problem of Christmas [. . .]," *RD,* 23 December 1865 (first quotation); "Christmas," *RD* 25 December 1865 (second quotation).
20. S.M.O., "A Letter from Richmond, Va.," *CR,* 20 January 1866 (quotation).
21. "Virginia," *NYT,* 29 December 1865.
22. "The Operation of the Freedmen's Bureau in Virginia," *RD,* 30 December 1865 (quotation).
23. Foner, *Second Founding,* 39–54; "The Consummation!" *NYT,* 19 December 1865.
24. Carter, *When the War Was Over,* 91–94; O'Brien, *From Bondage to Citizenship,* 282–83, 298; L. Q. Washington to R. M. T. Hunter, 25 December 1866, Hunter Papers, VMHC (quotation).
25. Isabel Maury to Mary "Molly" Herndon (Maury) Werth, 1 January 186[6], VMHC.

12. THE BOX OF PANDORA IS OPENED

1. "Freedmen's Celebration to Commemorate Their Emancipation," *RD,* 2 January 1866.
2. Ibid.
3. Ibid.
4. O'Brien, *From Bondage to Citizenship,* 303–5.
5. Ibid.
6. "Mr. Bott's Address," *RD,* 3 August 1867.
7. *RR,* 11 January (quotation), 13 January 1866.
8. Hamm, *Murder, Honor, and Law,* 25 (first quotation); Dawson, *Reminiscences,* 122 (second quotation); "Shooting in the Capitol," *Staunton Spectator,* 9 January 1866; Carter, *When the War Was Over,* 18–19.
9. "A 'Special Correspondent' Cowhided," *RD,* 13 January 1866; "The Recent Editorial Fracas," *NYT,* 15 January 1866.
10. Dawson to mother, 11 June 1866, cited in Carter, *When the War Was Over,* 22.
11. B. D. Simpson, *Let Us Have Peace,* 115–18, 126; Downs, *After Appomattox,* 105–6.
12. B. D. Simpson, *Let Us Have Peace,* 130 (first quotation); "Officers' Hop in Richmond," from *RE,* quoted in *Norfolk Post,* 6 February 1866 (second and third quotations); "City Intelligence," *RR,* 14 February 1866.
13. B. D. Simpson, *Let Us Have Peace,* 130–31; Grant to Terry, 9 February 1866, in Grant, *Papers of Ulysses S. Grant,* 16:71 (quotation); Johnson to Grant, 17 February 1866, in Johnson, *Papers of Andrew Johnson,* 10:110; Varon, *Appomattox,* 228.
14. Terry to Rawlins, 23 March 1866, in Grant, *Papers of Ulysses S. Grant,* 16:72.
15. *RT,* 16 January 1866, cited in Alderson, "Freedmen's Bureau," 64 (first quotation); Anna R. Sherrard to Elizabeth T. Munford, April 7, 1866, cited in Carter, *When the War Was Over,* 214 (second quotation); Isabel Maury to Mary "Molly" Herndon (Maury) Werth, 1 January 186[6], VMHC (third quotation).
16. Siviter, *Recollections,* 234–43.
17. Ayers, *Thin Light of Freedom,* 385–94; Lowe, "Testimony from the Old Dominion," 374–75.
18. John W. Turner, testimony, 23 January 1866, *Jt. Comm.,* 2:1–6 (quotation 2).
19. Alfred H. Terry, testimony, 20 February 1866, *Jt. Comm.,* 2:141–44 (quotation 141).

20. *Jt. Comm.*, 2:141–44 (quotation 143).
21. John C. Underwood, testimony, 31 January 1866, *Jt. Comm.*, 2:6–10 (quotation 7).
22. Daniel Norton (first quotation, 52), Richard R. Hill (second quotation, 56), Thomas Bayne (third quotation, 59), testimony, 3 February 1866, *Jt. Comm.*, 2:51–60.
23. John Minor Botts, testimony, 15 February 1866, *Jt. Comm.*, 2:120.
24. *Jt. Comm.*, 2:114–23 (first quotation 122; second quotation 121).
25. James W. Hunnicutt, testimony, 21 February 1866, *Jt. Comm.*, 2:149–51.
26. Pryor, *Six Encounters with Lincoln*, 11–12, 41–44; Robert E. Lee, testimony, 17 February 1866, *Jt. Comm.*, 2:129–36 (first and second quotations 130, third quotation 136); Varon, *Appomattox*, 220–24; Guelzo, *Robert E. Lee*, 394.
27. John Brown Baldwin, testimony, 10 February 1866, *Jt. Comm.*, 2:106.
28. Ibid., 2:102–9 (first and second quotations 108); Ayers, *Thin Light of Freedom*, 389–91.
29. B. R. [Peachy] Grattan, testimony, 10 February 1866, *Jt. Comm.*, 2:163.
30. "Report of the Reconstruction Committee," *RD*, 30 April 1866 (quotation); "General Terry before the Committee of Fifteen" and "Testimony of Officers of the Freedmen's Bureau in Virginia," *RW*, 31 March 1866.
31. Orlando Brown, testimony, 15 February 1866, *Jt. Comm.*, 2:123–28 (quotation 124).

13. WINTER INTO SPRING

1. Martha H. Chace, "From Richmond," *Freedmen's Record*, 1 April 1866.
2. "To the Public," *Central Presbyterian*, 2 February 1865 (quotation); "Meeting for the Relief of the Poor," *RD*, 12 January 1866; "City Intelligence," *RR*, 27 February 1866.
3. "Virginia," *NYT*, 22 January 1866.
4. "Robbery," *RR*, 13 Jan. 1866; "The Released Convicts and the Vagrancy Law," *RD*, 27 July 1866.
5. "The Police Force of Richmond," *RD*, 17 February 1866; "Miscegenation," *RR*, 13 January 1866.
6. "Mayor's Court," *RD*, 13 August 1866; "Mayor's Court," *RD*, 10 January 1866.
7. "The Disturbances at Chimborazo on Friday Last," *RD*, 9 March 1866 (quotation); O'Brien, *From Bondage to Citizenship*, 216–17.

8. C. A. Jones, *Intimate Reconstructions*, 2, 33, 103–6, 110, 118, 150; entry for 31 May 1865, Julia Wilbur Diary, IHOR.
9. "The City," *RW*, 4 April 1865.
10. O'Brien, "Albert R. Brooks (c. 1817–1881)," EV; Deal, Julienne, and Tarter, *Justice for Ourselves*, 62.
11. Dew, *Ironmaker*, 303–10; "Affairs in the South," *NYT*, 9 April 1866 (quotation).
12. "The Gallego Mills," *RD*, 16 May 1866.
13. Luebke, "William Mahone (1826–1895)"; Blake, *William Mahone*, 76–85.
14. "Medical College of Virginia," *RW*, 29 June 1865; "Medical College of Virginia," *RW*, 7 October 1865; "City and Suburban" (quotation) and "Medical College of Virginia," *RW*, 6 March 1866; Schildt, *Hunter Holmes McGuire*, 97.
15. "At a Meeting of the Bar of the City," *RD*, 10 October 1866.
16. Theodore, "Ida Vernon," 41–48; "Amusements: New Richmond Theatre," *RW*, 14 October 1865.
17. Lankford, *Richmond Burning*, 152.
18. George Bagby to George William Bagby, 24 May 1865, Bagby Family Papers, VMHC (first quotation); King, *Dr. George William Bagby*, 120–28 (second quotation 126); Watson, "George William Bagby (1828–1883)," EV.
19. "Letters from Richmond," 21 November 1865, *CR*, 2 December 1865 (quotation); Dew, *Ironmaker*, 313–15.
20. "Emigration to Virginia," *RNN*, 22 March 1866.
21. "Henry A. Wise," *Norfolk Post*, 2 February 1866.
22. "Virginia," *NYT*, 9 April 1866.
23. "The Governor's Reception," *RR*, 1 March 1866.

14. OBSERVED AND REMEMBERED

1. Nash, "The Devil Let Loose Generally," 298–333.
2. "City and Suburban," *RW*, 23 February 1866; "The Twenty-Second among the Negroes," *RD*, 23 February 1866.
3. "Third of April in Richmond 1866," *RNN*, 12 April 1866.
4. Richmond freedmen to mayor of Richmond, 21 March 1866, quoted in O'Brien, *From Bondage to Citizenship*, 334–35.
5. "Third of April in Richmond 1866," *RNN*, 12 April 1866 (quotation); "The Negro Celebration on the Third of April," *RW*, 10 March 1866;

"The Proposed Celebration of the Negroes on the Third of April," *RW,* 20 March 1866; "At a Mass Meeting," *RW,* 30 March 1866.

6. "At a Mass Meeting," *RW,* 30 March 1866 (first and second quotations); O'Brien, *From Bondage to Citizenship,* 337.
7. William Lyons et al. to Brown, n.d., cited in O'Brien, *From Bondage to Citizenship,* 335–36.
8. Ibid., 336–38; "The Negroes' Celebration," *RD,* 30 March 1866; "At a Mass Meeting," *RW,* 30 March 1866.
9. Terry to Maj. Gen. John A. Rawlins (quotation) and Grant to Terry, 29 March 1866, in Grant, *Papers of Ulysses S. Grant,* 16:142.
10. "Our Country," *CR,* 7 April 1866; L. W. Smith, "Richmond during Presidential Reconstruction," 260–61; *New-York Tribune,* 31 March 1866; O'Brien, *From Bondage to Citizenship,* 339 (quotation).
11. "The Second African Church Burned Down," *RD,* 10 April 1866 (first quotation); "Notice!" Broadside 1866:13, VMHC (second quotation).
12. O'Brien, *From Bondage to Citizenship,* 339; "Third of April in Richmond 1866," *RNN,* 12 April 1866; "Virginia," *NYT,* 9 April 1866 (quotation); "Local Matters," *RD,* 9 April 1866.
13. "Local Matters," *RD,* 9 April 1866 (first and second quotations); O'Brien, *From Bondage to Citizenship,* 328–29; Blair, *Cities of the Dead,* 38.
14. "Another Threat—Horrible to Think!" *RNN,* 12 April 1866 (quotation).
15. Blair, *Cities of the Dead,* 38–40; "Local Matters," *RD,* 9 April 1866; "Third of April in Richmond 1866," *RNN,* 12 April 1866.
16. "Local Matters," *RD,* 9 April 1866 (quotation); "Wonderful Results," *RNN,* 7 March 1867.
17. Rachleff, *Black Labor,* 39; "Third of April in Richmond 1866," *RNN,* 12 April 1866 (first quotation); "Local Matters," *RD,* 9 April 1866 (second quotation).
18. R. M. Manly to William Hawkins, 4 April 1866, cited in L. W. Smith, "Richmond during Presidential Reconstruction," 239, 261.
19. "Local Matters," *RD,* 9 April 1866 (quotation); *Petersburg Daily Index,* 11 April 1866, cited in Blair, *Cities of the Dead,* 41.
20. "Views of Ex-Governor Wise," *RW,* 19 April 1866.
21. "Negro Celebration on the Third of April," *RW,* 10 April 1866 (first quotation); *Richmond Citizen,* 4 April 1866, cited in Rachleff, *Black Labor,* 39 (second quotation).
22. Blair, *Cities of the Dead,* 40 (first quotation); O'Brien, *From Bondage to Citizenship,* 342 (second quotation).

23. "A Colored Fair," *RD,* 13 April 1866.
24. "Colored People's Concert," *RD,* 30 May 1866 (quotation), from University of Richmond, "Reconstructing Virginia: The Richmond Daily Dispatch, 1866–1871."
25. "The Norfolk Riot and Murders," *RD,* 20 April 1866 (first quotation); "The Norfolk Murders," *RD,* 21 April 1866; "The Nigger Riot at Norfolk," *RE,* 21 April 1866 (second quotation).
26. "The Norfolk Riot and Murders," *RD,* 20 April 1866.

15. THE HEROIC DEAD REIGNED SUPREME

1. Entry for 21 May 1866, Richard Eppes Diary, Eppes Family Papers, VMHC (quotation); Blair, *Cities of the Dead,* 52–53; Janney, *Burying the Dead,* 46–49; Faust, *Republic of Suffering,* 238; "Heroes Not Forgotten—Honours to Confederate Dead," *RE,* 5 May 1866.
2. Janney, *Burying the Dead,* 46–68.
3. "Honor to the Dead," *RD,* 19 April 1866; R. K. Smith, *Death and Rebirth,* 167; Kinney, "If Vanquished I Am Still Victorious," 237–42.
4. "Our Honored Dead," *RD,* 11 May 1866 (first quotation); Janney, *Burying the Dead,* 63 (second quotation).
5. "Our Honored Dead," *RD,* 11 May 1866 (all quotations); Krasnoff, "Contributions," 36.
6. "Hollywood Memorial Association of the Ladies of Richmond, Va.," *RD,* 4 May 1866; R. K. Smith, *Death and Rebirth,* 167; Peters, *Richmond's Hollywood Cemetery,* 55–56.
7. "Our Honored Dead," *RD,* 29 May 1866.
8. "Appeal by the Hollywood Memorial Association," *RD,* 29 May 1866.
9. "The Confederate Dead," *RD,* 1 June 1866
10. Ibid.
11. Harris to Bell, 5 July 1866, cited in O'Brien, *From Bondage to Citizenship,* 349; Janney, *Burying the Dead,* 60–62; Blair, *Cities of the Dead,* 54–55; R. K. Smith, *Death and Rebirth,* 169.
12. Janney, *Burying the Dead,* 62–65; R. K. Smith, *Death and Rebirth,* 151.
13. Dawson, *Reminiscences,* 128.

16. THE FIRES OF MALICE

1. "United States Circuit Court," *RD,* 6 June 1866.

2. "Trial of Davis," *NYT,* 6 June 1866 (first quotation); "Judge Underwood's Charge to the Grand Jury Yesterday," *RD,* 6 June 1866 (second quotation); "Trial of Jeff. Davis," *NYT,* 8 June 1866.
3. "Trial of Davis," *NYT,* 6 June 1866.
4. "Laying of the Corner-Stone of the Second African Church," *RD,* 22 May 1866.
5. O'Brien, *From Bondage to Citizenship,* 344.
6. Ibid., 301, 369 (first quotation), 375; "Views of Ex-Governor Wise," *RW,* 19 April 1866 (second quotation).
7. Reynolds, "The New Orleans Riot of 1866, Reconsidered," 5; Ayers, *Thin Light of Freedom,* 403.
8. "Virginia," *NYT,* 9 July 1866; "The Fourth of July in Richmond," *RD,* 6 July 1866.
9. "The Fourth of July in Richmond," *RD,* 6 July 1866; Van Lew to Gov. John A. Andrew, 5 July 1866, Andrews Papers, Massachusetts Historical Society (quotation), courtesy of Steve Engle; "City Intelligence," *RE,* 6 July 1866; Benjamin Butler comments on Wardwell, no date, private collection, courtesy of Terry Alford.
10. John M. Palmer to Malinda A. Palmer, 6 July 1866, in O'Brien, *From Bondage to Citizenship,* 356–57; "The Fourth of July in Richmond," *RD,* 6 July 1866 (first quotation); "The Enquirer and Negroes—False Statement of the Former," *RNN,* 19 July 1866 (second quotation); *RT,* 6 July 1866 (third quotation), cited in O'Brien, *From Bondage to Citizenship,* 357; "Free Press in Richmond Virginia," *RNN,* 30 August 1866 (fourth quotation).
11. "Virginia," *NYT,* 2 July 1866; "A Barbecue on the Fourth," *RD,* 6 July 1866 (quotation).
12. "Virginia," *NYT,* 2 July 1866.
13. Emberton, *Beyond Redemption,* 149; "Virginia," *NYT,* 2 August 1866; O'Brien, *From Bondage to Citizenship,* 363; "The Navy Hill 'Irrepressibles,'" *RD,* 30 July 1866.
14. "Great Mass Meeting," *RNN,* 26 July 1866 (first quotation); O'Brien, *From Bondage to Citizenship,* 370–73 (second quotation 373); "The Whipping Post and the Lash," *RNN,* 23 August 1866.
15. O'Brien, *From Bondage to Citizenship,* 372.
16. Varon, *Southern Lady, Yankee Spy,* 206–9.
17. "Death of Charles Palmer," *RD,* 1 August 1866; Alexander Rives to Dr. William Palmer, 3 August 1866, VMHC; Stuart, "Colonel Ulric Dahlgren," 188 (quotation).

18. Botts, *Great Rebellion,* 224, 226.
19. "Visit to Richmond," *RD,* 4 July 1866; "Base Ball," *RD,* 15 August 1866; "Runaway," *RD,* 13 September 1866.
20. "Cholera in Richmond," *RD,* 16 August 1866; Williams, *Century of Service,* 15–16.
21. "General Schofield," *RNN,* 30 August 1866.
22. "General Schofield," *RD,* 22 August 1866 (first quotation); O'Brien, *From Bondage to Citizenship,* 381 (second quotation).
23. Lowe, *Republicans and Reconstruction,* 66–67.
24. Krasnoff, "Contributions of Edward A. Pollard," 29–49.
25. Pollard, *Lost Cause,* 693 (first quotation), 749 (second quotation).
26. "Great Gathering of Virginians at Winchester," *NYT,* 26 October 1866 (quotation); Janney, *Burying the Dead,* 66–67; Blair, *Cities of the Dead,* 90–94.

17. OBLITERATE ALL DISTINCTIONS

1. "The Election," *RD,* 7 November 1866.
2. Boney, "John Letcher," 59–60; McDonough, *Schofield,* 166–67; Schofield, "Memoranda of reasons for the refusal to grant the petition of Counsel for the discharge of Dr. Jas. L. Watson, furnished to Maj. Layton, J. Av. of Milty. Commission for his information," [December 1866?], Schofield Papers, LC.
3. "The General Assembly of Virginia," *RD,* 3 December 1866 (first and second quotations); Ayers, *Thin Light of Freedom,* 416–17; Maddex, *Virginia Conservatives,* 43–45.
4. "Public Meetings," *RNN,* 3 January 1867; O'Brien, *From Bondage to Citizenship,* 416–17; Rachleff, *Black Labor,* 40; "Francis H. Pierpont and the Provisional Government," *RNN,* 10 January 1867 (quotation).
5. Foner, *Reconstruction,* 276–77; Foner, *Second Founding,* 89–90; Lowe, "Virginia's Reconstruction Convention," 341–42; Tarter, *Virginians and Their Histories,* 278–83; "District No. 1—General Orders," *RD,* 14 March 1867.
6. Foner, *Reconstruction,* 281, 290.
7. "Evacuation Day—Grand Celebration," *RD,* 4 April 1867.
8. "In and about the City," *RSO,* 18 July 1867; "Evacuation Day—Grand Celebration," *RD,* 4 April 1867.
9. "Public Meeting at the Theatre To-Night," *RD,* 15 April 1867.

10. *RD,* 16 April 1867 (quotation); "Great Conservative Rally," *REnq,* 16 April 1867.
11. "Local Matters," *RD,* 16 April 1867; O'Brien, *From Bondage to Citizenship,* 423.
12. "Local Matters," *RD,* 16 April 1867; "Address to the Colored People," *RD,* 22 April 1867 (quotations).
13. Foner, *Reconstruction,* 304 (quotation); Rachleff, *Black Labor,* 41; "Local Matters," *RD,* 18 April 1867.
14. "Speech of Senator Wilson," *RD,* 23 April 1867; Lowe, *Republicans and Reconstruction,* 83.
15. "Almost a Row," *RD,* 24 April 1867.
16. "The Street Railway Case," *RD,* 25 April 1867; "Another Street Car Difficulty," *RD,* 30 April 1867; "The Street-car Question," *RD,* 1 May 1867; "A Negro Man Attempts to Ride in One of the Ladies' Cars," *RD,* 8 May 1867; Chesson, *Richmond after the War,* 102–3, 140–41; "Local Matters," *RNN,* 25 April 1867.
17. "Serious Disturbance," *RD,* 10 May 1867; "Lawlessness of Negroes at Richmond Va.," *NYT,* 10 May 1867.
18. "Incendiary Meeting," *RD,* 11 May 1867.
19. Schofield to Grant, 14 May 1867, in Grant, *Papers of Ulysses S. Grant,* 17:139n; "More Resistance to the Law by Colored Men," *RD,* 13 May 1867.

18. THE PRISONER

1. Dispatch of 6 April 1865, in Blackett, *Chester,* 294 (first quotation); Campbell to B. R. Curtis, 20 July 1865, in *Century Magazine* 38:6 (October 1889): 952 (second quotation); Pollard, *Life of Davis,* vii (third quotation).
2. Lankford, *Cry Havoc!* 2 (first quotation); "Grand Commemoration at Hollywood Cemetery," *RD,* 1 June 1866 (second quotation).
3. Nicoletti, *Secession on Trial,* 192–204; Schofield to Underwood, 30 March 1867 (quotation), Schofield Papers, LC.
4. Nicoletti, *Secession on Trial,* 63–83; Cooper, *Jefferson Davis, American,* 540.
5. Nicoletti, *Secession on Trial,* 182–87.
6. "United States Circuit Court," *RD,* 7 May 1867 (first and second quotations); *New York Herald,* quoted in "The Northern Press on Underwood's

Charge," *RD,* 10 May 1867 (third quotation); *New York Nation,* cited in "Some First-Rate Notices of Underwood," *RD,* 11 May 1867.

7. Varina Davis, *Jefferson Davis: Ex-President of the Confederate States of America, A Memoir,* 2 vols. (New York: Belford, 1898), 794.
8. "Jefferson Davis," *NYT,* 14 May 1867.
9. Nicoletti, *Secession on Trial,* 164–65; "Jefferson Davis Indicted," *NYT,* 12 May 1866.
10. "Meeting at the African Church," *RD,* 15 May 1867.
11. "Mr. Davis Released on Bail—A Great Day for the Nation," *RD,* 14 May 1867; "Telegraphic Dispatches," *New Orleans Tribune,* 14 May 1867.
12. R. K. Smith, *Death and Rebirth,* 169; Blair, *Cities of the Dead,* 64–65; James H. Gardner to Mary Gardner Florance, 1 June 1867, VMHC.
13. "Decorating the Graves of the Dead of the Confederate Army in Richmond," *NYT,* 3 June 1867 (quotation); "A Day with Our Dead!" *RD,* 1 June 1867; Blair, *Cities of the Dead,* 64–65.

19. FIT THEM FOR CITIZENSHIP

1. "Freedmen's Bureau—Teachers Wanted," *RD,* 27 May 1867 (first quotation); W to Matthew Fontaine Maury, 23 August 1867, Maury Papers, LC (second quotation).
2. "Registering Officers," *RD,* 6 April 1867; "General Schofield's Order as to Registration," ibid., 16 May 1867; "Registration of Freedmen," ibid., 31 May 1867; Schofield to O. O. Howard, 26 March 1867, Schofield Papers, LC.
3. McDonough, *Schofield,* 174–75.
4. Lowe, *Republicans and Reconstruction,* 122; Schofield to Grant, 5 October 1867, Schofield Papers, LC.
5. "Registration," *RD,* 26 June 1867; "The Registry Intimidation," ibid., 27 June 1867 (quotation); Maddex, *Virginia Conservatives,* 50–55.
6. "Freedmen's Meeting at Amelia Courthouse," *RD,* 25 May 1867.
7. "Almost a Riot," *RD,* 31 July 1867; "The Twenty-Fifth Street Disturbance," ibid., 1 August 1867.
8. "John Oliver and Fields Cook Arraigned for Disloyalty," *RD,* 1 August 1867.
9. "Virginia Republican Convention," *Loyal Georgian,* 10 August 1867; "Colored Men Dissatisfied," *RD,* 3 August 1867.

10. "Local Matters: The Mass Convention Repudiated" and "Meeting at Republican Hall Last Night," *RD,* 2 August 1867 (quotation); "Subsequent Mass Meeting—Speeches and Resolutions," *NYT,* 3 August 1867.
11. "A Mass Meeting," *RD,* 3 August 1867 (first quotation); "Meeting of the United States Ex-Officers, Soldiers, and Sailors Association," ibid., 12 August 1867 (second quotation).
12. Blake, *William Mahone,* 81–83; Chesson, *Richmond after the War,* 136; "From Richmond to the Ohio," *RD,* 10 May 1867 (quotation); Fitzhugh, "Cui Bono?—The Negro Vote," 289.
13. "Lecture by a Mulatto Woman in the Capitol," *RD,* 6 August 1867.
14. Levine, *Failed Promise,* 139–42 (first quotation 140); Varon, *Appomattox,* 257–58; "Lecture by a Mulatto Woman in the Capitol," *RD,* 6 August 1867 (second quotation).
15. "Nat. Turner's Massacre," *RD,* 12 August 1867.

20. THE DISGRACE IS INFLICTED

1. Lowe, *Republicans and Reconstruction,* 122–23.
2. McDonough, *Schofield,* 175–76; "Elections for the Convention," *RD,* 25 September 1867.
3. O'Brien, "Albert R. Brooks (c. 1817–1881)," EV.
4. "Virginia," *NYT,* 18 October 1867.
5. Gen. John Schofield, "Personnel of the Virginia Convention," Schofield Papers, LC.
6. "Virginia," *NYT,* 18 October 1867.
7. "Sentiments of a Radical Candidate for the Convention," *RD,* 17 October 1867.
8. Whitley, "Joseph Cox (ca. 1835–1880)," EV; Lowe, "Virginia's Reconstruction Convention," 347; "Virginia," *NYT,* 18 October 1867.
9. "John Oliver and Fields Cook," *RD,* 1 August 1867.
10. "Nominations for the Convention," *RD,* 16 October 1867; "City Members of the Convention," ibid., 19 October 1867.
11. Quoted from *Enquirer* and *Examiner* in *Chicago Tribune,* 28 October 1867 (first quotation); *RD,* 21 October 1867 (second quotation).
12. "Attempt to Hold a Republican Meeting," *RD,* 19 October 1867.
13. Lyons to Johnson, 16 October 1867, in Johnson, *Papers of Andrew Johnson,* 13:175–76.
14. "The Times and the Remedies," *NYT,* 17 October 1867.

15. "The Virginia Election," *NYT,* 5 October 1867; "Gen. Schofield's Order," *NYT,* 7 October 1867; "Voting by Ballot," *RD,* 10 October 1867.
16. "The Election," *RD,* 23 October 1867; "The Election," ibid., 24 October 1867; "Last Day of the Election," ibid., 25 October 1867; "Virginia," *NYT,* October 18, 1867 (quotation).
17. Lowe, *Republicans and Reconstruction,* 122–29; "Special Correspondence of the Herald," *New York Herald,* 30 October 1867; "The Election in Richmond—The Destructives Victorious!" *RD,* 25 October 1867 (quotation).
18. Gilmer to editors, *RD,* 28 October 1867; Gilmer to Schofield, ibid., 29 October 1867; "Reply by General Schofield to Mr. Gilmer's Complaint," ibid., 30 October 1867; "Aspect of Affairs," *NYT,* 29 October 1867; calendar, 11 November 1867, in Grant, *Papers of Ulysses S. Grant,* 18:379. (A month later, Gilmer learned that the army was about to muster Brown out of the service. A good hater, he again wrote the president and thanked him "for the order decapitating General O. Brown." His congratulations were premature, and Brown remained on post [Gilmer to Johnson, 6 December 1867, in Johnson, *Papers of Andrew Johnson,* 13:315].)
19. "The Wise—Pollard Affair," *Alexandria Gazette,* 16 November 1867 (quotation); "Wise vs. Pollard," *RD,* 16 November 1867.

21. DEUX EX MACHINA

1. "Radical Meeting on the Capitol Square," *RD,* 30 October 1867.
2. "Virginia," *NYT,* 10 November 1867 (first quotation); McDonough, "John Schofield," 248 (second quotation); "Radical Mass Meeting," *RD,* 1 November 1867 (third quotation).
3. "Radical Mass Meeting," *RD,* 12 November 1867; "Arrest of Lindsay in Richmond," *Alexandria Gazette,* 14 November 1867.
4. "From Richmond—Arrest of Hunnicutt," *Alexandria Gazette,* 30 November 1867; "The Arrest of J. W. Hunnicutt in Richmond, Va.," *NYT,* 29 November 1867.
5. "The State Constitutional Convention," *RD,* 4 December 1867 (first quotation); Foner, *Reconstruction,* 316 (second quotation).
6. "Virginia," *NYT,* 7 December 1867 (first quotation); "The Unconstitutional Convention," *RD,* 5 December 1867 (second quotation).
7. "Organization," *RD,* 6 November 1867; "Call for a State Conservative Convention," ibid., 13 November 1867; cited in *Staunton Spectator,* 5 November 1867 (quotation).

8. "The Convention," *RD,* 12 December 1867.
9. Maddex, *Virginia Conservatives,* 54–56.
10. "The Conservative Convention," *RD,* 13 December 1867.
11. "The Convention of the Conservative Press of Virginia," *Staunton Vindicator,* 20 December 1867.
12. "Personnel of the Late Convention," *RD,* 1 May 1868.
13. *NYT,* 26 March 1868 (first quotation); Schofield, "Personnel of the Virginia Convention, City of Richmond," Schofield Papers, LC (second quotation); Deal, Julienne, and Tarter, *Justice for Ourselves,* 98.
14. Rachleff, *Black Labor,* 47; "Latest from the Unconstitutional Convention," *RD,* 14 December 1867.
15. "Local Matters," *RD,* 7 April 1868; "A Pow-Wow over the Mixed School Question," ibid., 8 April 1868 (quotation); Rachleff, *Black Labor,* 49.
16. "The Virginia Convention—Councilmen Appointed in Richmond," *NYT,* 11 April 1868; McDonough, "Schofield," 252–53; McDonough, *Schofield,* 184–85; Schofield to Mayo, 2 May 1868, and Mayo to President Johnson, 17 June 1868, Schofield Papers, LC.
17. Ambler, *Pierpont,* 306–9, 328–33 (quotation 308); Schofield to Grant, 2 April 1868, and Pierpont to Grant, 15 April 1868 (calendar), in Grant, *Papers of Ulysses S. Grant,* 18:218–19, 547; Schofield to Grant, 15 April 1868, Schofield Papers, LC.
18. Tarter, *Virginians and Their Histories,* 280–84.
19. John Brown Baldwin, testimony, 10 February 1866, *Jt. Comm.,* 2:106; Tarter, *Virginians and Their Histories,* 282–83; Lowe, *Republicans and Reconstruction,* 120, 221n; *RD,* 17 January 1868.
20. Tarter, *Virginians and Their Histories,* 280–83; Ayers, *Thin Light of Freedom,* 446–47; Schofield, *Forty-Six Years in the Army,* 402 (quotation).
21. Schofield to Grant, 18 April 1868, in Grant, *Papers of Ulysses S. Grant,* 18:222; "The Constitutional Convention," *REnq,* 18 April 1868.
22. "Virginia," *NYT,* 20 April 1868; "The Constitution—General Schofield—The Negro," *RD,* 18 April 1868; Schofield to Grant, 18 April 1868, in Grant, *Papers of Ulysses S. Grant,* 18:221–22 (quotation); "The Virginia Convention," *RD,* 18 April 1865.
23. Schofield to Grant, 18 April 1868, in Grant, *Papers of Ulysses S. Grant,* 18:222.
24. Ayers, *Thin Light of Freedom,* 446–52; Tarter, *Constitutional History of Virginia,* 152–56.

22. LEFT UNDONE

1. Mayo to Johnson, 17 June 1868, Schofield Papers, LC; "The Police Difficulties," *RD*, 11 June 1868; "Mayor's Court," *RD*, 16 June 1868; "Fourth of July," ibid., 4 July 1868.
2. "The Grand Concert To-night," *RD*, 26 June 1868.
3. Chesson, *Richmond after the War*, chaps. 5 and 6; Foner, *Reconstruction*, 82.
4. Deal, Julienne, and Tarter, *Justice for Ourselves*, 116.
5. Lowe, *Republicans and Reconstruction*, 159–63 (quotation 160).
6. Maury to F. W. Tremlett, 7 November 1865, cited in Hanna, "The Role of Matthew Fontaine Maury," 119–20.
7. "Virginia Conference African Methodist Episcopal Church," "Dedication of African Methodist Church at Rocketts," *RD*, May 14, 1867; West, "The Harris Brothers," 130.
8. Susan Hoge to Elizabeth H. Howard, 28 October 1865, Hoge Family Papers, VMHC.
9. Varon, *Southern Lady, Yankee Spy*, 209, 216–17, 246–47.
10. K. Green, *Devil's Half Acre*, 207–9, 219–21.
11. Hamm, *Murder, Honor, and Law*, chap. 1.
12. C. M. Simpson, *Good Southerner*, 304 (quotation), 314.
13. Guzman-Stokes, "A Flag and a Family."
14. "Freedmen's Celebration to Commemorate Their Emancipation," *RD*, 2 January 1866 (quotation); entry for "John Oliver (col'd) Clerk," FB records, Ancestry.com; Chesson, *Richmond after the War*, 97; Chesson, "John Oliver (d. 1899)."
15. John Oliver to editor, *RE*, 21 May 1867, reprinted in *New Orleans Tribune*, 8 June 1867.

EPILOGUE

1. "The Confederate Dead at Hollywood," *RD*, 3 June 1869.
2. Lowe, *Republicans and Reconstruction*, 177, 184–95.
3. "Burning Yet," *RD*, 7 February 1866.

BIBLIOGRAPHY

PUBLISHED PRIMARY SOURCES

Abbott, Martin, ed. "A Southerner Views the South, 1865: Letters of Harvey M. Watterson." *VMHB* 68:4 (October 1960): 478–89.

Alexander, General Edward Porter. *Fighting for the Confederacy: The Personal Recollections of General Edward Porter Alexander.* Edited by Gary W. Gallagher. Chapel Hill: University of North Carolina Press, 1989.

Berlin, Ira, Joseph P. Reidy, and Leslie Rowland, eds. *Freedom: A Documentary History of Emancipation, 1861–1867.* Ser. 2, *The Black Military Experience.* Cambridge: Cambridge University Press, 1982.

Blackett, R. J. M., ed. *Thomas Morris Chester, Black Civil War Correspondent: His Dispatches from the Virginia Front.* Baton Rouge: Louisiana State University Press, 1989.

Botts, John Minor. *The Great Rebellion: Its Secret History, Rise, Progress, and Disastrous Failure.* New York: Harper and Brothers, 1866.

Bratton, Mary J., ed. "Fields's Observations: The Slave Narrative of a Nineteenth-Century Virginian." *VMHB* 88:1 (January 1980): 75–93.

Butler, Benjamin F. *Private and Official Correspondence of Gen. Benjamin F. Butler.* 5 vols. Privately issued, 1917.

Conolly, Thomas. *An Irishman in Dixie: Thomas Conolly's Diary of the Fall of the Confederacy.* Edited by Nelson D. Lankford. Columbia: University of South Carolina Press, 1988.

Corbin, Diana Fontaine Maury. *A Life of Matthew Fontaine Maury, U.S.N., C.S.N.* 1888. Middleton, DE: Lucy Booker Roper, 2014.

Dawson, Francis W. *Reminiscences of Confederate Service, 1861–1865.* Charleston, SC: News and Courier Book Presses, 1882. Reprinted with annotations and introduction by L. P. Roper, 2020.

Dennett, John Richard. *The South as It Is: 1865–1866.* Edited by Henry M. Christman. New York: Viking, 1965.

Divine, William J. *Richmond City Directory, 1866.* Richmond: E. P. Townsend, 1866.

Duke, Maurice, and Daniel P. Jordan, eds. *A Richmond Reader, 1733–1983.* Chapel Hill: University of North Carolina Press, 1983.

Ezekiel, Herbert T., and Gaston Lichtenstein. *The History of the Jews of Richmond from 1769 to 1917.* Richmond: Herbert T. Ezekiel, 1917.

Fitzhugh, George. "Camp Lee and the Freedmen's Bureau." *De Bow's Review,* ser. 2, vol. 2 (July-December 1866): 346–55.

———. "Cui Bono?—The Negro Vote." *De Bow's Review,* ser. 2, vol. 4 (July-December 1867): 289–92.

Fitzpatrick, Marion Hill. *Letters to Amanda: The Civil War Letters of Marion Hill Fitzpatrick, Army of Northern Virginia.* Edited by Jeffrey C. Lowe and Sam Hodges. Macon, GA: Mercer University Press, 1998.

Flournoy, H. W., ed. *Calendar of Virginia State Papers and Other Manuscripts from January 1, 1836, to April 15, 1869; Preserved in the Capitol at Richmond.* Vol. 11. Richmond: n.p., 1893. Photocopy reprint. Xerox by Micro Photo, 1967.

Foner, Philip S. and George E. Walker, eds. *Proceedings of the Black State Conventions, 1840–1865.* Philadelphia: Temple University Press, 1979–80.

Garidel, Henri. *Exile in Richmond: The Confederate Journal of Henri Garidel.* Edited by Michael Bedout Chesson and Leslie Jean Roberts. Charlottesville: University Press of Virginia, 2001.

Gilmer, John H. *War of Races: By Whom Is It Sought to Be Brought About.* Richmond: n.p., 1867.

Grant, Julia Dent. *The Personal Memoirs of Julia Dent Grant [Mrs. Ulysses S. Grant].* Edited by John Y. Simon. Carbondale: Southern Illinois University Press, 1975.

Grant, Ulysses S. *The Papers of Ulysses S. Grant.* Edited by John Y. Simon et al. 24 vols. Carbondale: Southern Illinois University Press, 1967–2000.

Harrison, Mrs. Burton [Constance Cary]. *Recollections Grave and Gay.* London: Smith, Elder, 1912.

Hoge, Moses Drury. *Moses Drury Hoge: Life and Letters.* Edited by Peyton Harrison Hoge. Richmond: Presbyterian Committee of Publication, 1899.

Hollywood Memorial Association. *Register of the Confederate Dead, Interred in Hollywood Cemetery.* Richmond: Gary, Clemmitt & Jones, 1869.

Hunnicutt, James W. *The Conspiracy Unveiled; or, The Horrors of Secession.* Philadelphia: Lippincott, 1863.

Johnson, Andrew. *The Papers of Andrew Johnson.* Edited by Leroy P. Graf, Ralph W. Haskins, and Paul H. Bergeron. 16 vols. Knoxville: University of Tennessee Press, 1967–2000.

Jones, John Beauchamp. *A Rebel War Clerk's Diary: At the Confederate States Capital.* Edited by Howard Swiggett. 2 vols. New York: Old Hickory Bookshop, 1935.

Jones, Wilbur Devereux, ed. "A British Report on Postwar Virginia." *VMHB* 69:3 (July 1961): 346–52.

Kreutzer, William. *Notes and Observations Made during Four Years of Service with the Ninety-Eighth N.Y. Volunteers in the War of 1861.* Philadelphia: Grant, Faires & Rodgers, 1878.

Manarin, Louis H., ed. *Richmond at War: The Minutes of the City Council, 1861–1865.* Chapel Hill: University of North Carolina Press, 1966.

McGuire, Judith W. *Diary of a Southern Refugee during the War, Annotated Edition.* Edited by James I. Robertson Jr. Lexington: University of Kentucky Press, 2014.

Mugleston, William F., ed. "The Freedmen's Bureau and Reconstruction in Virginia: The Diary of Marcus Sterling Hopkins, A Union Officer." *VMHB* 86:1 (January 1978): 45–102.

Myers, Gustavus A. "Abraham Lincoln in Richmond: Memoranda." *VMHB* 41:4 (October 1933): 318–22.

Patrick, Marsena Rudolph. *Inside Lincoln's Army: The Diary of Marsena Rudolph Patrick, Provost Marshal General, Army of the Potomac.* Edited by David S. Sparks. New York: Thomas Yoseloff, 1964.

Perdue, Charles L., Jr., Thomas E. Barden, and Robert K. Phillips, eds. *Weevils in the Wheat: Interviews with Virginia Ex-Slaves.* Charlottesville: University Press of Virginia, 1976.

Pollard, Edward A. *Life of Jefferson Davis, with a Secret History of the Southern Confederacy Gathered "Behind the Scenes in Richmond"* [. . .]. Philadelphia: National Publishing, 1869.

———. *The Lost Cause; A New Southern History of the War of the Confederates.* New York: E. B. Treat, 1866.

———. *Southern History of the War.* New York: Charles B. Richardson, 1866.

Rachal, William M. E., ed. "The Occupation of Richmond, April 1865: The Memorandum of Events of Colonel Christopher Q. Tompkins." *VMHB* 73:2 (April 1965): 189–98.

Randolph, Peter. *From Slave Cabin to the Pulpit.* Boston: James H. Earle, 1893.

Reese, George H., ed. *Proceedings of the Virginia State Convention of 1861.* 4 vols. Richmond: Virginia State Library, 1965.

Reid, Whitelaw. *After the War: A Southern Tour. May 1, 1865, to May 1, 1866.* London: Sampson Law, Son, & Marston, 1866.

———. *A Radical View: The "Agate" Dispatches of Whitelaw Reid, 1861–1865.* Edited by James G. Smart. 2 vols. Memphis: Memphis State University Press, 1976.

Ripley, C. Peter, et al., eds. *The Black Abolitionist Papers.* Vol. 5, *The United States, 1859–1865.* Chapel Hill: University of North Carolina Press, 1992.

Ripley, Edward H. *The Capture and Occupation of Richmond, April 3rd, 1865.* New York: G. P. Putnam's Sons, 1907.

Robertson, James I., Jr., ed. "English Views of the Civil War: A Unique Excursion to Virginia, April 2–8, 1865" [account of Edward Moseley]. *VMHB* 77:2 (April 1969): 201–12.

Ruffin, Edmund. *The Diary of Edmund Ruffin.* Edited by William Kauffman Scarborough. Vol. 3, *A Dream Shattered: June, 1863–June, 1865.* Baton Rouge: Louisiana State University Press, 1989.

Schofield, John M. *Forty-Six Years in the Army.* New York: Century, 1897.

Simpson, Brooks D., LeRoy P. Graf, and John Muldowny, eds. *Advice after Appomattox: Letters to Andrew Johnson, 1865–1866.* Knoxville: University of Tennessee Press, 1987.

Siviter, Anna Pierpont. *Recollections of War and Peace, 1861–1868.* New York: G. P. Putnam's Sons, 1938.

Stevens, S. W. *A Trip to Richmond: or Notes by the Way.* Lowell, MA: Stone & Huse, 1865.

Strong, George Templeton. *The Diary of George Templeton Strong.* Edited by Allan Nevins and Milton Halsey Tomas. Vol. 3, *The Civil War, 1860–1865.* New York: Macmillan, 1952.

Swint, Henry L., ed. *Dear Ones at Home: Letters from Contraband Camps.* Nashville: Vanderbilt University Press, 1966.

Teamoh, George. *God Made Man, Man Made the Slave: The Autobiography of George Teamoh.* Macon, GA: Mercer University Press, 1990.

Trowbridge, J. T. *A Picture of the Desolated States; and the Work of Restoration, 1865–1868.* Hartford, CT: L. Stebbins, 1868.

———. *The South: A Tour of Its Battlefields and Ruined Cities, a Journey through the Desolated States, and Talks with the People* [. . .]. Hartford, CT: L. Stebbins, 1866.

United States Congress. *Report of the Joint Committee on the Conduct of the War, at the Second Session Thirty-Eighth Congress.* Washington, DC: Government Printing Office, 1865.

———. *Report of the Joint Committee on Reconstruction at the First Session Thirty-Ninth Congress.* Washington, DC: Government Printing Office, 1866.

United States War Department. *The War of the Rebellion: A Compilation of the Official Records of the Union and Confederate Armies.* 128 vols. Washington, DC: Government Printing Office, 1880–1901.

Van Lew, Elizabeth L. *A Yankee Spy in Richmond: The Civil War Diary of "Crazy Bet" Van Lew.* Edited by David D. Ryan. Mechanicsburg, PA: Stackpole, 1996.

Virginia. *The Debates and Proceedings of the Constitutional Convention of the State of Virginia.* Richmond: New Nation, 1868.

———. *Documents of the Constitutional Convention of the State of Virginia.* Richmond: New Nation, 1867 [1868].

Weitzel, Godfrey. *Richmond Occupied: Entry of the United States Forces into Richmond, Va. April 3, 1865; Calling Together of the Virginia Legislature and Revocation of the Same.* 1881. Edited by Louis H. Manarin. Richmond: Richmond Civil War Centennial Commission, 1965.

SELECTED ONLINE RESOURCES

Civil War Richmond: https://www.civilwarrichmond.com/.

Encyclopedia Virginia. Online resource on Virginia history and biography; joint partnership of Virginia Humanities and Library of Virginia: https://www.encyclopediavirginia.org.

Last Seen: Finding Family after Slavery: https://informationwanted.org.

Library of Congress. Historic American Newspapers database: https://chroniclingamerica.loc.gov.

Library of Virginia. Online Exhibition. Remaking Virginia: Transformation through Emancipation: https://www.virginiamemory.com/online-exhibitions/exhibits/show/remaking-virginia.

Library of Virginia. Newspaper Database: https://www.virginiachronicle.com.

Michael D. Gorman's Civil War Richmond: https://www.mdgorman.com.

National Archives and Records Administration. Civil War military records: https://www.archivesgov/research/military/civil-war.

National Park Service. Civil War Soldiers and Sailors System (CWSS): https://www.nps.gov/civilwar/soldiers-and-sailors-database.htm.

Philadelphia Area Consortium of Special Collections Libraries (PACSCL). In Her Own Right: A Century of Women's Activism, 1820–1920: https://www.inherownright.org.

Smithsonian Institution. Smithsonian Online Virtual Archives: https://sova.si.edu/.

University of Maryland. Freedmen and Southern Society Project: https://www.freedmen.umd.edu.

University of Richmond. Reconstructing Virginia: The Richmond Daily Dispatch, 1866–1871: https://reconstructingvirginia.richmond.edu/.

University of Virginia. The Valley of the Shadow: Two Communities in the American Civil War: https://www.iath.virginia.edu/vshadow2/.

SECONDARY SOURCES

Abbott, Richard H. *The Republican Party and the South, 1855–1877: The First Southern Strategy.* Chapel Hill: University of North Carolina Press, 1986.

Abrahamson, James L. *The Men of Secession and Civil War, 1859–1861.* Wilmington, DE: Scholarly Resources, 2000.

Alderson, William T. "The Freedmen's Bureau and Negro Education in Virginia." *North Carolina Historical Review* 29:1 (January 1952): 64–90.

———. "The Influence of Military Rule and the Freedmen's Bureau on Reconstruction in Virginia, 1865–1870." PhD diss., Vanderbilt University, 1962.

Alford, Terry. *Fortune's Fool: The Life of John Wilkes Booth.* Oxford: Oxford University Press, 2015.

Ambler, Charles H. *Francis H. Pierpont: Union War Governor of Virginia and Father of West Virginia.* Chapel Hill: University of North Carolina Press, 1937.

Ash, Stephen V. *Rebel Richmond: Life and Death in the Confederate Capital.* Chapel Hill: University of North Carolina Press, 2019.

———. *When the Yankees Came: Conflict and Chaos in the Occupied South, 1861–1865.* Chapel Hill: University of North Carolina Press, 1995.

———. "White Virginians under Federal Occupation, 1861–1865." *VMHB* 98:2 (April 1990): 169–92.

Ayers, Edward L. *In the Presence of Mine Enemies: War in the Heart of America, 1859–1863.* New York: Norton, 2003.

———. *The Thin Light of Freedom: The Civil War and Emancipation in the Heart of America.* New York: Norton, 2017.

Barber, Edna Susan. "'Sisters of the Capital': White Women in Richmond, Virginia, 1860–1880." PhD diss., University of Maryland, 1997.

Barksdale, Kevin. "Francis Harrison Pierpont (1814–1899)." Encyclopedia Virginia. Accessed 12 February 2021.

Bayliss, Mary Lynn. *The Dooleys of Richmond: An Irish Immigrant Family in the Old and New South.* Charlottesville: University of Virginia Press, 2017.

Bearss, Sara B. "Restored and Vindicated: The Virginia Constitutional Convention of 1864." *VMHB* 122:2 (2014): 156–81.

Belsches, Elvatrice Parker. *Richmond, Virginia.* Black America Series. Charleston, SC: Arcadia, 2002.

Berlin, Ira. *The Long Emancipation: The Demise of Slavery in the United States.* Cambridge, MA: Harvard University Press, 2015.

Berman, Myron. *Richmond's Jewry, 1769–1976: Shabbat in Shockoe.* Charlottesville: University Press of Virginia for the Jewish Community Federation of Richmond, 1979.

Blackford, L. Minor. *Mine Eyes Have Seen the Glory: The Story of a Virginia Lady, Mary Berkeley Minor Blackford, 1802–1896, Who Taught Her Sons to Hate Slavery and to Love the Union.* Cambridge, MA: Harvard University Press, 1954.

Blair, William A. *Cities of the Dead: Contesting the Memory of the Civil War in the South, 1865–1914.* Chapel Hill: University of North Carolina Press, 2004.

———. "Finding the Ending of America's Civil War." *American Historical Review* 120:5 (December 2015): 1753–66.

———. "Justice Versus Law and Order: The Battles over the Reconstruction of Virginia's Minor Judiciary, 1865–1870." *VMHB* 103:2 (April 1995): 157–80.

———. *The Record of Murders and Outrages: Racial Violence and the Fight over Truth at the Dawn of Reconstruction.* Chapel Hill: University of North Carolina Press, 2021.

Blake, Nelson Morehouse. *William Mahone of Virginia: Soldier and Political Insurgent.* Richmond: Garret & Massie, 1935.

Blanton, Wyndham B. *The Making of a Downtown Church: The History of the Second Presbyterian Church, Richmond, Virginia, 1845–1945.* Richmond: John Knox, 1945.

Blight, David W. *Frederick Douglass, Prophet of Freedom.* New York: Simon & Schuster, 2018.

———. *Frederick Douglass' Civil War.* Baton Rouge: Louisiana State University Press, 1989.

———. *Race and Reunion: The Civil War in American Memory.* Cambridge, MA: Belknap Press of Harvard University Press, 2001.

Blum, Edward J. *Reforging the White Republic: Race, Religion, and American Nationalism, 1865–1898.* Baton Rouge: Louisiana State University Press, 2005.

Boney, F. N. "John Letcher and Reconstruction in Virginia." *Mississippi Quarterly* 19:2 (Spring 1966): 53–65.

Broadus, John A. *Memorial of James Thomas, Jr.* Richmond: Everett Waddey, 1888.

Bromberg, Alan. "Joseph R. Anderson (1813–1891)." Encyclopedia Virginia. Accessed 12 February 2021.

———. "The Virginia Congressional Elections of 1865: A Test of Southern Loyalty." *VMHB* 84:1 (January 1976): 75–98.

Broomall, James. *Private Confederacies: The Emotional Worlds of Southern Men as Citizens and Soldiers.* Chapel Hill: University of North Carolina Press, 2019.

Brown, Elsa Barkley. "Uncle Ned's Children: Negotiating Community and Freedom in Postemancipation Richmond, Virginia." PhD diss., Kent State University, 1994.

Brumbaugh, Thomas B. "The Evolution of Crawford's 'Washington.'" *VMHB* 70:1 (January 1962): 2–29.

Butchart, Ronald E. *Northern Schools, Southern Blacks, and Reconstruction: Freedmen's Education, 1862–1875.* Westport, CT: Greenwood, 1980.

Carey, Hampton D. "New Voices in the Old Dominion: Black Politics in the Virginia Southside Region and the City of Richmond, 1867–1902." PhD diss., Columbia University, 2000.

Carmichael, Peter S. *The Last Generation: Young Virginians in Peace, War, and Reunion.* Chapel Hill: University of North Carolina Press, 2005.

Carter, Dan. T. "The Anatomy of Fear: The Christmas Day Insurrection Scare of 1865." *JSH* 42:3 (August 1976): 345–64.

———. *When the War Was Over: The Failure of Self-Reconstruction, 1865–1867.* Baton Rouge: Louisiana State University Press, 1985.

Censer, Jane Turner. *The Reconstruction of White Southern Womanhood, 1865–1895.* Baton Rouge: Louisiana State University Press, 2003.

Chesson, Michael B. "John Oliver (d. 1899)." *Dictionary of Virginia Biography.* Richmond: Library of Virginia, 2021.

———. *Richmond after the War, 1865–1890.* Richmond: Virginia State Library, 1981.

Christian George L. "John Harmer Gilmer." *Virginia Law Register* 14:9 (1909): 28.

Christian, W. Asbury. *Richmond: Her Past and Present.* Richmond: L. H. Jenkins, 1912.

Cimbala, Paul A. *The Freedmen's Bureau: Reconstructing the American South after the Civil War.* Malabar, FL: Krieger, 2005.

Cimbala, Paul A., and Randall M. Miller. *The Freedmen's Bureau and Reconstruction: Reconsiderations.* New York: Fordham University Press, 1999.

Cooper, William J., Jr. *Jefferson Davis, American.* New York: Knopf, 2000.

Coski, John. "Isabel Maury, Museum Pioneer." *Museum of the Confederacy Magazine,* Summer 2012, 18–22.

Cresap, Bernarr. *Appomattox Commander: The Story of General E. O. C. Ord.* San Diego: A. S. Barnes, 1981.

Crofts, Daniel W. *Reluctant Confederates: Upper South Unionists in the Secession Crisis.* Chapel Hill: University of North Carolina Press, 1989.

Dabney, Virginius. *Pistols and Pointed Pens: The Dueling Editors of Old Virginia.* Chapel Hill: Algonquin, 1987.

———. *Richmond: The Story of a City.* Garden City, NY: Doubleday, 1976.

———. *Virginia: The New Dominion.* 1971. Charlottesville: University Press of Virginia, 1983.

Dailey, Jane. *Before Jim Crow: The Politics of Race in Postemancipation Virginia.* Chapel Hill: University of North Carolina Press, 2000.

Davenport Insurance Corporation. *The Experience of a Century: A Narrative Report of the Century 1848–1948 as It Has Dealt with the Davenport Insurance Corporation.* Richmond: Whittet & Shepperson, 1948.

Davis, Robert Scott. "The Georgia Odyssey of the Confederate Gold." *Georgia Historical Quarterly* 86:4 (2002): 569–86.

Davis, William C. *Jefferson Davis: The Man and His Hour.* Baton Rouge: Louisiana State University Press, 1991.

Deal, John G., Marianne E. Julienne, and Brent Tarter. *Justice for Ourselves: Black Virginians Claim Their Freedom after Slavery.* Charlottesville: University of Virginia Press, 2024.

Deans, Bob. *The River Where America Began: A Journey along the James.* Lanham, MD: Rowman & Littlefield, 2007.

Dew, Charles B. *Ironmaker to the Confederacy: Joseph Reid Anderson and the Tredegar Iron Works.* New Haven, CT: Yale University Press, 1966.

Dimmick, Lauretta. "'An Altar Erected to Heroic Virtue Itself.'" *American Art Journal* 23:2 (1991): 4–73.

Donald, David Herbert. *Lincoln.* New York: Simon & Schuster, 1995.

Dorris, Jonathan Truman. *Pardon and Amnesty under Lincoln and Johnson: The Restoration of the Confederates to Their Rights and Privileges, 1861–1898.* Chapel Hill: University of North Carolina Press, 1953.

Downs, Gregory P. *After Appomattox: Military Occupation and the Ends of War.* Cambridge, MA: Harvard University Press, 2015.

Dozier, Graham T., comp. *Virginia's Civil War: A Guide to Manuscript Collections at the Virginia Historical Society.* Richmond: Virginia Historical Society, 1998.

Duggan, Richard M. "The Military Occupation of Richmond, Virginia." Master's thesis, University of Richmond, 1965.

Egerton, Douglas R. *The Wars of Reconstruction: The Brief, Violent History of America's Most Progressive War.* New York: Bloomsbury, 2014.

Emberton, Carole. *Beyond Redemption: Race, Violence, and the American South after the Civil War.* Chicago: University of Chicago Press, 2013.

Escott, Paul D. *Lincoln's Dilemma: Blair, Sumner, and the Republican Struggle over Racism and Equality in the Civil War Era.* Charlottesville: University of Virginia Press, 2014.

Ezekiel, Herbert T., and Gaston Lichtenstein. *The History of the Jews of Richmond from 1769 to 1917.* Richmond: Herbert T. Ezekiel, 1917.

Fahrner, Alvin A. "William 'Extra Billy' Smith, Governor of Virginia, 1864–1865." *VMHB* 74:1 (January 1966): 68–87.

Farmer-Kaiser, Mary. *Freedwomen and the Freedmen's Bureau: Race, Gender, and Public Policy in the Age of Emancipation.* New York: Fordham University Press, 2010.

———. "With a Weight of Circumstances Like Millstones about their Necks." *VMHB* 115:3 (2007): 413–42.

Faust, Drew. *This Republic of Suffering: Death and the American Civil War.* New York: Vintage, 2008.

Foner, Eric. *Freedom's Lawmakers: A Directory of Black Officeholders during Reconstruction.* New York: Oxford University Press, 1993.

———. *Reconstruction: America's Unfinished Revolution, 1863–1877.* New York: Harper Perennial, 2014.

———. *The Second Founding: How the Civil War and Reconstruction Remade the Constitution.* New York: Norton, 2019.

Foner, Eric, and Olivia Mahoney. *America's Reconstruction: People and Politics after the Civil War.* New York: Harper Perennial, 1995.

Foster, Gaines. *Ghosts of the Confederacy: Defeat, the Lost Cause, and the Emergence of the New South, 1865 to 1913.* New York: Oxford University Press, 1987.

Furgurson, Ernest B. *Ashes of Glory: Richmond at War.* New York: Knopf, 1996.

Gaines, William H., Jr. *Biographical Register of Members, Virginia State Convention of 1861.* Richmond: Virginia State Library, 1969.

Gibson, Langhorne, Jr. *Cabell's Canal: The Story of the James River and Kanawha.* Richmond: Commodore, 2000.

Glymph, Thavolia. *Out of the House of Bondage: The Transformation of the Plantation Household.* New York: Cambridge University Press, 2008.

Gottlieb, Matthew, and *DVB*. "James W. Hunnicutt (1814–1880)." Encyclopedia Virginia. Accessed 7 December 2020.

Graham, Christopher Alan. *Faith, Race, and the Lost Cause: Confessions of a Southern Church.* Charlottesville: University Press of Virginia, 2023.

Green, Hilary. "Educational Reconstruction: African American Education in the Urban South, 1865–1890." PhD diss., University of North Carolina, 2010.

———. "Ralza M. Manley (1822–1897)." Encyclopedia Virginia. Accessed 12 February 2021.

Green, Kristen. *The Devil's Half Acre: The Untold Story of How One Woman Liberated the South's Most Notorious Slave Jail.* New York: Seal, 2022.

Guelzo, Allen C. *Robert E. Lee: A Life.* New York: Knopf, 2021.

Guzman-Stokes, Theresa M. "A Flag and a Family: Richard Gill Forrester, 1847–1906." *VC* (Spring 1998): 52–63.

Hadden, Sally E. *Slave Patrols: Law and Violence in Virginia and the Carolinas.* Cambridge, MA: Harvard University Press, 2001.

Hamm, Richard F. *Murder, Honor, and Law: Four Virginia Homicides from Reconstruction to the Great Depression.* Charlottesville: University of Virginia Press, 2003.

Hanna, A. J. "The Role of Matthew Fontaine Maury in the Mexican Empire." *VMHB* 55:2 (April 1947): 105–25.

Harwell, Richard Barksdale. *Brief Candle: The Confederate Theatre.* Worcester, MA: American Antiquarian Society, 1971.

Heinemann, Ronald L., et al. *Old Dominion, New Commonwealth: A History of Virginia, 1607–2007.* Charlottesville: University of Virginia Press, 2009.

Heite, Edward F. "Judge Robert Ould: His Struggle for Justice Continued Long after the War Was Over." *VC* 14:4 (1965): 10–19.

Heizer, Ruth Bradfute. *Bradfute Beginnings.* Baltimore, MD: Gateway, 1988.

Hettle, Wallace. "The 'Self-Analysis' of John C. Rutherfoord: Democracy and the Manhood of a Virginia Secessionist." *Southern Studies* 5 (Spring and Summer 1994): 81–116.

Hildebrand, John R. *The Life and Times of John Brown Baldwin, 1820–1873: A Chronicle of Virginia's Struggle with Slavery, Secession, Civil War, and

Reconstruction. Staunton, VA: Published for the Augusta County Historical Society by Lot's Wife Publishing, 2008.

Hizer, Trenton, ed. *Guide to the Personal Papers Collection at the Library of Virginia.* Richmond: Library of Virginia, 2008.

Hodes, Martha. *Mourning Lincoln.* New Haven, CT: Yale University Press, 2015.

Hoole, Wm. Stanley. *Lawley Covers the Confederacy.* Confederate Centennial Studies, No. 26, Tuscaloosa, AL: Confederate Publishing, 1964.

Hume, Richard L. "The Membership of the Virginia Constitutional Convention of 1867–68: A Study of the Beginnings of Congressional Reconstruction in the Upper South." *VMHB* 86:4 (October 1978): 461–84.

Irons, Charles F. "And All These Things Shall Be Added unto You: The First African Baptist Church, Richmond, 1841–1865." *VC* 47:1 (Winter 1998): 26–35.

Irvine, Dallas D. "The Fate of the Confederate Archives." *American Historical Review* 44 (July 1939): 823–41.

Janney, Caroline E. *Burying the Dead but Not the Past: Ladies' Memorial Associations and the Lost Cause.* Chapel Hill: University of North Carolina Press, 2008.

———. *Ends of War: The Unfinished Fight of Lee's Army after Appomattox.* Chapel Hill: University of North Carolina Press, 2021.

Janney-Lucas, Caroline Elizabeth. "If Not for the Ladies: Ladies' Memorial Associations and the Making of the Lost Cause." PhD diss., University of Virginia, 2005.

Johns, Frank S., and Anne Page Johns. "Chimborazo Hospital and J. B. McCaw, Surgeon-in-Chief." *VMHB* 62:2 (April 1954): 190–200.

Jones, Catherine A. *Intimate Reconstructions: Children in Postemancipation Virginia.* Charlottesville: University of Virginia Press, 2014.

Jordan, Ervin L., Jr. *Black Confederates and Afro-Yankees in Civil War Virginia.* Charlottesville: University of Virginia Press, 1995.

Kachun, Mitch. *Festivals of Freedom: Memory and Meaning in African American Emancipation Celebrations, 1808–1915.* Amherst: University of Massachusetts Press, 2003.

Kimball, Gregg D. *American City, Southern Place: A Cultural History of Antebellum Richmond.* Athens: University of Georgia Press, 2000.

King, Joseph Leonard, Jr. *Dr. George William Bagby: A Study of Virginian Literature, 1850–1880.* New York: Columbia University Press, 1927.

Kinney, Martha E. "'If Vanquished I Am Still Victorious': Religious and Cultural Symbolism in Virginia's Confederate Memorial Day Celebrations, 1866–1930." *VMHB* 106:3 (Summer 1998): 237–66.

Krasnoff, Justin F. "The Contributions of Edward A. Pollard's *The Lost Cause* to the Myth of the Lost Cause." Master's thesis, Eastern Michigan University, 2021.

Krowl, Michelle A. "African American Women and the United States Military in Civil War Virginia." In *Afro-Virginian History and Culture,* edited by John Saillant. New York: Garland, 1999.

Lang, Andrew F. "Republicanism, Race, and Reconstruction: The Ethos of Military Occupation in Civil War America." *Journal of the Civil War Era* (December 2014): 559–89.

Lankford, Nelson D. *Cry Havoc! The Crooked Road to Civil War, 1861.* New York: Viking, 2007.

———. *Richmond Burning: The Last Days of the Confederate Capital.* New York: Viking, 2002.

Latimore, Carey H. *The Role of Southern Free Blacks during the Civil War Era: The Life of Free African Americans in Richmond, Virginia, 1850 to 1876.* Lewiston, NY: Edwin Mellen, 2015.

Leveen, Lois. "Mary Richards Bowser (fl. 1846–1867)." Encyclopedia Virginia. Accessed 7 December 2020.

Levine, Robert S. *The Failed Promise: Reconstruction, Frederick Douglass, and the Impeachment of Andrew Johnson.* New York: Norton, 2021.

Litwack, Leon F. *Been in the Storm So Long: The Aftermath of Slavery.* New York: Knopf, 1979.

Long, E. B. *The Civil War Day by Day: An Almanac, 1861–1865.* With Barbara Long. Garden City, NY: Doubleday, 1971.

Longacre, Edward G. *Army of Amateurs: General Benjamin F. Butler and the Army of the James, 1863–1865.* Mechanicsburg, PA: Stackpole, 1997.

Love, Richard. *Founded upon Benevolence: A Bicentennial History of the Mutual Assurance Society of Virginia.* Richmond: The Valentine, the Museum of the Life and History of Richmond, 1994.

Lowe, Richard G. "Francis Harrison Pierpont: Wartime Unionist, Reconstruction Moderate." In *The Governors of Virginia, 1860–1978,* edited by Edward Younger and James Tice Moore. Charlottesville: University Press of Virginia, 1982.

———. "The Freedmen's Bureau and Local Black Leadership." *JAH* (December 1993): 989–93.

———. "The Freedmen's Bureau and Local White Leaders in Virginia." *JSH* 64:3 (August 1998): 455–72.

———. "Local Black Leaders during Reconstruction in Virginia." *VMHB* 103:2 (April 1995): 181–206.

——. *Republicans and Reconstruction in Virginia, 1856–70.* Charlottesville: University Press of Virginia, 1991.

——. "Testimony from the Old Dominion before the Joint Committee on Reconstruction." *VMHB* 104:3 (Summer 1996): 373–97.

——. "Virginia's Reconstruction Convention: General Schofield Rates the Delegates." *VMHB* 80:3 (1972): 341–60.

Luebke, Peter. "William Mahone (1826–1895)." Encyclopedia Virginia. Accessed 22 December 2021.

Maddex, Jack P., Jr. "Pollard's *The Lost Cause Regained:* A Mask for Southern Accommodation." *JSH* 40:4 (November 1974): 595–612.

——. *The Reconstruction of Edward A. Pollard: A Rebel's Conversion to Postbellum Unionism.* Chapel Hill: University of North Carolina Press, 1974.

——. *The Virginia Conservatives, 1867–1879: A Study in Reconstruction Politics.* Chapel Hill: University of North Carolina Press, 1970.

Majeske, Penelope K. "Your Obedient Servant: The United States Army in Virginia during Reconstruction, 1865–1867." PhD diss., Wayne State University, 1980.

Marchant, Anyda. "Maury's New Virginia." *Southwest Review* 48:4 (Autumn 1963): 370–76.

Marszalek, John F. *Commander of All Lincoln's Armies: A Life of General Henry W. Halleck.* Cambridge, MA: Belknap Press of Harvard University Press, 2004.

McDonough, James L. "John Schofield as Military Director of Reconstruction in Virginia." *Civil War History* 15 (1969): 237–56.

——. *Schofield: Union General in the Civil War and Reconstruction.* Tallahassee: Florida State University, 1972.

McFeely, William S. *Yankee Stepfather: General O. O. Howard and the Freedmen.* New Haven, CT: Yale University Press, 1968.

McPherson, James M. *Battle Cry of Freedom: The Civil War Era.* New York: Ballantine, 1989.

Meacham, Jon. *And There Was Light: Abraham Lincoln and the American Struggle.* New York: Random House, 2022.

Mehrländer, Andrea. *The Germans of Charleston, Richmond and New Orleans during the Civil War Period, 1850–1870: A Study and Research Compendium.* Berlin: De Gruyter, 2011.

Mitchell, Mary H. *Hollywood Cemetery: The History of a Southern Shrine.* Rev. ed. Richmond: Library of Virginia, 1999.

Moore, Louis. "The Elusive Center: Virginia Politics and the General Assembly, 1869–1871." *VMHB* 103:2 (April 1995): 207–36.

Morton, Richard L. *The Negro in Virginia Politics, 1865–1902.* Charlottesville: University of Virginia Press, 1919.

Naragon, Michael Douglas. "Ballots, Bullets, and Blood: The Political Transformation of Richmond, Virginia, 1850–1874." PhD diss., University of Pittsburgh, 1996.

Nash, Steven E. "'The Devil Let Loose Generally': James W. Hunnicutt's Conceptualization of the Union in Fredericksburg." *VMHB* 126:3 (2018): 298–333.

National State and City Bank. *Fifty Years of Service, 1870–1920.* Richmond: Garrett & Massie, 1920.

Neff, John R. *Honoring the Civil War Dead: Commemoration and the Problem of Reconciliation.* Lawrence: University Press of Kansas, 2005.

Nelson, Scott Reynolds. *Iron Confederacies: Southern Railways, Klan Violence, and Reconstruction.* Chapel Hill: University of North Carolina Press, 1992.

Neumann, Brian. "'Long Tried Patriotism': The Republican Politics of UVA's Alexander Rives." https://naucenter.as.virginia.edu.

Nicoletti, Cynthia. *Secession on Trial: The Treason Prosecution of Jefferson Davis.* New York: Cambridge University Press, 2017.

O'Brien, John. "Albert R. Brooks (c. 1817–1881)." Encyclopedia Virginia. Accessed 12 February 2021.

O'Brien, John T. "Factory, Church, and Community: Blacks in Antebellum Richmond." *JSH* 44:4 (November 1978): 509–36.

———. *From Bondage to Citizenship: The Richmond Black Community, 1865–1867.* New York: Garland, 1990.

———. "Reconstruction in Richmond: White Restoration and Black Protest, April-June 1865." *VMHB* 89:3 (July 1981): 259–81.

O'Brien, John T., and *DVB*. "Fields Cook (1817–1897)." Encyclopedia Virginia. Accessed 7 December 2020.

O'Grady, Joseph P. "Immigrants and the Politics of Reconstruction in Richmond, Virginia." *Records of the American Catholic Historical Society of Philadelphia* 83:2 (June 1972): 87–101.

Perman, Michael. *Reunion without Compromise: The South and Reconstruction, 1865–1868.* Cambridge: Cambridge University Press, 1973.

Perry, James M. *A Bohemian Brigade: The Civil War Correspondents—Mostly Rough, Sometimes Ready.* New York: John Wiley & Sons, 2000.

Peters, John O. *Richmond's Hollywood Cemetery.* Richmond: Valentine Richmond History Center, 2010.

Phillips, Jason. *Diehard Rebels: The Confederate Culture of Invincibility.* Athens: University of Georgia Press, 2007.

Pryor, Elizabeth Brown. *Reading the Man: A Portrait of Robert E. Lee through His Private Letters.* New York: Viking, 2007.

——. *Six Encounters with Lincoln: A President Confronts Democracy and Its Demons.* New York: Viking, 2017.

Quatman, G. William. *A Young General and the Fall of Richmond: The Life and Career of Godfrey Weitzel.* Athens: Ohio University Press, 2015.

Rabinowitz, Howard N. *Race Relations in the Urban South, 1865–1890.* New York: Oxford University Press, 1978.

——, ed. *Southern Black Leaders of the Reconstruction Era.* Urbana: University of Illinois Press, 1982.

Rachleff, Peter. *Black Labor in Richmond, 1865–1890.* Urbana: University of Illinois Press, 1989.

Redkey, Edwin S. "Black Chaplains in the Union Army." *Civil War History* 33:4 (1987): 331–50.

Reynolds, Donald E. "The New Orleans Riot of 1866, Reconsidered." *Louisiana History* 5:1 (Winter 1964): 5–27.

Richardson, E. Allen, "Architects of a Benevolent Empire: The Relationship between the American Missionary Association and the Freedmen's Bureau in Virginia, 1865–1872." In *The Freedmen's Bureau and Reconstruction: Reconsiderations,* edited by Paul A. Cimbala and Randall M. Miller. New York: Fordham University Press, 1999.

Roark, James L. *Masters without Slaves: Southern Planters in the Civil War and Reconstruction.* New York: Norton, 1977.

Robert, Joseph C. *The Story of Tobacco in America.* New York: Knopf, 1949.

——. *The Tobacco Kingdom: Plantation, Market, and Factory in Virginia and North Carolina, 1800–1860.* Durham, NC: Duke University Press, 1938.

Rood, Daniel. "Bogs of Death: Slavery, the Brazilian Flour Trade, and the Mystery of the Vanishing Millpond in Antebellum Virginia." *JAH* 101:1 (June 2014): 19–43.

Ryan, David D. *Four Days in 1865: The Fall of Richmond.* Richmond: Cadmus, 1993.

Saunders, Robert, Jr. *John Archibald Campbell, Southern Moderate, 1811–1889.* Tuscaloosa: University of Alabama Press, 1997.

Schermerhorn, Calvin. "George Fitzhugh (1806–1881)." Encyclopedia Virginia. Accessed 12 February 2021.

Schildt, John W. *Hunter Holmes McGuire: Doctor in Gray.* Chewsville, MD: J. W. Schildt, 1986.

Schwarz, Philip J. *St. Paul's Episcopal Church: 150 Years, 1845–1995.* Richmond: Pine Tree, 1995.

Schweninger, Loren. "The Roots of Enterprise: Black-Owned Businesses in Virginia, 1830–1880." *VMHB* 100:4 (October 1992): 525–42.

Scott, Mary Wingfield. *Houses of Old Richmond.* New York: Bonanza, 1941.

Sefton, James E. *Andrew Johnson and the Uses of Constitutional Power.* Boston: Little, Brown, 1980.

———. *The United States Army and Reconstruction, 1865–1877.* Baton Rouge: Louisiana State University Press, 1967.

Shaffer, Donald R. *After the Glory: The Struggles of Black Civil War Veterans.* Lawrence: University of Kansas Press, 2004.

Sheehan-Dean, Aaron. "The Long Civil War: A Historiography of the Consequences of the Civil War." *VMHB* 119:2 (2011): 106–53.

Simpson, Brooks D. *Let Us Have Peace: Ulysses S. Grant and the Politics of War and Reconstruction, 1861–1868.* Chapel Hill: University of North Carolina Press, 1991.

Simpson, Craig M. *A Good Southerner: The Life of Henry A. Wise of Virginia.* Chapel Hill: University of North Carolina Press, 1985.

Smith, D. T. "Tobacco and Its Role in the Life of the Confederacy." Master's thesis, Old Dominion University, 1993.

Smith, James Douglas. "The Virginia Constitutional Convention of 1867–1868." Master's thesis, University of Virginia, 1956.

———. "Virginia during Reconstruction, 1865–1870: A Political, Economic and Social Study." PhD diss., University of Virginia, 1960.

Smith, Leslie Winston. "A Historical Study of the Role of the Industrialist in the Tobacco, Flour and Textile Industries of Virginia, 1860–1890." Master's thesis, University of Richmond, 1963.

———. "Richmond during Presidential Reconstruction, 1865–1867." PhD diss., University of Virginia, 1974.

Smith, Ryan K. *Death and Rebirth in a Southern City: Richmond's Historic Cemeteries.* Baltimore, MD: Johns Hopkins University Press, 2020.

Stampp, Kenneth M. *The Era of Reconstruction, 1865–1877.* New York: Vintage, 1965.

Stanley, Philip, and *DVB*. "Lewis Lindsay (1843–1908)." Encyclopedia Virginia. Accessed 7 December 2020.

Sternhell, Yael A. *Routes of War: The World of Movement in the Confederate South.* Cambridge. MA: Harvard University Press, 2012.

Stuart, Meriwether. "Colonel Ulric Dahlgren and Richmond's Union Underground: April 1864." *VMHB* 72:2 (April 1964): 152–204.

———. "Of Spies and Borrowed Names: The Identity of Union Operatives in Richmond Known as 'The Phillipses' Discovered." *VMHB* 89:3 (July 1981): 308–27.

Summers, Mark Wahlgren. *The Ordeal of the Reunion: A New History of Reconstruction.* Chapel Hill: University of North Carolina Press, 2014.

Takagi, Midori. *"Rearing Wolves to Our Own Destruction": Slavery in Richmond, Virginia, 1782–1865.* Charlottesville: University Press of Virginia, 1999.

Tarter, Brent. "Conference with President Andrew Johnson (June 16, 1865)." Encyclopedia Virginia. Accessed 7 December 2020.

———. *Constitutional History of Virginia.* Athens: University of Georgia Press, 2023.

———. "The New Virginia Bookshelf." *VMHB* 104:1 (Winter 1996): 7–102.

———. *A Saga of the New South: Race, Law, and Public Debt in Virginia.* Charlottesville: University of Virginia Press, 2016.

———. *Virginians and Their Histories.* Charlottesville: University of Virginia Press, 2020.

Tarter, Brent, and *DVB.* "John C. Underwood (1809–1873)." Encyclopedia Virginia. Accessed 12 February 2021.

Taylor, Alrutheus Ambush. "Giving Virginia a Democratic Constitution." *Journal of Negro History* 11:3 (July 1926): 478–93.

———. *The Negro in the Reconstruction of Virginia.* Washington, DC: Association for the Study of Negro Life and History, 1926.

Theodore, Terry. "Ida Vernon: America's Forgotten Star." *Nineteenth Century Theatre Research* 6:1 (Spring 1978): 41–48.

Thomas, Emory M. *The Confederate State of Richmond: A Biography of the Capital.* Austin: University of Texas Press, 1971.

Townes, A. Jane. "The Effect of Emancipation on Large Landholdings, Nelson and Goochland Counties, Virginia." *JSH* 45:3 (August 1979): 404–12.

Trefousse, Hans L. *Andrew Johnson: A Biography.* New York: Norton, 1989.

Trent, Hank. *The Secret Life of Bacon Tait: A White Slave Trader Married to a Free Woman of Color.* Baton Rouge: Louisiana State University Press, 2017.

Trexler, Harrison A. "The Davis Administration and the Richmond Press, 1861–1865." *JSH* 41:2 (May 1950): 177–95.

Turner, Nicole Myers. "Independent Black Church Conventions, 1866–1868." Chapter 2 of *Soul Liberty: The Evolution of Black Religious Politics in Postemancipation Virginia,* by Myers. Chapel Hill: University of North Carolina Press, 2020.

Tyler-McGraw, Marie. *At the Falls: Richmond, Virginia, and Its People.* Chapel Hill: University of North Carolina Press, 1994.

Varon, Elizabeth R. *Appomattox: Victory, Defeat, and Freedom at the End of the Civil War.* New York: Oxford, 2014.

———. *Southern Lady, Yankee Spy: The True Story of Elizabeth Van Lew, a Union Agent in the Heart of the Confederacy.* New York: Oxford University Press, 2003.

Watson, Ritchie. "George William Bagby (1828–1883)." Encyclopedia Virginia. Accessed 22 December 2021.

Weis, Tracey. "Negotiating Freedom: Domestic Service and the Landscape of Labor and Household Relations in Richmond, Virginia, 1850–1880." PhD diss., Rutgers University, 1994.

West, Earle H. "The Harris Brothers: Black Northern Teachers in the Reconstruction South." *Journal of Negro Education* 48:2 (Spring 1979): 126–38.

Whitley, William. "Joseph Cox (ca. 1835–1880)." Encyclopedia Virginia. Accessed 12 February 2021.

Williams, Frances Leigh. *A Century of Service: Prologue to the Future; A History of the First & Merchants National Bank.* Richmond: n.p., 1965.

Work Projects Administration. *The Negro in Virginia: Compiled by Workers of the Writers' Program of the Work Projects Administration in the State of Virginia.* Sponsored by Hampton Institute. New York: Hastings House, 1940.

Wyatt-Brown, Bertram. *The Shaping of Southern Culture: Honor, Grace, and War, 1760s–1890s.* Chapel Hill: University of North Carolina Press, 2001.

INDEX

Page numbers in italics refer to illustrations.

RECENT BOOKS IN THE SERIES

A Nation Divided: Studies in the Civil War Era

From Dakota to Dixie: George Buswell's Civil War
Edited by Jonathan W. White and Reagan Connelly

Reconstruction beyond 150: Reassessing the New Birth of Freedom
Orville Vernon Burton and J. Brent Morris, editors

Dueling Cultures, Damnable Legacies: Southern Violence and White Supremacy in the Civil War Era
James Hill Welborn III

The Civil War Political Tradition: Ten Portraits of Those Who Formed It
Paul D. Escott

The Weaker Sex in War: Gender and Nationalism in Civil War Virginia
Kristen Brill

Young America: The Transformation of Nationalism before the Civil War
Mark Power Smith

Black Suffrage: Lincoln's Last Goal
Paul D. Escott

The Cacophony of Politics: Northern Democrats and the American Civil War
J. Matthew Gallman

My Work among the Freedmen: The Civil War and Reconstruction Letters of Harriet M. Buss
Edited by Jonathan W. White and Lydia J. Davis

Colossal Ambitions: Confederate Planning for a Post–Civil War World
Adrian Brettle

Newest Born of Nations: European Nationalist Movements and the Making of the Confederacy
Ann L. Tucker

A Vastly Different World: Confederate Planning for a Postwar Global Role
Adrian Brettle

The Worst Passions of Human Nature: White Supremacy in the Civil War North
Paul D. Escott

Preserving the White Man's Republic: Jacksonian Democracy, Race, and the Transformation of American Conservatism
Joshua A. Lynn

American Abolitionism: Its Direct Political Impact from Colonial Times into Reconstruction
Stanley Harrold

A Strife of Tongues: The Compromise of 1850 and the Ideological Foundations of the American Civil War
Stephen E. Maizlish

The First Republican Army: The Army of Virginia and the Radicalization of the Civil War
John H. Matsui

War upon Our Border: Two Ohio Valley Communities Navigate the Civil War
Stephen I. Rockenbach

Gold and Freedom: The Political Economy of Reconstruction
Nicolas Barreyre, translated by Arthur Goldhammer

Daydreams and Nightmares: A Virginia Family Faces Secession and War
Brent Tarter

Intimate Reconstructions: Children in Postemancipation Virginia
Catherine A. Jones

Lincoln's Dilemma: Blair, Sumner, and the Republican Struggle over Racism and Equality in the Civil War Era
Paul D. Escott

Slavery and War in the Americas: Race, Citizenship, and State Building in the United States and Brazil, 1861–1870
Vitor Izecksohn

Marching Masters: Slavery, Race, and the Confederate Army during the Civil War
Colin Edward Woodward